The controversy aroused
*manae Vitae,* the papal encyclical
on birth control, reached a peak
with the publication in 1977 of
*Human Sexuality,* a report commissioned by the Catholic Theological Society of America that
contradicted much official Catholic
teaching on sex. In this book, several prominent biblical and theological scholars critically evaluate
the arguments and conclusions of
*Human Sexuality.* What is needed,
they argue, is a fresh appreciation
of the close bond between body
and spirit that will support a positive view of sexuality as an expression of the total personality.

Gathered together here, from
the broad spectrum of Christian
University of Würzburg, where his
thesis was the first English-lan-
guage volume to be published in
a prestigious series of monographs
on the history of Catholic moral
theology. He is also the author of
*Divorce and Remarriage: Resolv-
ing a Catholic Dilemma* (Abbey
Press, 1974) and of numerous articles in scholarly and popular
journals.

# DIMENSIONS OF
# *HUMAN SEXUALITY*

# DIMENSIONS OF
# *HUMAN SEXUALITY*

## Edited by Dennis Doherty

✿

DOUBLEDAY & COMPANY, INC.
GARDEN CITY, NEW YORK
1979

Grateful acknowledgment is made to the following publishers for permission to quote material from their published works:

America Press for portions of *Documents of Vatican II*, edited by W. M. Abbott, copyright © 1966 by America Press, 106 West 56th Street, New York, New York 10019.

Catholic Theological Society of America for portions of *Human Sexuality: New Directions in American Catholic Thought*, copyright © 1977 by the Catholic Theological Society of America, Manhattan College, Bronx, New York 10471.

Helicon Press, Inc., 1120 North Calvert Street, Baltimore, Maryland 21202 for portions of *Law for Liberty: The Role of Law in the Church Today*, ed. James Biechler, copyright © 1967 by the Canon Law Society of America.

Orbis Books for portions of Juan Luis Segundo's *Theology for Artisans of a New Humanity*, Vol. 5, *Evolution and Guilt*, copyright © 1967 by Orbis Books, Maryknoll, New York 10545.

Library of Congress Cataloging in Publication Data
Main entry under title:

Dimensions of human sexuality.

Includes bibliographical references and index.
1. Sex (Theology)—Addresses, essays, lectures.
I. Doherty, Dennis.
BT708.D55      241
ISBN: 0-385-15040-7
Library of Congress Catalog Card Number 79–7046

FOR
DAVID

# CONTENTS

# CONTENTS

# INTRODUCTION

The authors of *Human Sexuality: New Directions in American Catholic Thought*[1] conclude their Preface with the hope that others will join them "in the continuing search for more satisfactory answers to the mystery of human sexuality" (p. xv). This is echoed in the Postscript when they invite "serious criticism" of their work and further "scholarly dialogue" (p. 241). The present volume is an acceptance of that invitation.

Because *Human Sexuality* received advance publicity, some persons anticipated the invitation, not so much to join in the search but simply to reiterate the official Catholic teaching. When the book was released, critics showered the authors with both bouquets and brickbats. Even the Catholic Theological Society of America (CTSA), which commissioned the Study,[2] and the publishing house as well, were praised and condemned. The furor was understandable enough. Suggested "new directions" ran counter to authoritative teachings of long standing. Such an approach was (is) seen as challenging to authority and as disturbing to many Catholics whose sensitivities have been shaped by the Church's clear-cut teaching on sexual conduct. To challenge authority is, in the minds of many, to subvert *the* source of truth. To map out new directions is to pervert the sexual order in a society which already allegedly exists in a sexual wilderness.

From a very human standpoint a non-traditional approach necessarily creates a certain tension for those who have "borne the heat of the day" in trying to adhere to the traditional code. Tension is no less a part of religious teaching than it is of life itself. Indeed, for believing Christians Vatican II's *Dogmatic Constitution on the Church* hardly lessens the tension when it declares that salvation is attainable also by those "who through no fault of their own do not know the gospel of Christ or His Church, yet sincerely seek God and, moved by grace, strive by their deeds to do His will as it is known to them through the dictates of conscience. Nor does divine Providence deny the help necessary for salvation to those who, without blame on their part, have not yet arrived at an explicit knowledge of God, but who strive to live a good life, thanks to His grace."[8] The problem is as old as the gospel account of the Last Judgment (Mt. 25:31–46). Persons are awarded or denied eternal life by the standard of simple human kindness; there is no apparent need for an explicit faith in Christ. Hence, those who make such a profession of faith must surely wonder at times why they believe at all. And when by reason of affiliation with a particular Christian denomination (in context, Roman Catholic) they are confronted with a strict sexual code whose prohibitions are said to bind under pain of eternal damnation, the tension can only be greater. There is a paradox here. On the one hand, there is a real security in identifying oneself as a believer and in knowing clearly what one's Church teaches. On the other, believers must wonder what such a teaching on sexuality has to do with the Good News of salvation, how such a detailed approach is possibly encompassed in the works of mercy (as spoken of in the Last Judgment description), and why all other Christians do not see things alike if the truth is supposedly so obvious and if salvation is at stake.

This should be tension enough for anyone to attempt to cope with. Nonetheless, it is intensified all the more for some when theologians and others within a given denomination ask about the current value of a specific teaching, one especially that is highly volatile. Hence it is that the authors of *Human Sexuality* have caused a certain tension. But tension can be creative; one always profits by coming to grips with an issue if he thereby gains a better appreciation of reality. The task of the contributors to the present volume is to argue the views advanced in *Human Sexuality* in

a way that critics to date have not done. While this is our common task—which is, in a word, an attempt to apply the admonition of St. Paul to "test all things and keep what is good"
(1 Thess. 5:21)—we do not agree among ourselves on the value of
the positions taken by the authors of the CTSA Report.

This is a major difference between their work and ours. Working together as a committee for several years, they produced a
study which "is not a collection of separate essays authored by
different members"; rather, "the entire work was . . . approved by
the committee as a whole . . . without substantial disagreement
or objection" (p. xiv). Accordingly, that work is marked by an intrinsic coherence. By contrast, the unity of the present study is
our common concern to evaluate what they have written and in
so doing to try to advance the arguments which they have proposed. For this reason the disposition of chapters in this volume
loosely parallels the structure of *Human Sexuality*. Fr. Kosnik and
his co-authors describe their study as "a position somewhere between that of a highly technical, cumbrously footnoted work of
speculative theology and a practical, experience-oriented work of
pastoral theology" (p. xii). Our own overall approach is similar.
And Fr. Kosnik himself is evaluating our several approaches.

The attempt to advance the arguments of *Human Sexuality* is
made from both the traditional and new-directions orientation
of the present contributors, according to the personal conviction
and professional vantage point of each. We are all engaged in
"free inquiry," that sincere endeavor in which persons "explain to
one another the truth they have discovered, or think they have
discovered, in order thus to assist one another in the quest for
truth." And it is reassuring to recall, from the same passage of
Vatican II's *Declaration on Religious Freedom*, that "as the truth
is discovered, it is by a personal assent that men are to adhere to
it."[4] That assent is to be *personal* highlights the dignity of the individual (and the *Declaration* just referred to begins with the
words "Dignitatis humanae personae"). When "truth" is proposed authoritatively, dissent is naturally inevitable and often
enough necessary; it is also theologically respectable. In my judgment, therefore, the reduction of every issue to authoritative declarations, with discussions on the nature and extent of ecclesiastical authority and of religious submission, is the bane of so much

"theologizing." Persons not open to views which do not restate official teaching need to be reminded that if an authoritative declaration of whatever genre is the ultimate norm (of truth), it is in effect the only norm and there is no need to discuss anything—except, perhaps, in an effort to somehow justify official teaching. In this they remind one of the situation of the medieval dialecticians described by John of Salisbury (at the end of the twelfth century) and recounted by E. Gilson: "When he revisited the schools of Paris after an absence of twelve years, John says that he still found there the very same professors saying the very same things. None of them had either learned or unlearned anything—a striking illustration indeed of what happens to philosophy when it attempts to live by logic alone. Other centuries than the twelfth would be well advised to remember the lesson."[5] The lesson is what happens to moral theological teaching when it attempts to live by the extrinsic evidence of authority alone. To the contrary, the writers in this volume who espouse the official teaching, whether in whole or in part, argue the intrinsic merits of that teaching.

In this regard the contribution made by Archbishop Joseph Bernardin is singular—a combination of the speculative and pastoral and deserves special mention here. In theoretical treatises on the beauty of God's plan regarding marriage and human sexuality, on the glory of the Paschal mystery, on a moral theology grounded in the Incarnation and nourished by Sacred Scripture, and so on, many "practical" ramifications are understandably not considered. These speculative approaches could be very satisfying to many since, by way of comparison, a simple direct map is usually more readable than one which details every feature of the terrain. But the moral climate of our tradition and of our times provokes many practical questions—as *Human Sexuality* itself proves. Even official teachings which moralize in intimate detail about certain questions usually occasion more questions. In consequence, people are left wondering about many things. Some of these are the substance of the topics presented for comment to Archbishop Bernardin, a distinguished member of the American hierarchy and a fellow theologian, who would have preferred to write an essay on a positive theological approach to human sexuality but who agreed by return mail to meet this challenge head on. (Perhaps other members of the hierarchy will be encouraged to speak as forthrightly to these and related issues, at least in their own diocesan media.)

Recalling again the conciliar passage on the quest for truth, I share the conviction of many that moral truth is not "discovered" in the same way that an archeological treasure is unearthed; "truth naturally knowable" (to borrow a phrase from Cardinal Cajetan[6]) emerges in the dynamics of human living from a whole constellation of value factors. Moral truth is fashioned (discovered) by persons as they endeavor to shape a mode of existence which they regard to be human or a type of conduct which they judge to be humanizing. Insights will vary from culture to culture and, within a given culture, from era to era; Catholic moral teaching through the centuries is replete with examples of different perceptions of truth. Hence it is that our understanding of what is human or moral or good or true with regard to sexuality at least qualifies for reconsideration. That human sexuality is a mystery-laden phenomenon is reason enough to probe it.

Seeking the truth in whatever regard, and living it in love, will make and keep us free (cf. John 8:32; Gal. 5:6).

DENNIS J. DOHERTY
Marquette University
28 December 1978
Feast of the Holy Innocents

## NOTES

1. A. Kosnik, W. Carroll, A. Cunningham, R. Modras, J. Schulte (New York: Paulist Press, 1977); referred to throughout this volume as *Human Sexuality* or the CTSA Report or the CTSA Study or, simply, the Report.
2. Our work, it should be noted, is completely independent of the Catholic Theological Society of America. However, at the thirty-third annual convention held in Milwaukee, Wisconsin, in June of 1978, officials of the Society considered the possibility of publishing a volume of reviews of the Report (more precisely, a simple collection of such reviews) in an effort to acknowledge those who criticized the So-

ciety for commissioning it. When the board members learned of this project they abandoned the idea.

3. *Lumen Gentium*, Art. 16; translation: *The Documents of Vatican II*, ed., W. Abbott, S.J. (New York: America Press, 1966), p. 35. (Except where otherwise noted, all passages from these documents in the present volume are taken from this translation.)

4. *Dignitatis Humanae*, Art. 3, p. 681. One might here recall a view of St. Thomas Aquinas, *Summer Theol.* I–II, 57, 5 ad 2: When one acts on the force of personal conviction, he is acting more perfectly as a person; the good that is done will be done "simply well, which is what to live well really means."

5. E. Gilson, *History of Christian Philosophy in the Middle Ages* (New York: Random House, 1955), pp. 153f.

6. Writing in 1498 Cajetan noted (translation mine) that "only those things which are matters of faith are subject to the judgment of the Supreme Pontiff inasmuch as he has been constituted by Christ as teacher and guide of the faithful as faithful, not of persons as persons; and to him has been promised all truth regarding whatever is necessary for the salvation of the faithful, not all truth that is naturally knowable or moral." In this latter regard "reason holds the primacy." See *De Monte Pietatis*, in P. Zammit, ed., *Thomas de Vio Cardinalis Caietanus: Scripta philosophica, opuscula oeconomico-socialia* (Romae: 1934), nn. 74–75.

## Chapter One

✣

# THE RELEVANCE OF THE OLD TESTAMENT

JOSEPH JENSEN, O.S.B.
CARROLL STUHLMUELLER, C.P.

## I. A Different Methodological Approach:
### Joseph Jensen, O.S.B.

Although much of my evaluation will be critical in nature, I
would like to emphasize at the outset what needs to be said in
favor of the Report. In many places the positive scriptural teachings on sexuality are treated with great sensitivity. Furthermore,
the Report does have the merit of calling Christians to a mature
responsibility to evaluate their actions in the light of all the
relevant factors, clearly rejecting any approach that suggests Christian morality can be outlined in a collection of do's and don'ts. It
ought by now to be a truism that Christian morality is not one of
commandment, yet this is far from being the case. Not only do
extreme right-wing Catholics often take emphasis on the Decalogue as the very touchstone of orthodoxy in their evaluations of
catechisms, textbooks, and moral theologians, but even pronouncements of the hierarchical magisterium seldom stray far
from the legal mentality much of the New Testament is intent on
rejecting. It is no doubt in large part against this very kind of approach that the Report was reacting.

It may seem something of a contradiction to speak in these

terms and then to criticize the Report from the very area from which much of the legalism condemned by the New Testament arises, namely, the Old Testament. The explanation includes four points:

1. The New Testament itself, even while not accepting the binding force of Old Testament law on the Christian, nevertheless is deeply influenced by its content.[1]

2. The Old Testament moral teaching is far broader than the legal tradition since this teaching is contained also in the historical books as well as in the prophetic and wisdom traditions.

3. The Report itself has an extended discussion of the Old Testament and therefore any critique of the Report necessarily has to pass judgment on the use it makes of this material, considered from a scholarly point of view.

4. Beyond these considerations is the fact that the Old Testament introduces us to a community ethic based on covenant. Israel was aware that it was called to be a holy, priestly, consecrated people in a way that set it apart from the profane cultures around it, from which, in fact, Israel was explicitly forbidden to draw its standards of behavior. Members of the covenant community recognized the right of the community to establish the sort of standards that ought to prevail among them and to enact sanctions. In this sense, at least, the Old Testament is relevant and beyond any charge of legalism, for the situation is very similar in the New Testament community. Little of this is apparent, however, in the approach taken by the Report.

The Report's use of Scripture is superficial and tendentious. One does not have the impression that the Bible has been objectively evaluated in order to discover its teaching; rather, the impression emerges that area after area is being dealt with in order to stay up conclusions already arrived at. Although individual texts are frequently cited, the weight attributed to them derives not from careful exegesis and attention to context, but from a handful of questionable principles: prohibitions of adultery reflect concern for the husband's right to a clear line of descent; rape laws relate to a father's financial stake in his daughter's virginal state when it comes time to present her for marriage; pagan rites are mainly responsible for condemnations of prostitution, sodomy, and bestiality.[2] But when all the evidence has been weighed, such positions can only be termed simplistic.

Positions such as those in the preceding list can be termed "inaccuracies in general characterizations"; since they rest on inadequate exegesis or, more frequently, on *no* exegesis of relevant texts, the label of "tendentiousness" is invited. Other shortcomings in the use of Scripture in the Report are more properly methodological, though all tend toward depriving the Bible of the power to say anything relevant to our modern situation. For example, the Report makes much of the fact that biblical statements in the area of sexuality are culture- and time-conditioned and that they cannot therefore be considered to provide absolute norms (pp. xii, 7, 20), that the "plurality" of statements and attitudes found in Scripture makes it impossible to reach conclusions concerning the morality of particular sexual acts (p. 31), and that the biblical authors did not ask our questions and so we cannot expect answers to our problems from them (p. 31).

All of this would leave very little for the Bible to say to us in the area of sexual morality (see p. 7) and one wonders why the authors of the Report spent so many pages on it. Did the effort spring from the sort of respect which prompts one to attend the wake of the once powerful man who ended his days in senility? Indeed, the Report's attempt to separate out what is "revealed and lasting" (p. xii) begets results that are meager and disappointing in the extreme. The summary that follows the statement "This is not to say, however, that the Bible leaves us without ideals or any guidance whatever" (p. 31) is about as brief and general as can well be imagined: "the biblical authors consistently give witness to the nature of God as gracious and loving, and to the ideal of fidelity as a foremost expression of our loving response. . . . [The Bible] declares that intercourse is good, always to be seen, however, within the larger context of personhood and community" (pp. 31f.).

But to say that all biblical statements concerning sexual matters are time- and culture-conditioned is hardly enlightening; the same is true of all human discourse, whether in or out of the Bible, but it is not thereby deprived of all power to speak to our present situation.[3] Again, once it is conceded that biblical pluralism[4] in any area makes it impossible to "approve or reject" anything in that area (p. 31), theologizing must come to an end. Would anyone assert that the variety of New Testament christological statements makes it impossible to "approve or reject" anything in the area of Christology? Furthermore, to take a last example, it is too easy an out to say "our questions simply were not asked by the biblical authors; hence answers to these questions should not be expected from them" (p. 31). This may be true of some of the items listed (e.g., birth control), but it can hardly be true of all. For example, the problem of "premarital sexual intercourse," as old as the institution of marriage, does come up in a number of biblical texts, and the moral question in the days of Sirach or Paul was not all that different from our own.

In its use of individual Scripture texts (we will return to methodology shortly), the Report often resembles the old proof text method of following an assertion with a string of texts which relate, perhaps only peripherally, to the matter at hand and often do not support the assertion at all. See, e.g., the use of Am. 2:7, Hos. 4:14, and Jer. 2:20ff. on p. 9, of Ez. 16:40 and Deut. 22:22 on p. 14. None of the six texts cited on p. 17 demonstrates that "ritual precepts became subordinated to moral requirements"; rather, some of them say that the sacrifice of the unrighteous is unacceptable. The intention of the law of Deut. 24:1–4 (the Report cites only v. 1) is not "to circumscribe the arbitrariness of a husband and protect his wife" (p. 20), for v. 4 gives the reason he may not take her back, namely that she has become defiled; see also Jer. 3:1. On p. 16 it is asserted that "wisdom literature equated secular prostitution with practices of ritual intercourse, and the wise men of Proverbs directed their longest and most dire warnings against prostitutes (Prov. 6:23–35; 7:1–27; 9:13–18)." The baselessness of the former assertion is seen in the fact that wisdom literature seldom or never even mentions cultic prostitution. As to the "most dire warnings," the first two passages cited deal with adultery rather than prostitution; in the third, the personification of Dame Folly is comparable to a harlot in her open solicitation (as is true also of the adulteress in the first two passages), but the references to "stolen water" and "bread gotten secretly" (v. 17) suggest adultery.

The Report falls short methodologically in that its use of Scripture is atomistic (as in the proof text approach just referred to), neglecting any attempt at a diachronic and synchronic approach. The emphasis is almost solely on legal texts, and there is no attempt to read them synchronically in relation to the historical books, prophets, or wisdom literature, and little attempt to see diachronically the sort of development that takes place through the centuries;[5] further, there is no attempt to ask why *these* particular texts found their way into the canon of Scripture and what function they fulfill in the canon.

Methodology is again at issue in the Report's heavy reliance on "pagan practice" as a reason for explaining away biblical prohibitions and their force (invoked in the cases of prostitution, homosexuality, and bestiality). In fact, it is *not* sufficient to say "connected with pagan practice, therefore forbidden." Much of Israel's cultic practice—agricultural feasts, altars, blood rites, specific names for God, etc.—came directly from pagan, Canaanite background; one of the unique features of Israel's religion was its ability to determine what was of value in the surrounding culture and to assimilate and transform it. So frequently did this happen that where objection is raised to a pagan rite, some reason *other* than its pagan associations must be sought. The authors of the Report would not want to assert that infant sacrifice was forbidden simply because of its pagan aspects, or that, once the pagan associations were removed, it could be found acceptable. The argumentation is clearly simplistic.

Most of my further comments will illustrate points raised above and will attempt to show how better results can be obtained in one particular area, namely, Old Testament teaching concerning adultery, through a synchronic and diachronic approach, leaving other areas to be dealt with elsewhere.[6] The Report states: "Adultery was prohibited to Israelite men . . . but only when the wife of a fellow Israelite was involved" (p. 14); and "only adultery with the wife or betrothed of a fellow Israelite was consistently condemned, and this in such a way as to make it clear that the reason for the condemnation is to be found not in the nature of human sexuality but in the familial and societal responsibilities owed to members of the same community" (p. 30).[7] A broader approach than simply through legislation, i.e., one that includes historical narrative and the wisdom tradition, not simply as seen in Israel but in continuity with that of Egypt, promotes a somewhat different understanding.

An obvious text is the story of Joseph and Potiphar's wife. It refutes the contention both that only wives of Israelites were off limits and that religious morality was not a prime concern in this area. Joseph's response to the woman's solicitation was that it would be "great wickedness" and a "sin against God" (Gen. 39:9). Similarly, in the Abimelech story, the behavior expected of the man was not predicated on who was or was not an Israelite, and it was to God that accountability was owed. Abimelech, the pagan, is depicted as protesting to God that he acted "in the integrity of my heart and the innocence of my hands" in regard to Sarah (Gen. 20:5) and Abraham gives as his excuse for misleading Abimelech the suspicion that "there is no fear of God in this place" (v. 11). It is hardly to be supposed that Israelites would have looked for such probity (integrity, innocence, fear of God) in pagans if moral dispositions were not involved, nor would they have considered themselves exempt from obligations they expected pagans to recognize.

Whether or not one accepts von Rad's thesis concerning wisdom influence in the Joseph narrative,[8] the story reflects very well the sort of behavior which is consistently urged upon the man who would be wise and virtuous in the wisdom literature. And the point at issue there *is* precisely wise and virtuous living, *not* primarily the safeguarding of the fellow Israelite's right to a line of inheritance. That the exhortations in the wisdom literature do not simply reflect the legal tradition and its concerns is seen from the way in which the warnings against adultery fit into the context of similar warnings in Egyptian wisdom literature, many instances being older than Israel herself.[9] If the primary concern were "familial and societal responsibilities owed to members of the same community," the warnings would not so often regard the "strange woman" (*zārâ*—Prov. 2:16; 5:3, 20; 7:5; 22:14), a theme that again comes up in Egyptian wisdom, where the temptress is specified as from abroad, not known in her own town, a woman away from her husband.[10]

It is especially in this area that the Report is at fault in neglecting the diachronic development. Although the wisdom tradition helps put Israel's early legislation in perspective, it clearly goes beyond it. If the Report could assume Israel's legislation concerned primarily legitimacy of offspring, Sir. 23:22f. places this as a third consideration after "disobeyed the law of the Most High" and "wronged her husband." The religious note is found again in Prov. 2:17, where the crime of the adulteress consists in "forgetting her covenant with her God." In the light of a text such as this, one views with astonishment the Report's claim that "it is not altogether clear that these warnings were morally based" (p. 16)—warnings the Report takes to be against prostitution rather than adultery. Here it is relevant to mention that Egyptian wisdom can use the term "abomination" for a man's sexual misconduct.[11] Finally, it can be pointed out that Sir. 23:18 can threaten the *man* "who dishonors his marriage bed."

A brief concluding word on the Report's treatment of homosexuality will barely scratch the surface.[12] The Report's claim that sodomy was condemned in the Old Testament only because of its connection with pagan cult rests on no secure basis. The terminology in the Leviticus prohibitions (18:22; 20:13) is not cultic. Since purely secular homosexuality was known in Mesopotamia, there is no reason to suppose that the Bible has the purely cultic forms in mind.

Most especially I would like to point out that the attempt to place sole responsibility on the Bible for the opprobrium associated with homosexuality (p. 188) hardly reflects the true situation. The Old Testament viewed sodomy as a serious sin and attached a death penalty to it, as it did to other acts considered serious sins (e.g., adultery and breaking the Sabbath). However, it was in morally "tolerant" Mesopotamia that we find the homosexual first termed "dog" (used only once in the Old Testament, Deut. 23:19, and here the context *is* cultic); where he is considered "half a man"; where by transvestism and other means (e.g., symbolically carrying the spindle) he becomes a parody of a woman; where he is, in fact, considered a man who has been turned into a woman by the curse of Ishtar[13]—a proposition equally insulting to women.

It is true that the Old Testament does not distinguish between homosexual behavior and homosexual orientation, but it is unlikely that the motive for condemning homosexual acts goes beyond the nature of the act itself. But it needs to be noted that the Old Testament, unlike Mesopotamia and other cultures, says nothing to diminish the dignity of the individual.

## II. Prophetic Ideals and Sexual Morality: Carroll Stuhlmueller, C.P.

For many reasons I looked forward to the publication of *Human Sexuality*. When it appeared, I wrote:

> It is very biblical to interact vigorously as the book . . . does, with the real world of problems and tensions, and to recognize the role of conflict and traumatic transitions in the formulation of divine revelation and moral precepts. The Bible is more a history of struggle, collapses and new beginnings, than it is an orderly manual of dogmatic and moral theology.[14]

In the same review, however, I voiced serious disappointment. I confined my remarks to three areas.

1. Conclusions were reached without sufficiently evaluating the distinctive literary styles and various moral expectations in the Bible. For instance, most scholars recognize that the "Elohist" author of Genesis 20 is more sensitive to moral questions than the "Yahwist" author of Genesis 12.[15] It can be argued that the former passage was meant by the redactor of the book of Genesis to correct the moral ambiguity of the latter.

2. Sexual sin is reduced too simplistically to ritual misdemeanors.[16] The authors of *Human Sexuality* even stated that the book of Proverbs condemned prostitution as ritual acts from Canaanite liturgy.[17] Major works on Israel's wisdom literature by Gerhard von Rad, William McKane, and Leo G. Perdue reached

a radically different conclusion.[18] The first two works were available to the authors of *Human Sexuality,* yet they were never quoted nor even mentioned.

3. Prophetic ideals are not given equal time. Here is where I will now delay and hopefully make an independent contribution to a biblical inquiry into sexual morality.

The book under discussion frequently discounts or neutralizes biblical condemnations of sexual offenses as simply a rejection of improper liturgy, an intrusion of Canaanite fertility cults into Israelite worship. The evil of extramarital intercourse, according to this interpretation of the Old Testament, was to be located not in the "secular" fact of carnal relations with a person other than one's spouse, but with its performance within the "sacred" setting of temple or sanctuary. We begin, therefore, by summarizing the interaction between the secular and the sacred, between "reality" as observable in the daily life of home, neighborhood, and work, and the cultic or ceremonial "symbolization" of that reality.[19] Still another reason for this excursus into the secular and the sacred is prompted by the firm positioning of the classical prophets within the secular; from this attitude they judged Israel's infidelity to the covenant and its sexual morality.

Biblical religion did not originate in a paradise setting (Genesis 1–3 are not among its first compositions) nor with the foundation of a temple, city, and sacred dynasty (as other ancient Near Eastern religions explained their inception)[20] but rather in a secular situation of migrations (Genesis 11:17–12:9; Deut. 26:5–9; Josh. 24:2–15), oppression (Ex. 3:7–10; 20:3), and military or political action (1 Sam. 8:5; 2 Sam. 6–7). These political or economical moves, however, left no mark on the archives or records of Mesopotamia or Egypt and therefore would never have qualified as "history." If these exploits are still remembered as Israelite history—while most of Egyptian and Mesopotamian history is generally forgotten!—the reason lies in their religious celebration at sanctuaries and eventually at the Jerusalem temple. Liturgy imparted a continuous existence to these single and often insignificant deeds of the past.

Israel, during the "secular" and rather elementary existence in the Sinaitic desert, possessed very little liturgical richness. Upon entering Canaan and establishing herself in this, her promised land, the people unashamedly acculturated themselves to Canaanite styles in liturgy as in agriculture and language.[21] Yet, once religion no longer fulfilled its purpose of inspiring the liberation of the oppressed and offering their praise to the Lord, prophets proclaimed God's detestation of "new moons and [other religious] festivals" and spoke out in behalf of orphans and widows (Is. 1:2–3, 10–20). Israel then could bear with a considerable amount of Canaanite polytheism (Pss. 29, 82, 89), but was aggressively intolerant of any liturgy, no matter how correct or orthodox, if used to shield privileged people in their oppression of the poor. According to Claus Westermann, God summoned prophets to speak as his personal messengers when "no higher authority [was] capable of intervening against [someone like] the king."[22] Furthermore, the prophets were not only "profoundly alive to the historical environment of their own day,"[23] but they sought to correct these "secular" violations of Israel's "religious" covenant with Yahweh by reaching back to the stern, desert morality of Moses' day. They appealed to the apodictic laws, like the Ten Commandments, which originated in the Mosaic period before the rich liturgical development under Canaanite influence took place.[24]

Before providing examples from the prophetical books, we summarize our position thus far:

Israelite religion originated in secular liberation. It celebrated freedom from Egyptian slavery and the exodus-way toward a land flowing with milk and honey. A stern, desert morality was received from this period in the form of apodictic laws.

When liturgical celebration no longer inspired liberation but was used by privileged groups to suppress the poor—when, therefore, the religious covenant was broken by what happened in the secular arena of life—God summoned his messengers the prophets.

Prophets appealed to the ancient apodictic laws in order to purify religion by a vigorous reformation in the secular area and to restore religion's divine purpose, the worship of a God merciful and trustworthy (Ex. 34:6–7).

Sexual immorality then was condemned along with other acts of oppression as a violation of the covenant. Intercourse with persons other than one's spouse was judged evil and an abuse of religion because of ancient laws which originated in, and basically remained a part of, secular life. We turn to the prophets for specific examples.

Summoning foreign nations and Israel to trial (Am. 1:3–2:16), the prophet Amos began each new indictment with the phrase:

> *For three crimes [from the Hebrew pešaʻ]*
> *of Damascus [or Gaza, or Tyre, etc.] or four,*
> *I will not turn back my word [or verdict].*[25]

The word *pešaʻ* carries a technical meaning of an offense against a covenant, a treaty, or a clan tradition.[26] Amos was implicitly recognizing for the gentile nations some kind of bond with the Lord, independent of the Mosaic or Sinaitic covenant and of its laws. They are being tried for "secular" or non-cultic crimes against humanity: excessive cruelty in times of war (1:3); buying captive soldiers and selling them into slavery at a profit (1:6, 9); desecrating graves (2:1). Israel is now summoned to trial and handed the charge of violating her treaty with Yahweh. The references in this case are to the Sinaitic covenant and to Yahweh, "who brought you up from the land of Egypt and who led you through the desert for forty years" (2:10).[27] Israel too had sinned against humanity, and once again "secular" or non-cultic crimes violated the ancient apodictic laws:

> *They have sold the innocent person for silver*
> *and the poor one for a pair of sandals, . . .*
> *a man and his father copulate with the (same)*
> *maiden.*[28]

Amos listed other crimes, more religious in nature, in this trial speech against Israel, yet these opening lines refer to secular crimes, indeed hideous ways of oppressing the poor. To ensure obedience to a law that debts be paid, a poor man is sold into slavery for something as insignificant as a single pair of sandals.[29] The action was similar to kidnaping (Ex. 21:16) and ran against clan regulations for restricting slavery (Ex. 21:2–11). The sexual offense in this same passage of Amos is not associated with ritual prostitution. Amos avoided the technical word for cult prostitute, *qĕdēšâ* (from the root *qādaš*, to be holy). The following liturgical phrase, "profaning my holy name," is a late addition to Amos' words from Ezekiel and the Holiness Code of Leviticus.[30] Amos is protesting against the disgusting practice of pressing a young woman (*na'ărâ*) into service for male sexual gratification and seriously impairing her prospects for marriage. H. W. Wolff adds:

> By engaging in sexual congress with a young maiden, the young man obligates himself to marry her, while the man's father is prohibited from having intercourse with her, just as he is with his daughter-in-law. Hence what we have here in Amos is, in effect, a radicalizing of the apodictic stipulation in Lev. 18:15 (cf. Lev. 20:12).[31]

Jeremiah, like Amos, considered Israel's sexual transgressions to be a rupture—*peša'*—of the covenant with Yahweh. Again the religious covenant is violated, not because of contamination from Canaanite fertility rites but because of a disgusting and flagrant violation of sex *per se*. We read in Jer. 5:6b–8.

> *For they have multiplied their violations [peša']*
>  *their rebellions are numerous. . . .*
> *They swear [šb'] by no-gods.*
> *I gave them their fill [šb']*[32]
>  *yet they committed adultery*[33]
>  *and tarried*[34] *at the harlot's house.*
> *Stallions fat and ruttish they are,*
>  *each neighs after the neighbor's wife.*

Covenant language occurs in the presence of *peša'* and in the notion of swearing by no-gods. Covenant infidelity is gauged by the physical, literal aspects of sexual debauchery. Jeremiah's language is crude, as he compares the Israelites to animals in rut. Even if he were speaking against cultic prostitution (which I deny), still his violent reply manifests an angry disgust at the betrayal of sex.

Cultic language is much more apparent in Jer. 13:20–27. The

phrase "to strip off a woman's skirt" is found in treaty-curses of the ancient Near East. It symbolizes a curse against a country and its rulers for breaking a treaty.[35] The final lines condemn Israel for sexual orgies, not simply for liturgical violations:

> *Your adulteries and your rutting!*
> *your shameless prostitutions!*

Other prophetic passages strike out explicitly against a series of "secular" crimes, oppressing the poor in their everyday life and contradicting the basic apodictic laws of the covenant. We refer to Hos. 4:1–3; Jer. 7:8–9; 23:13–15; 29:23; Ez. 22:10–12.

In Hos. 4:1–3 Hosea situates Israel's sins within a covenant context; he refers to those special covenantal virtues of Yahweh: *'emet* (trustworthy), *ḥesed* (devoted love within a blood relation), *da'at 'ĕlōhîm* (knowledge of the Lord, unique to his chosen people).[36] The *religious* covenant is fractured when Israel breaks the apodictic laws in her *secular* life. In the following citations the references in each case draw attention to appropriate apodictic laws that have been violated:

| | |
|---|---|
| *'ālōh* | cursing (Ex. 20:7) |
| *kāḥēš* | lying (Lev. 19:11) |
| *rāṣōaḥ* | premeditated murder (Ex. 20:13) |
| *gānōb* | stealing; kidnaping (Ex. 20:15; 20:16; Lev. 19:11) |
| *nā'ōp* | adultery (Ex. 20:14; Lev. 20:10) |

Even if "the vocabulary and word order do not precisely correspond with the Decalogue, [still] all the offenses have to do with one's neighbor"[37] in the secular aspects of life. H. W. Wolff concludes: "The malicious deeds mentioned by the prophet . . . led to an early form of capitalism and at the same time produced a social crisis of the first order."[38] One of the social abuses, the sensual side of wealth, is the crime of adultery.

Turning to Jeremiah, we hear "the prophet [in 7:8–9 as he] cries out in dismay at the sins committed by the people, . . . He is alluding to certain prohibitions, well-known to the people, against larceny, murder, adultery, perjury, and the worship of strange gods." E. Hammershaimb writes further: "The resem-

blance to the Decalogue is so striking that it cannot be a coinci-
dence, even though the order of the commandments . . . is
different."[39] Other scholars too, like Bright, Couturier, and
Rudolph,[40] connect this list of offenses in Jer. 7:8–9 with the covenant's apodictic laws. These sins are principally secular in scope.
Even if Jeremiah's speech in chapter 7 centers on the Jerusalem
temple and its inviolability, the prophet zooms in almost exclusively upon secular issues like stealing, murder, adultery, and perjury to determine the possibility of the temple's survival. That
these conditions go back to the desert, pre-conquest period of Israel's origins is clearly stated by Hammershaimb.[41]

Finally, the crimes enumerated by Ezekiel in chapter 22 mingle
cultic with social abuses. The prophet, in an introductory statement, bluntly labels them "filthy" (*Jerusalem Bible* translation),
"abominations" (*New American Bible*), or "abhorrent deeds"
(*Jewish Publications Society*, 1978). The Hebrew word here,
*tô'ăbôt*, originally referred to an offense "*in ritual*," but as
Koehler-Baumgartner's *Lexicon* points out, the exclusive connection with the cult was lost and "*thereafter* [it was used] *also in
moral a*[nd] *general sense.*"[42] As we read the list of sins in Ezekiel
22, we see that "moral and cultic sins are thus linked together as
indissolubly associated expressions of hostility to God. . . . The
prophet regards the law of God as a single integral whole."[43]
Ezekiel addresses "the murderous city" thus:

. . . where people despise their fathers and mothers; where they
ill-treat the settlers; where they oppress the widow and the
orphan; where you have no reverence for my sanctuaries and
profane my sabbaths; where informers incite to bloodshed;
where there are people who eat on the mountains and couple
promiscuously; where men uncover their father's nakedness;
where they force women in their unclean condition; where one
man engages in filthy practices with his neighbour's wife, another defiles himself with his daughter-in-law, another violates
his sister, his own father's daughter; where people take bribes
for shedding blood; you charge usury and interest, you rob your
neighbour by extortion, you forget all about me—it is the Lord
Yahweh who speaks. (Ez. 22:7–12)

It is evident that many secular crimes are condemned as immoral *in se* and not for any cultic connection. Adultery and incest were wrong, like extortion and robbery, not because of any connection with Canaanite worship but because of Israel's apodictic laws.[44] Because of these secular offenses, the holy city and its temple were doomed.

These selections from the preaching of the pre-exilic prophets, ranging from Amos and Hosea in the mid-eighth century to Jeremiah and Ezekiel in the seventh and sixth centuries, bring us to the following conclusions:

1. Sexual sins like adultery and prostitution, whether involving gentile or Israelite people, are condemned along with other social abuses as evil *in se* and not simply as Canaanite fertility rites which invaded Israelite sanctuaries.

2. These *social* or *secular* offenses constituted the principal reasons why Israel's *religious* covenant with the Lord was broken. The classical prophets rose to defend the covenant not because of major interest in liturgical reform but because of their compassion for the oppressed. They would have impressed their hearers as very secular.

3. The norm for judging social abuses was traced back by the prophets to ancient collections of apodictic laws which originated in the desert days of the exodus and covenant. They implied a period of liberation from slavery and an initial organization of political and religious life. They were a basic charter of clan tradition. The prophets then did not judge by cultic standards which emerged in a later Canaanite setting but by these earliest law codes.

4. Prophets spoke out against kings and priests when these highest civil and religious authorities no longer defended the rights of the oppressed and even became oppressors themselves by their own immorality. As such, prophets were not liturgical ministers (symbolic representatives of God) but his direct messengers, summoned personally for the work at hand. "The lion roars: who can help feeling afraid? The Lord Yahweh speaks: who can refuse to prophesy?" (Am. 3:8).

For all these reasons we conclude that the prophets condemned all adultery and prostitution, literally as such.

We end with an insight into prophetic morality, not developed in this essay but one with which we can re-examine the biblical texts cited here. The prophets lived in heroic days of stark simplicity; the stakes were as high as life or death, reformation or destruction. Heroic decisions were almost the order of the day. Such drastic and vigorous demands cannot become daily obligations, hammered into "casuistic laws" which interpret and apply the ideals of the people. Still the ideals must be sustained as apodictic laws which set the policy[45] and can be called upon in crucial moments of social and religious reform. Each individual person is summoned to the heroic at key moments of life in order to fulfill the divine ideal for sexual and social fulfillment. The Church ought to be compassionate and adaptable in "casuistic" or case laws, heroic and traditional in "apodictic" laws of sexual morality.

## NOTES

1. On the question of the interplay of the two testaments in Christian moral foundations, see J. Jensen, "Old Testament, New Testament, and Christian Morality," *The Living Light* 12 (1975), 487–507.

2. See especially pp. 14, 16, 30, 189f., 244.

3. On this see the comments of George T. Montague, "A Scriptural Response to the Report on Human Sexuality," *America* (October 29, 1977), 284f.

4. The accuracy of the assertion of biblical inconsistency and "plurality" in this area must itself be challenged. There is no biblical text, for example, that condones what is understood to be adultery. The only variable is the understanding of what constitutes adultery. Far from being inconsistent, the term undergoes a development by becoming stricter and more inclusive, so that the husband, too, can be guilty of adultery against his wife (Luke 16:18).

5. When assertions are made concerning chronological development, they usually rest on questionable assumptions. See, e.g., the statement on p. 17 that "under the impact of the prophets, cultic notions of pu-

rity were interiorized and transformed into profound moral concepts."
This reflects a Wellhausenian idea of the development of Israel's
religion that few moderns would accept so uncritically. Most of the
cultic laws of the Old Testament are found in P, which reached its
present form centuries after the great pre-exilic prophets. Much of its
material is undoubtedly earlier, but most of the cultic *emphasis* is attributable to P and datable to post-exilic times. On the other hand
much of Israel's earliest legislation, antedating the great prophets,
shows a deep moral sensitivity; cf. Ex. 22:21–24, 25–27; 23:1f., 4f.,
6–8, 9. The same sort of moral sensitivity is found in Israel's wisdom
tradition, which in part at least antedates the prophets and may be
the origin of prophetic teaching on many points, including their polemic against insincere sacrifice (cf., e.g., Prov. 15:8; 21:3, 27), a position found in the wisdom tradition outside of Israel at least as far
back as the twenty-second century in Egypt. See "The Instructions of
Meri-ka-re." ANET 417. See further O. S. Rankin, *Israel's Wisdom
Literature: Its Bearing on Theology and the History of Religion*
(New York: Schocken Books, 1969 [c. 1936]), p. 15; Johannes Hem-
pel, *Das Ethos des Alten Testaments* (BZAW 67; Berlin: Töpel-
mann, 1964), pp. 28, 224; S. Terrien, "Amos and Wisdom," *Israel's
Prophetic Heritage, Essays in Honor of James Muilenburg*, eds.,
B. W. Anderson and W. Harrelson (New York: Harper & Row,
1962), pp. 108–15; J. W. Whedbee, *Isaiah & Wisdom* (Nashville:
Abingdon, 1971), pp. 14–22; J. Jensen, *The Use of tôrâ by Isaiah: His
Debate with the Wisdom Tradition* (CBQMS 3; Washington, D.C.:
The Catholic Biblical Association of America, 1973), pp. 73–83.

6. In a joint critique, undertaken with Scripture colleagues, I hope to
comment on other matters dealt with in the Report. Publication plans
are presently only tentative, so no closer specification can be given at
this point. Relevant material will be found in my article "Does *Porneia* Mean Fornication? A Critique of Bruce Malina," *NovT* 20
(1978), 161–84.

7. The ability of the authors of the Report to uncover motivations
behind complicated complexes of laws is truly astounding. Their own
position, stated in the first sentence of Chapter 1, is that "the Sacred
Scriptures are not concerned with sexuality as such" (p. 7), and the
present disclaimer ("not in the nature of human sexuality") coheres
with this. In the light of what follows, the a priori assertion collapses.

8. G. von Rad, "The Joseph Narrative and Ancient Wisdom," in *The
Problem of the Hexateuch and Other Essays*, tr. E. W. T. Dicken
(New York: McGraw-Hill, 1966), pp. 292–300.

9. See, for example, "The Instructions of the Vizier Ptah-hotep,"
ANET 412, and "The Instructions of Ani," ANET 420. In each case
the warning against adultery is followed shortly by rules for the care of
one's own wife—the same pattern that is found in Prov. 5:1–11,
15–20.

10. See "The Instructions of Ani," *ANET* 420, and compare it with Prov. 7:18–21. Both texts refer to the repeated urgings, the absence of the husband.

11. "The Instructions of the Vizier Ptah-hotep," *ANET* 413. The Egyptian term is the sense-equivalent of the Hebrew *tôʿēbâ*, though they are not etymologically related. The Report's faulty discussion of *tôʿēbâ* will have to be dealt with elsewhere.

12. This area, too, I hope to cover in greater detail in the joint critique referred to above, n. 6.

13. See especially J. Bottéro and H. Petschow, "Homosexualität," *Reallexikon der Assyriologie und Vorderasiatischen Archäologie* 4 (Berlin/New York: Walter de Gruyter, 1972–75), pp. 459–68.

14. C. Stuhlmueller, "Human Sexuality—A Biblical Appraisal: The Old Testament." *The Bible Today* 93 (1977), 1437.

15. Cf. H. W. Wolff, "The Elohistic Fragments in the Pentateuch," in *The Vitality of Old Testament Traditions,* eds., W. Brueggemann and H. W. Wolff (Atlanta: John Knox Press, 1975), pp. 70–71: "Thus we see that the Elohist has made a very involved theological problem of guilt out of the unambiguous failing of the patriarch."

16. *Human Sexuality* frequently states that certain sexual acts are condemned not for their sexual connotation but for their association with Canaanite worship; see n. 2 above.

17. P. 16.

18. G. von Rad, *Wisdom in Israel* (Nashville: Abingdon, 1972), pp. 187–88; W. McKane, *Proverbs* (Philadelphia: Westminster Press, 1970), p. 284; L. G. Perdue, *Wisdom and Cult* (Society of Biblical Literature Dissertation Series, 30; Missoula: Scholars Press, 1977), pp. 154–55. The first two authors are quoted in *The Bible Today, art. cit.,* 1441; Perdue writes: "But the warning against cultic involvement in the fertility religions known to the Israelites is not based upon sacral law issuing forth from the Yahwistic polemic against the Canaanite and Mesopotamian fertility cults, but rather upon the sapiential ethos in which certain sexual relationships were completely rejected as being out of step with the righteous order of society expressed in social mores and customs." The prophets, as we shall see later in this chapter, associated sexual offenses more closely with the Mosaic covenant, yet the norm of judgment came from the secular, not the ritual domain.

19. Cf. C. Stuhlmueller, "History as the Revelation of God in the Pentateuch," *Chicago Studies* 17 (Spring 1978), 29–43.

20. Cf. R. de Vaux, "Jerusalem and the Prophets," in *Interpreting the Prophetic Tradition* (New York: Ktav, 1969), pp. 275–300, with an augmented revision in *Revue Biblique* 73 (1965), 481–509; J. Gray, "Kingship of God in the Prophets and in the Psalms," *Vetus*

*Testamentum* 11 (1961), 1–29; R. A. F. MacKenzie, "The City and Israelite Religion," *Catholic Biblical Quarterly* 25 (1963), 60–70.

21. Cf. C. Stuhlmueller, "The Process of Humanization," in *Thirsting for the Lord: Essays in Biblical Theology*, ed., M. Romanus Penrose (N.Y.: Alba House, 1977), pp. 217–29.

22. C. Westermann, *Basic Forms of Prophetic Speech* (Philadelphia: Westminster Press, 1967), p. 131.

23. N. W. Porteous, "The Basis of the Ethical Teaching of the Prophets," in *Studies in Old Testament Prophecy*, ed., H. H. Rowley (Edinburgh: Clark, 1949), p. 152.

24. Cf. Dennis J. McCarthy, *Old Testament Covenant. A Survey of Current Opinions* (Richmond: John Knox Press, 1972), pp. 17–20, where particular attention is drawn to W. Beyerlin, *Origins and History of the Oldest Sinaitic Traditions* (Oxford: Blackwell, 1965).

25. For this translation, see H. W. Wolff, *Joel and Amos* (Philadelphia: Fortress Press, 1977), p. 153.

26. Cf. ibid., pp. 152–53.

27. Cf. Am. 3:1; 9:7. In the latter passage Amos compares the exodus to other migrations in ancient Near Eastern history and asks the tantalizing question: is Israel's any different?

28. For this translation, see Wolff, op. cit., p. 133.

29. Ibid., p. 165.

30. Ibid., pp. 133–34.

31. Ibid., p. 167.

32. A few manuscripts read a different Hebrew word, *šbʿ*, which would translate here, "though I received their oath." The spelling of the two Hebrew words, *śbʿ* and *šbʿ* is so similar that confusion is possible. A number of authors prefer *šbʿ*: A. Weiser, *Der Prophet Jeremia* (Göttingen: Vandenhoeck & Ruprecht, 1960), p. 42; A. Penna, *Geremia* (Torino: Marietta, 1952), p. 68; J. Bright, *Jeremiah* (Garden City, N.Y.: Doubleday, 1965), p. 36. This allusion to an oath strengthens the covenant setting for this passage.

33. Bright, op. cit., p. 36, translates *nʾp* more generally as "they whored."

34. The Hebrew text reads *gdd*, "to gash oneself"—Jer. 16:6; 41:5—with cultic meaning (cf. Deut. 14:1; 1 Kgs. 18:28; Mic. 4:14). Most commentators change to *grr*, following the Greek Septuagint, with the meaning "to tarry" or "to delay."

35. Cf. D. R. Hillers, *Treaty-Curses and the Old Testament Prophets* (Rome: Pontifical Biblical Institute, 1964), pp. 58–62.

36. Cf. J. Scharbert, "Formgeschichte und Exegese von Ex. 34, 6f. und seiner Parallelen," *Biblica* 38 (1957), 130–50.

37. H. W. Wolff, *Hosea* (Philadelphia: Fortress Press, 1974), p. 67.

38. Ibid., p. 68.

39. E. Hammershaimb, "On the Ethics of the Old Testament Prophets," *Congress Volume Oxford 1959* (Leiden: Brill, 1960), p. 98.

40. Bright, op. cit., p. 56; G. P. Couturier, "Jeremiah," *Jerome Biblical Commentary* (Englewood Cliffs, N.J.: Prentice-Hall, 1968) 19:25; W. Rudolph, *Jeremia*, 3.Aufl. (Tübingen: Mohr, 1968), p. 53.

41. Art. cit., p. 98.

42. L. Koehler and W. Baumgartner, *Lexicon in Veteris Testamenti Libros* (Grand Rapids, Mich.: Eerdmans, 1958), p. 1022.

43. W. Eichrodt, *Ezekiel* (Philadelphia: Westminster Press, 1970), p. 309.

44. D. M. G. Stalker, *Ezekiel* (London: SCM Press, 1968), p. 185, lines up the references to apodictic laws.

45. According to G. E. Mendenhall, *Law and Covenant in Israel and the Ancient Near East* (Pittsburgh: The Biblical Colloquium, 1955), pp. 3–23.

## Chapter Two

✣

# THE WITNESS OF
# THE NEW TESTAMENT

### EUGENE A. LaVERDIERE, S.S.S.

Anthony Kosnik and his co-authors have raised a much needed
warning against the simplistic and uncritical application of New
Testament passages on sexual morality to modern situations. The
basis for their *cautio* is that all such New Testament statements
were occasional and historically conditioned by the various ancient contexts to which they responded. This applies to the teaching of Jesus as well as to that of St. Paul.[1]

It should be noted that the authors' contention concerning sexual ethics is not specific to this area but equally applicable to
every other aspect of life, doctrinal and ethical, which is treated in
the New Testament. They have thus affirmed a general principle
of contemporary New Testament scholarship, which recognizes
that the Scriptures must be studied historically and critically for
their modern-day relevance to emerge. Only then does it become·
possible to discern the implications of New Testament proclamation, prophecy, and teaching for life in a vastly altered situation of Church and world.

Recourse to the New Testament in developing a contemporary
sexual ethics thus includes two major investigative stages. By contemporary convention, the first, which deals with the text in its
ancient context, is broadly termed exegesis. The second stage,

which confronts the ancient text with our modern situation and translates it into contemporary theology, is called hermeneutics. Without the former, hermeneutics is pursued independently of any controls or limits provided by the text. Without the latter, exegesis may prove interesting to the historian of Christian origins, but the endeavor prescinds from the most important issue of the place of Scripture in the ongoing life of the Church.

In the short section of their book which formally addresses the sexual ethics of the New Testament, the authors were quite understandably unable to go much beyond their *cautio* and the affirmation of a few general principles. Their observations, however, were limited almost exclusively to the general area of exegesis. Because of this, one might be left with the impression that the New Testament is all but irrelevant in matters of sexual morality. Their effort to liberate contemporary sexual ethics from the limits imposed by past conditions which no longer obtain would thus result in an obvious injustice to the living faith of the Church which continues to draw life and inspiration from the New Testament writings.

This chapter takes up the invitation of the authors to continue and expand the discussion they have initiated. In the first section I shall explore the New Testament teaching on sexuality exegetically and historically. The second section is devoted to hermeneutics. Exploring the relationship between the Church today and the first stages of its emergence in earliest times, I shall attempt to draw out the meaning of New Testament teaching on sexual ethics for the modern situation.

## I. Sexual Ethics in the New Testament: Exegesis

Within the rather ample and varied body of New Testament writings, explicit references to sexual attitudes and behavior are quite meager. In this, the New Testament stands in sharp contrast with the modern world, where sexual mores and ethics constitute a major concern. It may be that the New Testament challenges and calls into question our preoccupation with sexual ethics and the central position it has taken in a wide range of human and Christian consciousness. The relative silence of the New Testament would thus be extremely significant.

In order to explore that significance and to define its challenge, however, we cannot remain at the level of general observations. We must first differentiate the various stages in the social development of the early Church and examine the special context of the community being addressed. As we shall see, greater or lesser attention to sexual mores was closely related to the Church's evolving identity, a process in which some levels of development exhibited far greater concern with sexual ethics than others. Second, one must consider the author's stance vis-à-vis the community along with his general theological perspective and presuppositions. Sexual issues will thus be situated in the broader context of Christian life and in relation to a work's special purpose and concerns.

In this section, I shall accordingly attempt to situate sexual ethics first in the earliest stage of ecclesial development when the Church was primarily a movement characterized by a strong apostolic and evangelical outward thrust. I shall then examine those texts which pertain to the early Christian communities or churches which resulted from this creative proclamation of the gospel. At this point, our primary focus will be on the Pauline letters. Finally, I shall explore the sexual ethics of the gospel narratives, literary syntheses associated with long-established churches and with the emergence of a universal Church. Since the teaching of Jesus was integrated, interpreted, and transmitted within these post-Easter literary documents, it will be examined as part of these gospel syntheses.

I recognize that the limits of this study make a comprehensive study impossible. I have consequently selected a number of important texts and shall emphasize methodology in my analysis. I thus hope to facilitate further investigation. Like the authors of *Human Sexuality*,[2] I invite the scholarly and pastoral community to join in an ongoing exploration and discussion.

FIRST EVANGELIZATION AND THE EARLY CHURCHES

The earliest Christian proclamation of the gospel did not focus on the heritage of Jesus' teaching but on the absolutely fundamental event of Jesus' death-resurrection and his expected return in glory. Following the shock of Jesus' death, the apostolic community had been quickened by its experience of the risen Lord. In light of these events, previous experiences in the company of the historical Jesus and many other concerns of daily living receded temporarily into the background. Accordingly, the apostolic proclamation addressed only the most fundamental issues of human life and death.

Jesus' death-resurrection had revealed the ultimate value of life and the meaningfulness of death as life-giving. By raising Jesus from the dead, God had shown that those who gave of themselves unto death found not death but new life. Infused by the Christ-experience of God's glory, that is by the appearances of the risen Jesus, the earliest proclamation thus consisted in a communication of radical hope. In this context, which can be recovered from the early creeds, hymns, and liturgical texts cited by Paul (e.g., 1 Cor. 15:3b–5; Rom. 1:3–4; Phil. 2:6–11; 1 Cor. 11:23–25), particular ethical questions had little or no place.

First evangelization, however, was not without ethical implications. As interpreted by Luke in the various discourses of Acts, it constituted a general invitation to conversion and life's reorientation. This bond between the gospel's proclamation and a Christian's ethical stance can also be discerned in Paul's writing when he exhorts his readers to model their behavior on the attitude attributed to Christ in the Philippians' hymn (Phil. 2:3–5) or when he argues for faith attitudes and behavior consistent with the Christian credal and liturgical formulas (1 Cor. 15:12–58; 11:26–34). From a very early time, therefore, if not from the beginning, Christians were aware that the fundamental gospel proclamation had ethical implications. Only gradually, however, would the latter unfold in relation to a variety of contextual challenges. We can thus understand why the most basic evangelization included no reference to sexual issues; just as other specific issues, they were displaced by primordial concerns. Consequently, silence cannot be interpreted as implying that these were insignificant or irrelevant.

The above considerations refer to the absolute beginnings of the Church in Jerusalem as well as to its relative beginnings in the broadening geographical sphere of the Mediterranean world, as the first apostolic figures gradually reached out to people who had not yet heard the good news of salvation and new life in Christ.

Those who first heard and accepted the gospel in any given social context were bonded into communities of Christian solidarity. Together the Christians gradually worked out the implications of gospel living. Relatively little primary data is available to demonstrate this process in the earliest days. However, thanks to Paul's first letter to the Christians of Thessalonica (*circa* A.D. 51) we do have some material on developments in that community, including an important passage which refers to sexual ethics (4:1–8).[3]

In a brief introduction (4:1–2), Paul first exhorts the Christians to develop along the lines he had already presented and personally demonstrated during his brief period of evangelization at Thessalonica. The unit is thus important not only as the earliest Pauline literary statement on the subject of sexuality, but as an indication of the rule played by sexual ethics in the apostolic teaching which spelled out the implications of the gospel's first proclamation. It may be that the earliest preaching at Jerusalem had not moved so quickly to particular issues. The Thessalonian mission, however, benefited from Christianity's twenty-year experience of evangelization.

Paul then summarizes his teaching as follows. Since God had given the Thessalonians the Holy Spirit, they were called to holy living (vv. 7–8), and sexual immorality was not consistent with the gift and call they had received (vv. 3–8). This gift, be it recalled, had come through Paul's word or gospel proclamation, a word which they had received, not as the word of men, but as it truly is, the word of God at work within the believers (2:13). The gospel thus constituted an internalized life principle[4] which called for certain attitudes and behavior in sexual matters. This new life or Christian nature was consequently the wellspring of right living as well as the point of departure for ethical reflection.

For sexual immorality, Paul uses the term *porneia*, a generic term whose specific meaning must be determined from the context. In vv. 4–6, he discusses two fairly specific but complex issues. First, each one must guard his body, taking a wife for himself, that is have sexual relations with his own wife, and he must do so in holiness and honor (v. 4), not in the passion and lust of the gentiles who do not know God (v. 5). Second, he must not transgress and wrong his brother in this matter (v. 6).

From the point of view of the Christians' relationship to God, sexual ethics is thus grounded in the will of God who called them to holiness (v. 3) as well as in the gospel gift of the Holy Spirit (v. 8) through which they know God (v. 5). From the point of view of the Christians' relationship to one another, sexual ethics is grounded in their specifically Christian nature, a nature which calls for honor and respect for one's marital partner, for oneself, and for one's brother and which therefore precludes adultery as a breach of Christian community solidarity. The passage thus approaches sexuality with a strong appreciation for human and Christian dignity and for interpersonal relationships within the Christian community.

While the passage is short, it does reveal that sexual ethical considerations were extremely important as a consequence of the gospel, even in a social context strongly focused on eschatological realities and the Lord's parousia (4:13–5:11). The remarkable thing is not so much that the passage is short, but that it is present at all in a brief exuberant letter which takes up none but the most pressing issues.

In the second letter to the Christians of Thessalonica (circa A.D. 52), which develops some of the issues taken for granted or inadequately treated in the first, Paul does not allude to sexual issues. In the letter to the Galatians (circa A.D. 54), however, where he argues strongly for the freedom which characterizes Christians and for the kind of behavior which springs from that freedom, he includes a number of sexual aberrations in a partial list of evils which proceed from the flesh (Gal. 5:19–21).[5] The terms which Paul uses in the list are rather general, evoking a whole range of overlapping attitudes and behavior. Concrete application to specific cases is then left open to the Christian sensitivity of the addressees.

The fruits of the internalized Spirit are listed in 5:22–23. They had already been summarized in 5:13–14, however, as Christian love of neighbor, in which each one is at the service of the others. The deeds of the flesh (5:19–21), on the other hand, had been summarized in 5:15, where Paul turned to graphic metaphors in warning against biting and devouring one another unto mutual destruction. Along with other evils, immorality (porneia), impurity (akatharsia), licentiousness (aselgeia), and carousing

(*komoi*) are consequently to be avoided because they are inconsistent with the nature of the Christian and destructive of the
new Christian self and of the community. As in 1 Thess. 4:1–8,
Christian dignity and community solidarity are thus given as the
norm of sexual attitudes and behavior.

Ultimately, human sexuality is governed by the biblically
founded Christian law of love (5:13–14). Everything which
stands contrary to genuine love of neighbor and of oneself must
be considered aberrant. When sexual behavior is a concrete expression of this love it is properly Christian and one of the fruits
of the Spirit. It is thus integrated in a life characterized by love,
joy, peace, kindness, goodness, faithfulness, gentleness, and self-
control (5:22). This does not occur, however, unless the unre-
deemed flesh has been crucified with Christ (5:24). In sexual
matters, as in other areas of life, Paul does not allow us to escape
the challenge of the crucifixion.

The first letter to the Corinthians 5–7 is the longest Pauline
treatment of sexuality. Called forth by a deeply troubled situation, the letter (*circa* A.D. 56–57) confronts a general community
context of factional and destructive divisiveness and lack of solidarity (1:10–17). In 5:1–13, a particular case leads Paul to deal
with the question of excluding immoral persons from the community. To appreciate the unit's significance, we must carefully distinguish the Church's development at Corinth from its first
evangelization. The party in question, who was having sexual relations with his father's wife, that is his stepmother (5:1–2), had already responded to Paul's gospel proclamation and was now a
member of the Christian community.

As we indicated earlier, the initial proclamation had been issued
to all without distinction, calling them to conversion and new life.
Those who accepted the gospel, however, were distinguished from
those who did not, and their membership in the community of
salvation placed certain demands on them and created legitimate
expectations in their regard on the part of others. When these
were unfulfilled, they returned to their pre-evangelical condition
and once again stood in need of evangelization. Recognizing that
they no longer served the community in its internal life and mis-
sionary efforts, they were to be excluded from the community and

treated as non-members. Toleration of their presence could only
weaken the community and its efforts for Christ. Exclusion from
the community, be it noted, was in view of the destruction or
crucifixion of the flesh that once again such persons might be
gifted with the Spirit and saved on the day of the Lord (5:5).

Paul's teaching is thus to be approached from the standpoint of
a community which had but recently been evangelized and which
retained a strong sense of its evangelical mission to the non-Christian world all about it. It did not stem from a Church with a
strong sense of its universality, which was politically and socially
established, and whose primary concern lay in its internal development. Had the latter been the case, Paul's teaching might have
been quite different.

Matters at Corinth had fallen to such a state that Christians
were even dragging one another into civil courts (6:1–8). This situation, however, was but one of many symptoms of disintegration
which Paul discusses in a warning against self-deception (6:9–20).

Along with idolaters, thieves, misers, drunkards, slanderers, and
robbers, Paul lists fornicators, adulterers, and sensually soft men
who lie with males (6:9–10). The behavior of all such men, summarized in the term unholy (cf. 1 Thess. 4:3, 7), is deemed unworthy of those who have been sanctified in baptism and justified
in the name of the Lord Jesus Christ and in the Spirit of our God
(6:11).

Unlike Gal. 5:19–21, the Corinthians list does not refer to the
vices themselves, but to categories of people who are characterized
by the vices. Nevertheless, it clearly approaches the latter from
the point of view of their relationships and behavior. Deceiving
themselves, some Corinthian Christians have committed themselves to an evil course of life, and consequently they will not inherit the kingdom of God (cf. Gal. 5:21).

The modern distinction between a person's basic sexual orientation and sexual behavior itself does not enter into this picture.
Paul's warning, therefore, cannot be interpreted as a condemnation of homosexuals as such, for example. In the case of all behavior, sexual or other, the question remains one of living according to one's fundamental Christian nature, which calls not for
self-service, but for the service of the community. Paul does not

consider homosexual behavior to be consistent with the nature of the Christian who has been freed by the gospel and whose life must unfold for the development of the community.

In 6:12–20, Paul turns to a particular case of immorality, that of sexual intercourse with a prostitute. General principles had sufficed to establish the need for moral living and for seeking what is right and good. A particular case, however, calls for further reflection and specification of these principles. Paul therefore points out that some forms of living in freedom are actually self-enslaving (v. 12). In this he responds to the Corinthians' self-deception which saw a normal link between the body and sexual expression, just as the stomach and food are made for one another (v. 13a). In a sense this was an argument from nature, not unlike Paul's own approach to such questions. The problem with it lay in the perception and appreciation of the Christian nature and in particular of the Christian body which is related to the Lord and which will join him in the resurrection (vv. 13b–14). Members of Christ, the Christians are members of one another and this excludes relationships which are incompatible with the members' Christian identity and solidarity.

Paul's point becomes extremely clear if the prostitution in question is sacred prostitution. The latter would then establish a relationship to a form of worship and religious allegiance other than Christian and would therefore work for the disintegration of the body of the Lord. Paul's mention of idolaters between fornicators and adulterers in 6:9 supports this interpretation, as also the manner he has linked relations with a prostitute (vv. 9–20) to recourse to the law courts of unbelievers (6:1–8), a link which remains otherwise enigmatic. The enslavement mentioned in v. 12 thus consists in a return to one's pre-Christian state from which the Christian had been liberated (cf. Gal. 5:13), that is cleansed, made holy, and justified (v. 11).

We must not conclude, however, that Paul tolerated other forms of prostitution. The list in 6:9–10 includes many categories which are enslaving of self and destructive of community, quite apart from incompatible relationships with the non-Christian political, juridical, and religious world of Corinth. In Pauline terms, the question thus remains whether relations with any prostitute can be considered consistent with the development unto resurrection (6:14) of one who has been redeemed at a price in view of God's glory (6:20) and whose body is sanctified by the Holy Spirit (6:19).

In chapter 7, Paul's entire teaching concerning marriage and various states of life is conditioned by the general rule that each one should remain in the state of life, married or other, in which he was at the time of the Lord's call (vv. 17, 20, 24). In v. 26 this general rule is reiterated in a statement which also discloses its basis: the Christians were living in a time of stress, a time which would be short (v. 29) and soon climax in the passing away of the world as we know it (v. 31). Given this eschatological view, it is thus better for Christians not to assume a new state of life and its responsibilities. The concerns and trials involved in changing their state would divide their attention and distract them from the affairs of the Lord (vv. 32–35). As Paul perceived it, the time in which they were living also called for detachment from all concerns, attitudes, and activities which were intrinsically associated with this passing world (vv. 29–31). In all these matters, Paul recognizes that the ideals he has presented are contingent on the experiential situation of his addressees and that their personal needs might call for another course of action (vv. 2, 9, 28, 36, 39). Although all have been gifted by God, all have not been gifted in the same way (v. 7). In all the cases discussed, save the question of divorce (vv. 10–11), Paul presents his teaching as his preference (v. 7) or opinion (v. 12) as one who by the Lord's mercy is trustworthy (v. 25). As Paul himself notes, such teaching must not be placed on the same level as those commands which are from the Lord (vv. 12, 25).

The above analysis and reflections illustrate how sexual issues arose and were treated in several of the early churches which emerged in response to the proclamation of the gospel. In each case, while local histories and contexts varied, sexual matters joined other areas of ethical concern as Christians gradually positioned themselves with regard to their world environment. In places as diverse as Thessalonica, Galatia, and Corinth, the fundamental determinant of sexual attitudes and behavior always remained the Christian nature of those who had accepted the gospel and were bonded by the Spirit in developing communities.

TOWARD A UNIVERSAL CHURCH

With the passing decades, the early evangelical movement and the emerging communities developed into consolidated churches with a carefully defined sense of their identity vis-à-vis the greater world and the challenge of history. The articulation of this identity can be found in each of the four gospel narratives and their presentation of the teaching of Jesus. Contextualized by Jesus' death-resurrection and his expected return in glory, the latter had been shaped and interpreted by tradition, that is by the very life of the churches which ever sought to affirm Jesus' message in its relevance to their concrete historical situation. In this process, the Gospels constituted syntheses of basic Christianity in which the various issues of life were presented in their relationship to the entire Christian challenge.

Apart from Mark (*circa* A.D. 70), these Gospels reveal a growing sense of the Church's universality. Matthew and Luke, writing in the ninth decade, and John, whose Gospel was completed in the tenth decade, thus prescind from questions of purely local or immediate concern and deal with issues of universal application. Although Mark may not have possessed this same awareness, his Gospel was received by communities as varied as those of Matthew and Luke, for whom the first gospel synthesis provided an important literary source. Mark thus constituted a transitional factor in the development of ecclesial universality. Accordingly, both the formulation and the relative position of sexual ethics in the four Gospels must be taken very seriously within the context of each Gospel's articulation of Christian identity.

The most important passage in Mark's Gospel concerning Christian sexuality is 10:2–12, where Jesus' careful response to a test of the Pharisees is situated in a long unit on discipleship as the way of Jesus' cross (8:27–10:52). In that unit, Jesus affirms the value of marriage and the evil of its dissolution. Husband and wife are one (10:8) as they follow in Jesus' steps (8:34), not seeking their own importance but as servants of all (9:35). The demands of the cross thus transcend the ethic of Moses, who allowed divorce (vv. 3–5). To accept this teaching without fear, however, those who accept Jesus' call must want to see and have their blindness removed by Christ (10:46–52).

Within the second part (9:30–10:31) of the unit on discipleship, the question of marriage is associated with Jesus' teaching on attachment to riches (10:17–27). In both matters, Christians must share the simplicity of a child as they accept God's reign (10:13–16). The Gospel thus addresses various aspects of life in the world, while recognizing that in the future risen life even the marriage relationship will be transcended (12:25). In this, as in the remainder of his Gospel, Mark responds to the apocalyptic tendencies of the community, for whom earthly realities and relationships held no hope and were about to be destroyed (13:5–7). His affirmation of the marriage bond is thus a positive value judgment on life in history. Passing through difficult times, the Christians must be faithful to the end. Responding to a crisis situation, the author presents all aspects of the Christian challenge in absolute terms calling for a renewed firm decision to follow Christ. Hence his unyielding position on the indissolubility of marriage (10:9–12), whose formulation betrays a marked egalitarian attitude toward men and women.

Mark's position on marriage and divorce (10:11–12) was retained by Luke, who included it in Jesus' teaching (16:18) along the great journey to Jerusalem (9:51–24:53). In Luke, however, the question received far less emphasis. Writing for communities called to a long-term insertion in history, Luke tempers the absoluteness of the Markan challenge (Mk. 8:34; Lk. 9:23). Confronting the day to day of Christian life in the world, Luke recognizes human lapses and places great emphasis on forgiveness and reconciliation in the teaching of Jesus (7:36–50). His pastoral intention is consequently directed, not so much to bringing the community to a radical and staunch decision and fidelity, but to the continual need to extend a gesture of peace and solidarity to those who drifted away and who returned with love (17:3–4). Going beyond hospitality, the community must actively seek out and find those who had been lost (15:1–31; 24:13–35). Although the Gospel shows little concern for specific sexual issues, it does reveal a general attitude toward all who have sinned, whether sexually or otherwise.

It should be noted that, unlike Mk. 10:29 and Mt. 10:37; 19:29, Luke includes the wife among those persons whom Christians must leave for the sake of the kingdom of God (18:29–30) For Luke, however, leaving is a matter of attitude and not of physical abandonment, as we observe from the story of Levi, who left everything to become Jesus' follower (5:28) but who then gave a large reception for Jesus in his house (5:29). Leaving everything or someone is thus a state of detachment in which values are respected and properly subordinated. To leave one's wife is consequently not necessarily an option for celibacy. Christians frequently appear as couples and families in the Lukan communities (e.g., Acts 5:1; 10:1, 44, 48; 18:2–3, 18–19, 26).

Matthew's teaching on sexual matters is included first in Jesus' discourse on the mount (5:27–32), a synthesis of Christian life attitudes which focused the community's identity in relation to the synagogue from which it had been ejected. At this point two important questions are treated, the need for a chaste interior attitude (vv. 27–30) and the matter of divorce (vv. 31–32). In 19:3–13, the author presents and adapts Mark's teaching (10:2–12) and discusses the difficulty of accepting it even in its modified form.

The community must disassociate itself from the hypocrites and not perform religious acts for others to see (6:1–18). The value of such acts stems from the Christians' hidden interior attitude which the Father both sees and rewards. The same principle applies to acts such as adultery, whose evil resides not in the act alone but in the interior disposition which precedes it and which it fulfills (cf. 15:17–20).

Adjustment to an ongoing mission to the gentile world (28:18–20) and to the realities of this challenge also led Matthew to temper Mark's position on divorce and adultery. While the prohibition of divorce remains the general rule, the author recognizes situations which may call for divorce and he accepts possible exceptions in cases where unchastity has disrupted marital solidarity. The same exception is introduced in 19:9, where it modifies Mark's unconditional view. In the latter context, Matthew goes on to respond to the objection that this teaching, even in its tempered application, is too difficult and makes marriage impossible.

To accept Jesus' demand concerning marriage, one must be gifted
to do so (19:11). Christians are thus asked to call on their nature
as Christians; so transformed they should be able to accept Jesus'
teaching in their new life context just as some of their fellows are
able to accept life outside of marriage (19:12). Like Paul (1 Cor.
7:7), Matthew thus recognizes a variety of gifts and corresponding life-styles within the Christian community.

From the above presentation, it appears that the Gospels considered marriage and fidelity to be extremely important in Christianity. At the same time, we note that the matter was but one of
many realities in Christian life. The synoptic Gospels reflect this
relative position of sexuality and concentrate their attention on issues which are of deeper import and which give meaning to the
marriage commitment. The same is even more striking in John's
Gospel, where little attention is paid to sexual matters apart from
the narrative of the wedding at Cana (2:1–11) and Jesus' discussion with the Samaritan woman at the well (4:16–18). The value
of marriage is implied in Jesus' very presence at the feast and marital fidelity affirmed by his observation that the woman's succes-
sive husbands were not really her husbands.

John's relative silence in relation to the other Gospels is understandable in light of the fundamental problem he meant to
counter. Addressing a community whose tendency was to escape
the flesh, his concern was not so much with the difficulties which
issued from the flesh as with the need to affirm its importance and
value. For John, the glory of God was manifested in the Word become flesh (1:14), a position which has profound implications for
the sexuality of all who receive that Word while living in the
flesh. The Christians' association with the Word become flesh
constitutes a deep interior source for ethical living and the point
of departure for reflection on what is right and what is wrong in
the area of sexual morality.

## II. The New Testament and the Life of the Church: Hermeneutics

A hermeneutical interpretation of the New Testament's teaching on Christian sexuality must respect the nature of its various
documents. Since without exception all New Testament writings

were fundamentally apostolic and pastoral by intent, their primary application must consequently reside in the area of apostolic and pastoral practice. Our task is thus to discern the position of the Church today in relation to that which underlies the various letters and Gospels which we accept as challenging and normative for Christian living. In light of this relationship, the significance of New Testament ethical teaching for modern life should emerge with considerable clarity.

Some general observations are warranted at the outset. First, at no time in the development of the New Testament did sexual issues displace the central message of Christianity from its position at the heart of the Church's efforts. There were situations, such as that which obtained at Corinth, where they drew more attention than usual. Even there, however, preoccupation with sexual matters was clearly related to deeper realities such as the gospel of the cross. Given the modern world's preoccupation with sexual gratification, does it not then become part of the Church's mission to strive for balance and perspective in human sexual attitudes?

Second, in all the passages we have examined, sexual ethics is grounded in a strong sense of the Christians' new identity in Christ as well as in their community solidarity. Human dignity and respect for other persons are constants of New Testament teaching concerning sexuality. In a world which manipulates human beings by subliminal appeals to the sex drive as isolated from the full reality of personhood, must the Church not use every means to emphasize the dignity of human beings?

Third, the New Testament approaches sexual issues by appealing to the Christian nature of its addressees, men and women gifted by the Spirit and transformed by the gospel which provided an interior principle of moral living and of discernment. All was not specified. Rather, Christians were expected to be able to recognize in individual cases what was in keeping with the Christian self and what was not. Too minute a specification constitutes a return to a law extrinsic to the human person and fails to recognize the new law which is inscribed in the heart. Our fundamental questions should then concern what actually reflects the Christian self in practice and what contributes to the development of a Church community with a mission to the world.

## FIRST EVANGELIZATION AND THE EARLY CHURCHES

As we learn from the New Testament, the Church's initial efforts at evangelization focused on the fundamental reality of the gospel and its call to conversion. Only later did the more specific ethical implications of the gospel come to the fore. At that point, appeal would be made to the Christians' internalized sense of gospel in sorting out moral options and orienting Christian life in the world. Does this not constitute a legitimate pattern for evangelization today? In recent times, the Church no longer assumes that populations which have known Christianity for a long time are actually evangelized. Ethical teaching to such populations has all too often been ineffective precisely because the basic gospel proclamation had not been heard and accepted. Without a personal experience of the Lord, the demands of the gospel in sexual matters make little or no sense.

Only after hearing the gospel and encountering Christ do Christians personally assume their Christianity. Membership in a Christian community then provides a point of insertion into the universal Church. It is there in the local community of believers that moral values develop and the challenge of living according to the gospel is first confronted. As in the case of evangelization, the Church has come to realize that the existence of a true community cannot be assumed. Without a sense of community solidarity, however, and the needed social context for developing one's Christian selfhood, the Christian sexual ethic, which is a personal and social ethic, has no experiential basis. The New Testament thus challenges the Church to build genuine communities in which sexual behavior can be recognized as disruptive or constructive of community life.

Our major difficulty in interpreting Pauline passages such as 1 Corinthians 5–7 lies not in Paul's actual teaching but in recognizing the community's level of development. The fact that Paul excludes an incestuous person from the community in order that this person might be open to salvation is especially difficult to understand. However, once we recognize that this community had no sense of the indelible character of baptism, Paul's position makes sense. For a Church which baptizes infants and maintains baptism's irrevocability, Paul does not provide a warrant for exclusion from the community. His message does imply, however, that a renewed effort at evangelization must be made.

In chapter 7, Paul's expectations with regard to the imminent passing of this world condition the entire statement concerning marriage and various states of life. In a Church which no longer has such expectations, Paul's positions consequently become highly relativized. They do remind us, however, of the ultimate realities which govern all of our life choices and introduce a note of seriousness as decisions are made in light of the passing of each one's world.

## TOWARD A UNIVERSAL CHURCH

Recent times have seen a resurgence of the Church's sense of its universal mission to the world. This renewed attitude gives the gospel syntheses and their effort to formulate a Christian ethic of universal scope great importance for our time. Like the early churches which gave birth to the Gospels, the modern Church is no longer preoccupied with its life as set apart from the world but with life as set apart for the world.

In a world which provides few supports for faithful married life and where family relationships have become tenuous or non-existent, the strong affirmation in all four Gospels of the value of married life, sex, and fidelity is extremely important. Mark's absolute rejection of divorce counters tendencies to take the marriage bond lightly. Luke challenges the Church to extend a welcoming hand of forgiveness and peace to those who have not lived up to their commitment. Matthew emphasizes interior dispositions for a world which values performance and productivity. At the same time, he opens our eyes to possible exceptions to the indissolubility of marriage.

Through the years, every effort has been made to explain away the exception clause which he included in his statement on the indissolubility of marriage. It appears better to accept the obvious and to recognize that Church practice is at variance with the openness which Matthew felt free to affirm even in the face of Mark's absolute position. Following Matthew, the Church would hold that while the marital intention must be unconditional and maintained until death in fidelity, conditions could well arise in which this intention is unfulfilled and the marriage relationship dissolves. Semantics aside, this is quite different from affirming that the marriage never existed.

Joining John's Gospel as well as the other Gospels in affirming the Christian value of married love, the Church is thus challenged to adopt an apostolic and pastoral attitude in sexual matters which is appropriate for its universal mission to the world.

# NOTES

1. *Human Sexuality*, pp. 17–29.
2. Ibid., pp. xiv–xv, 241.
3. The passage includes a number of interpretive difficulties. While in itself the reference to wronging one's brother *en to pragmati* (v. 6) could mean "in business," the context, which refers to sanctification (*hagiasmos,* v. 3) and opposes the latter to uncleanness or impurity (*akatharsia,* v. 7), renders this interpretation quite improbable. Wronging one's brother is thus related to matters of sexual immorality (*porneia,* v. 3). It is most unlikely, however, that the brother in question would have been a prostitute. Paul would not have referred to him as a brother without qualification. Paul could then have been referring to a Christian's forcing himself on his brother or to transgressing his marital rights. Since the text is open to both interpretations, we have no grounds for limiting it to one or the other.

In itself, the expression to *heautou skeuos ktasthai* (v. 4) could refer to control of one's own body, or member as well as to having sexual relations with one's own wife. Given Paul's subsequent reference to wronging or cheating one's brother, the latter is very likely the primary meaning. At the same time, a secondary meaning for what might well be an intentionally general or open expression should not be excluded, especially when the two meanings are so closely related.

4. Cf. 2 Cor. 3:1–3 and Jer. 31–34.
5. The "flesh" in this context must not be interpreted as a sensual or sexual reference. Rather it refers to the whole person from the point of pre-Christian existence and is opposed to the whole person as gifted by the Spirit of God.

## Chapter Three

# THE TRADITION
# IN HISTORY

### DENNIS J. DOHERTY

It is universally customary to congratulate a couple when they announce their engagement. It is customary too, indeed connatural, to rejoice with them on the occasion of their wedding, a celebration to which the Kingdom of Heaven has been likened by Christ himself (Mt. 22:2). But if traditional Catholic moralists are to be believed, both engagement and marriage are combinations of good news and bad.

The good news (Good News) is that an engaged couple publicly proclaim their intention to enter into a union which in common Christian teaching symbolizes that relationship of love between Christ and the Church, the "great mystery" that St. Paul speaks of in Ephesians (5:32f.). For baptized persons, the engaged couple is preparing to enter an institution which, to recall traditional Catholic phraseology, had been elevated by Christ to the dignity of a sacrament. The bad news is that engagement has been regarded by Catholic moralists, who choose their words with casuistic carefulness, as a "necessary proximate occasion of sin"[1] and marriage itself as a state in life in which husband and wife are "permitted" to engage in "shameful acts."[2]

Whence this dichotomy between sacramentality and sexuality? Why this emphasis on the sanctity of marriage and, at the same time, on the shamefulness of sex even within marriage? Pope Pius XII argued in 1951 that the marriage contract confers on spouses the right "to satisfy the inclinations of nature" and he asserted that since pleasure is intended by the Creator spouses "do no evil" in seeking and enjoying it.[3] These remarks about contractual rights guardedly acknowledge that sin is avoided—which is not the same as emphasizing that virtue is practiced; and they hardly resonate the joy ordinarily associated with conjugal intimacy. Twenty-five years later the bishops at Vatican II, in the context of conjugal love, would declare what had long been a matter of common awareness, namely that "This love is uniquely expressed and perfected through the marital act."[4] It took a long time for such an admission to be made in official teaching—and, at that, in the solemn deliberations of an ecumenical council. Why so long?

I alluded above to the universally common instances of engagement and marriage not simply because they go together but, rather, because what has been said of them together in Catholic moral teaching encapsulates virtually the whole Catholic tradition at least until recent years. In that tradition virginity is seen as preferable to marriage, virginal marriage as more noble than one blessed with children, conjugal intercourse as sinless (that, namely, ordered to procreation or to helping one's spouse avoid unchastity), carnal intercourse as at least venially sinful (that, namely, used as a means to avoid personal unchastity or to enjoy pleasure), all non-marital sex as immoral, and all sexual activity not procreatively intended as unnatural whether in or outside of marriage. "Everything is the sum of the past," wrote Teilhard de Chardin, "and nothing is comprehensible except through its history."[5] In this chapter I intend to look at the past in order to show that the traditional teaching on engagement and marriage—more precisely, on the place of human sexuality in the plan of God—is certainly comprehensible from the perspective of history. But I also hope to show that elements of that teaching are no longer tenable. Here I am not referring simply to the pessimism of the past since no one (we may hope) really holds that conjugal sexual activity is shameful.[6] However, the earlier mentality which alleged this shamefulness is what is important, for this same mentality pervades considerations of current questions in sexual ethics. It is perhaps the height of irony that a Church which proclaims the goodness of creation as well as the proneness to sin of fallen man has traditionally felt more at home with a negative attitude toward sex. With regard to human sexuality the goodness of creation came to mean the primacy of procreation. Man's fallen condition, redemption notwithstanding, made him especially prone "to satisfy the inclinations of nature," to recall Pius XII's expression. Accordingly, I hope to argue too that a more judicious evaluation of the historical data can support the theology of sexuality articulated by the authors of *Human Sexuality*.

These authors, to my reading, do a commendable enough job in simply recalling the Christian tradition in its Catholic orientation. But there are glaring lacunae. In the spate of reviews that have appeared not much is said of this chapter which deals with our roots. One writer finds it to be a "competent summary of old work." But she asks: ". . . who really wants to go over all of that ground once more and drag along through the centuries of theological and scriptural ins and outs: St. Paul's use of the word 'flesh,' what the story of Onan really means, how Augustine's pessimism and St. Thomas' bad science affected church teaching?"[7] The answer, of course, is everyone who is seriously interested in having as complete a perspective as possible. Even "old work" can be looked at anew: *non nova sed nove*. Another, an archbishop, finds certain problems with the book: "The first is the treatment of history and tradition. Both are too simplistically brushed aside, almost as if they were at best a weak reflection of human nature. . . . the impression is left that modern existential research suggests that no one in the past really understood human nature."[8] The impression is accurate. But it would be more accurate to hold that the real difficulty with the past is that we thought we really understood human nature; theologians abstracted it and derived moral imperatives from it said to be applicable to almost every situation. The impression is accurate also because no one in the present completely understands human nature either. In fact, referring to what he considers "the value of the Report," the archbishop, after just objecting to the impression left regarding the past, says (italics mine): "It [the Report] indicates that there has been an evolution of thought which has resulted in a change of perspective, a change in emphasis from the legalistic to the personal. It makes the point that the confessor, the counselor, the

teacher cannot be satisfied only with old tools while people are
developing *new understandings of human nature* and human
sexuality."[9]

For their purposes, an overall pastoral approach, the authors of
*Human Sexuality* found a survey or historical overview sufficient;
as a principal consultant I concurred with this since the history of
our sexual ethical teaching has been considered so extensively by
others.[10] So I do not think that it is fully accurate to charge that
"history and tradition . . . are too simplistically brushed aside"
even though they are surveyed without depth. For purposes of this
volume I think it appropriate now to comment on some things
which the *Human Sexuality* authors only touch on, to recall some
facts that they do not consider, and to suggest that a living tradition and the dynamics of history can support the "New Directions
in American Catholic Thought" which Fr. Kosnik and his co-
authors point the way to. More specifically, I intend to reinforce
their approach by stressing the pessimism of the past which they
simply allude to and in which our attitude of extreme restraint
has been rooted. And I intend, further, to probe some of the traditional casuistry for assistance in establishing a personalistic view
of natural law as this relates to sexual ethics.

## Motives for Sexual Intercourse

Although the *Human Sexuality* authors follow a strict chronological approach in their historical survey and are, for the most
part, on target in their assertions, it may be more helpful here to
consider things topically. A theologically controversial issue in
both the early and late Middle Ages was the problem of subjective motivation, namely the morality of the motives for sexual intercourse. That medieval song may be over but the melody has
lingered on. As recently as the turn of this century moralists were
arguing, and agreeing, that the personal (subjective) intention of
the spouses in having intercourse need not coincide with the (objective) intention of nature, namely procreation, as long as the
spouses did not contravene nature's own procreative intent.[11] In
brief, four motives eventually were distinguished and discussed by
theologians; in the earlier terminology they included: procreation,
rendering the debt, petitioning the debt, and pleasure.[12] Times

can change dramatically. In Augustine's time and before, Church writers were concerned about "justifying" procreation by sexual intercourse. Even in the thirteenth century Thomas Aquinas was asking whether in Paradise there would have been generation and whether it would have been through coitus (he answers both in the affirmative).[13] In recent years Catholic theologians and others have been concerned about the morality of procreation by means of artificial insemination; more recently yet, the actuality of *in vitro* fertilization and embryo implantation have become the focus of moral evaluation. The question arose earlier in the context of the place of venereal pleasure that is attendant on intercourse, or more generally the phenomenon of sexual excitability, in the plan of God. More precisely, discussions centered on the nature of concupiscence or disordered desire. Fundamental to medieval sexual ethics was Augustine's teaching on marriage as it existed in Paradise and on the subsequent relationship between concupiscence and original sin.[14]

*Procreation.* This was a most difficult question for Augustine, one that occupied his attention from time to time for many years. Sexual pleasure itself, he reasoned, could not be sinful properly speaking since sin requires freedom. The will can choose only to avoid stimulation. Anyone who would will to be sexually stimulated must be properly motivated, and the only morally good motive is procreation. This motive does not diminish the rebelliousness of the sexual appetite; rather, it justifies the enjoyment of the pleasure. Concupiscence itself, the disordered desire for venereal pleasure, is, according to Augustine, an evil but not in the sense of imputable sin; it is an imperfection in the present state.[15] What interests us in this context is not so much Augustine's negative attitude toward sex which is well documented in so many other sources but certain aspects of his exegesis concerning sexual excitation. I shall return to this in a moment. Suffice it to say here that it was Augustine's view on procreation that influenced theological thinking in the West in the millennium following. Procreation as a sinless motive for sexual intercourse was unanimously taught.

*The Debt.* The term "debt" (*debitum*) refers to Paul's admonition in 1 Cor. 7:3-6 which begins: "The husband must give the wife what is due to her, and the wife equally must give the hus-

band his due." At the start of the early scholastic era theologians
regarded intercourse to be sinless which was motivated by contractual justice.[16] This placed "rendering the debt" on a moral par
with procreation[17] and both motives properly classified sexual intercourse as "conjugal," "marital," "nuptial," "legitimate," and
even "necessary." In time the concept of "debt" was distinguished
—rendering the debt as opposed to petitioning the debt. This latter was considerably controverted. (Later casuistry would make a
further distinction between petitioning and *demanding* the debt.)
On the one hand, it was commonly regarded as a permissible motive for marriage but, on the other, it was not regarded as a morally good motive for the marriage act. To petition the debt—that
is, to request sexual intercourse—for the sake of avoiding a sin of
unchastity personally (masturbation or adultery) was seen by
most, following Augustine's lead, as a "concession" by St. Paul to
human weakness and hence was venially sinful.[18] This view was
echoed throughout the centuries by major and minor theologians
with the subsequent explanation that such a request—referred to
as "impetuous," "fragile," and "carnal" intercourse—was
superfluous indulgence. For there were other means available to
overcome the tendency to unchastity, namely prayer, fasting, etc.
Casuistry was rife in determining sinfulness regarding the rendering of the debt to or the petitioning of the debt by a spouse who
was pregnant, menstruating, diseased, bound by a vow of chastity, guilty of adultery (and it made a difference whether the
other spouse had knowledge of this), inclined to onanism, and so
on. Casuists were quick to ask how rendering the debt could be
sinless since it involved complicity in the sin of the one petitioning the debt. This was the famous "*casus perplexus*"—it was a
mortal sin to refuse the debt but a venial sin to cooperate—which,
it may be of historical interest to note here, led Albert the Great
to introduce to Catholic moral theology Aristotle's teaching on
*epikeia*.[19] All in all, these deliberations on the outer edge of morality served to enshrine an understanding of marriage in terms of
a twofold institution: one, *ad officium* (for procreation); the
other, *in remedium* (for the legitimate, albeit venially sinful, satisfying of sexual desire). That sexual pleasure as a motive for intercourse was sinful is already an obvious inference.

*Pleasure.* The only controversy in this regard looked to the precise sinfulness of "libidinous" or "voluptuous" intercourse, as it was called. While such intercourse was commonly regarded to be at least venially sinful, some theologians judged this motive to be mortally sinful. They recalled the account of Tobias (6:17; 8:9) to the effect that the devil is especially powerful over those who marry for the sake of lust (pleasure).[20] This emphasis in the biblical account on intercourse for procreation and on abstinence from intercourse for three days is attributed to St. Jerome, who translated the book of Tobias into Latin and in so doing apparently inserted his own views into the original text. Although hardly inspired in the biblical sense, his views on sexuality served to inspire theologians and popular preachers; the so-named "Tobias Night" was quite popular in medieval piety.[21] However, a greater impetus to regard such motivation as mortally sinful originated elsewhere with Jerome through his rendition and popularization of a Stoic epigram, namely (in Jerome's version) "a man who makes love to his wife too passionately is an adulterer" (*adulter est in suam uxorem amator ardentior*).[22] Incorporated into the *Concordance* of Gratian (more commonly known as the *Decree of Gratian*, the "Father of Canon Law," †*circa* 1143) and thence into the *Sentences* of Peter Lombard (archbishop of Paris, †1160) this citation enjoyed a tremendous popularity. It was repeated countless times and in various formulations. While most theologians and canonists agreed that intercourse motivated by the desire for excessive pleasure was mortally sinful, trying to determine what constituted excess was the subject of much debate. Possibilities included intercourse during forbidden times (e.g., days of feast and fast, Advent and Lent, before receiving Holy Communion; all told, during the Middle Ages marital intercourse was forbidden for twenty weeks of the year[23]—not to mention during menstruation, pregnancy and after childbirth); in forbidden places (e.g., churches—except, disputably, during times of siege); and in forbidden positions (with obvious reference to non-procreative intent). "Libidinous" intercourse was therefore effectively the same as "impetuous" (carnal) intercourse and in some instances either could be mortally sinful.

With regard to the classification and moral gravity of these four motives opposition was not wanting. All things considered, however, it was token. The far-reaching shadow cast by Augustine dimmed some of the illumination that might have penetrated the darkness of the teaching on sexuality, notably concerning the motives of petitioning the debt and pleasure. Abelard thought that requesting intercourse for the purpose of avoiding unchastity was too egocentric, too utilitarian. He positivized the motive by insisting that a person should marry so as to please God, not primarily so that he might overcome the tendency to personal incontinency or even have children for his own satisfaction. This emphasis on love for God as the guiding principle was a radical departure from Augustinian tradition.[24] Others reasoned that since sexual pleasure is not evil in itself, for otherwise it could not be the object of the virtue of temperance, avoiding unchastity was therefore a prudential judgment and hence reasonable and sinless. (It is possible too that "sinless" meant only that no mortal sin was involved since there was some confusion with terminology. For some authors mortal sin really meant venial sin but was used for pedagogical reasons to scare people into restraint.[25]) Robert Courson (†1219), who otherwise upheld a strict Augustinian approach, made a singular contribution to the whole discussion by asking whether married persons are expected to be able to distinguish the four motives—he denies it—and by observing for the first time that the usual reason spouses have intercourse is love.[26] Unfortunately, no one listened—at least in the ranks of the theologians.

Because the Augustinian view prevailed—and, indeed, for not a few authors was nuanced with a rigor not imputable to Augustine himself—it was impossible, and is still difficult, to have a perspective on sexuality apart from marriage and procreation. Some of the rigor, however, was mitigated in the course of time; ecclesiastical commandments (relating to forbidden times, etc.) eventually became counsels. One aspect of Augustine's own teaching, alluded to earlier, namely his exegetical views on concupiscence, should be recalled here since they are a focal point of later theologizing about sex. For Augustine, in the state of original innocence the will exercised the same control over the sex organs as over the hands and feet. He reasoned that since self-control is possible in other regards in our fallen condition—as is exemplified by persons who can wiggle their ears at will, cry and perspire at will, place themselves in suspended animation, and become insensitive to pain—*a fortiori* sexual excitation was subject to the control of the will in the state of innocence.[27] The inability of the will in the present state to directly regulate erections is the result of man's disobedience to God: "disobedience is the penalty for disobedience"; hence, unruly sexual passions are a constant reminder of Adam's original disobedience which is passed on to posterity through the instrumentality of sexual intercourse.[28] Aquinas would later use Aristotle's reasoning to corroborate this view of the non-subjection of man's genitalia to the will.[29]

However, there is no reason to hold that physiologically man was different in Paradise. Augustine himself accepts the notion that men are the same both before and after the Fall—except regarding sexual excitation.[30] His faulty exegesis is based on an (understandably) incomplete knowledge of neurology. We distinguish the central nervous system as voluntary and autonomic. The former has to do with voluntary muscle control, the latter with the workings of the glands, digestive system, and reproductive organs whose activity is involuntary. In one regard there is a gradual development of control; toilet training takes time. Augustine could concede, as noted earlier, only that the will can choose to avoid stimulation but, because of the Fall, not genital excitation. But we know that this excitation is due to the nervous system and there is no reason to suggest that this was affected by the Fall as understood by Augustine (and commonly; how the biblical story is to be exegeted is still debatable). Accordingly, there is no "shamefulness" and no reason to argue that this is "compensated" for by procreation or rendering the debt.

Whatever is positive in the patristic and scholastic approach to marriage is an emphasis on its reflection of the mystery of the union of the soul with God and of Christ's relationship to the Church. The approach does not encompass a healthy appreciation of its sexual nature since sex somehow got in the way of union with God. Although marriage eventually came to be regarded as a sacrament in the same sense as the other sacraments, as an effective sign of grace, it was long disputed precisely because of its carnal nature.[31] Even St. Thomas Aquinas, after reviewing the various opinions, concluded originally that marriage was "more probably" a sacrament; later he argued more positively.[32]

### The Purpose of Sexual Pleasure

Enough has been said about "voluptuous" intercourse—coitus for the purpose of pleasure—to show the common theological judgment that venereal pleasure always occasioned some degree of sin. But what about the purpose of sexual pleasure itself? Some held, as did Augustine originally, that it was intended by God in view of the Fall, which he foresaw, as a reward for the difficulties of rearing a family. Aquinas accepts Augustine's later view that sexual pleasure in Paradise would have been greater because reason would have been in perfect control; and in the state of innocence there would have been generation through coitus—when the hardships of this present state were non-existent.[33] All this is pure speculation, of course, but nonetheless it was a type of exegesis which was very influential. If we can prescind from it—even today, as noted, exegetes are not sure how to understand the Fall —and take another approach, we can get a different perspective on the morality of sexual pleasure. In consequence, we might also be better able to judge current issues in the area of sexual ethics.

One possible approach is to recall Aquinas' own highly positive analysis and synthesis of Aristotle's view of the nature of pleasure in general. Sexual pleasure is only one of many of life's enjoyments. Paradoxically, this approach is a rich source of insight within our own tradition.

For Aquinas pleasure (*delectatio*) is "something which is consequent upon happiness or a part of happiness because a person delights in having some good which he finds suitable, either here and now or in anticipation or at least in memory."[34] Pleasure has to do with the desire for good and is "nothing other than the quieting of an appetite in good."[35] (This is reminiscent of Freud's notion of libido as the quiescence which follows the discharge of energy.) The cause of pleasure is "the presence of a connatural good."[36] Pleasure is a further perfection of an operation in two ways: it is an added completion since as every good it is sought for itself; and indirectly, since people take pleasure in what they are doing they are more attentive to what they are doing.[37] Moreover, pleasure shares in the moral goodness or evil of an act.[38] As a further perfection pleasure is itself "somehow an end."[39] How? The question is crucial.

Cardinal Cajetan, St. Thomas' greatest commentator (†1534), explains how Aquinas intends this "somehow" to be understood. Since pleasure is attendant on an act, it is perfectly natural to desire and to engage in that activity precisely because it is pleasurable. The act and its accompanying pleasure are regarded as one desirable object; the sense appetites make no distinction between an act and its pleasurable dimension. They do not, because they cannot, see one as a means to the other. The experience of pleasure is sufficient in itself; and Aristotle himself, as Cajetan points out, thought it a foolish question to ask about the why of pleasure.[40] It is the intellect which can understand the nature of good and sees the relationship between pleasure and act. It is the intellect which knows that pleasure, although directly intended by the sense appetites, is in the designs of nature subordinate to the activity—i.e., is a means to an end. And it is reason which must determine the suitableness of an end, whether an intended end is the "presence of a connatural good." For example, the sense appetites can be turned on by a mouth-watering gourmet meal which is both visually lovely and gastronomically delightful despite the fact that the meal is laced with a toxic substance (e.g., strychnine) not perceptible to the senses. But the intellect, knowing this, will realize that this is not a connatural good. Moreover, because we are psychophysical creatures the receptivity of the senses can be sharpened or dulled depending on other circumstances; the same meal before one's execution is hardly as enjoyable as that on the occasion of a wedding banquet. Accordingly, it is reasonable (and hence virtuous) to desire or intend something precisely as pleasurable provided that that something is itself reasonable.

The intensity of a particular pleasure has nothing to do with the notion of moderation (with which the virtue of temperance is concerned); moderation does not look to quantity.[41] Rather, the norm of moderation is what is reasonable.[42] But what is normative of reasonableness? According to Aristotle and Aquinas necessity is the norm of what is reasonable whether it be absolute necessity or the necessity of convenience. Food is absolutely necessary to sustain life; gourmet meals, however, or snacks

between meals are not absolutely necessary but are "convenient"
—that is they are pleasurable, and as long as they do not adversely
affect one's health they are said to be enjoyed with moderation.
Nor does one have to eat with the intention of sustaining life in
order to virtuously enjoy the pleasure of eating and drinking.[43]

It would seem from every standpoint (logically, psychologically,
theologically) that all that is said of sensual pleasure in general
should be equally applicable to sexual pleasure in particular.
The climactic pleasure of orgasm should be moral quite apart at
least from the subjective intent to procreate. But in the tradition
this is not the case; temperance demands not only that nature's
intention to procreate be respected (i.e., not contravened) but
that it also be subjectively intended by those having intercourse.
In other words, gourmet sex ("the joy of sex" even with procreation in mind) and sexual snacks (affection this side of intercourse) are intemperate. Aquinas venerated Augustine too deeply
to think differently even though reason would have required this
application,[44] and others echo Aquinas. Today, the enjoyment of
sex apart from the personal intention to procreate is no issue. Current issues have to do with two considerations: whether the enjoyment of sexual pleasure, to be moral, must always be in circumstances open to the possibility of procreation; and whether
procreation apart from sexual intercourse can ever be moral. Since
past teachings, engrained in our collective psyche, are not easily
forgotten, current issues dealing with sexual conduct are especially
volatile. These same teachings are grounded not only in an anthropology that claims to be authentically biblical; they are rooted
as well in a peculiar view of natural law.

## The Natural Law of Human Sexuality

Here again St. Thomas Aquinas epitomized and furthered an
outlook of long standing. Borrowed from the Stoics and baptized
by Augustine (among others), it was confirmed by the scholastics
and eventually canonized in official teaching, most recently in the
Vatican's *Declaration on Certain Questions Concerning Sexual
Ethics* (of December 29, 1975). Thoughout, it was analyzed and
applied by casuists whose task it was to make the theory work.
The outlook, the so-named natural law argumentation, is decep-

tively simple and ought to be recalled, at least briefly: in a word, sexual intercourse is moral only within marriage. This is based on the nature of seed whose purpose is to bear fruit. A seminal ejaculation therefore requires a certain context: coitus, between human beings, of either sex, according to the natural (physiological) proportionality of the sexual organs (how one fits into the other). This means that a voluntary seminal ejaculation is unnatural, because non-procreative, in circumstances of masturbation, bestiality, homosexuality and of intercourse that is extravaginal (oral, sodomitic, onanistic) or intravaginal if the insemination is impeded in any way. Moreover, since a person is responsible for the outcome of his acts and since a child must of necessity be cared for (educated), procreation and education together as one are the primary purpose of sexual intercourse. This requires that a bond exist between those persons who would engage in this activity to ensure proper provision for offspring. This is the stability of marriage—indeed, coitus is the *marriage act* par excellence—and, hence, all non-marital (fornicatory and adulterous) sexual relations are immoral. And, by necessary extension or inclusion, all activity which would actuate the "seed of life" is morally reducible to the actual context in which that seminal ejaculation would take place; this includes the realm of sexual fantasizing as well. The male orientation of this approach is more apparent than real; in the tradition it was applied coequally to females (except in the instances of completed pre- or post-coital stimulation by a wife) since, according to the argumentation, venereal pleasure is bound up with generation on the part of both sexes.

The argument is perfect in its symmetry. It enunciates an "objective" order and provides a definite norm, procreativity, for sexual conduct. Philosophically, it is said to be a metaphysical (not physical) argument based on the nature of man as man (not on the genital apparatus) regardless of particular considerations in individual instances. Historically, it has always been held by the Church. Scripturally, it is said to be based on the divine blessing and command to increase and multiply (Gen. 1:28). Morally, it means that respect for this order is what chastity is all about and it makes any transgression to be mortally sinful since the capacity to beget life is in question. Canonically, to deny this is to vitiate the marital contract at its source. And theologically, overall, it is said to be the plan of the Creator.

However, from all of these standpoints the argument is vulnerable. The philosophical emphasis is on procreativity to which man by nature tends since nature intends the preservation of the species; it is not on procreation itself (rather, and most precisely, on heterosexual union) since procreation is often enough precluded by natural sterility whether permanent or periodic. Sexual activity is said to be, and therefore morally must be, "*per se* apt for procreation" or, in the language of *Humanae Vitae*, "open to the transmission of life." Those who hold this view must explain how coitus by persons naturally and permanently sterile is open to the transmission of life. The traditional reasoning is that their sterility is an accidental consideration; sexual intercourse *as such* is tendential to procreation. But here (in the context of procreativity, not pleasure) the male-centered approach is more real than perhaps apparent. With earlier biologists theologians accepted the notion that a woman was like a garden in which the seed could germinate; *per se* aptness for procreation meant unimpeded intravaginal insemination. But since coitus as such, in the sense just described, requires both male and female it cannot be defined primarily in terms of a seminal ejaculation; its procreative orientation is a unitary consideration. And since a woman's contribution to procreation is both active and essential and since from a metaphysical and moral standpoint there can be no double standard, the traditional "*per se* apt" argument cannot stand. Moreover, in the designs of nature female sterility is not an accidental consideration; it is the usual situation both during the continuum when it is impossible periodically for a woman to conceive and postmenopausally as well. Nor is her sterility during pregnancy an accident of nature. With regard to the effective use of the rhythmic cycles, which means scientifically pinpointing the time of ovulation in order that conception may be avoided, how intercourse during a woman's sterile (or "safe"!) periods is intercourse *per se* apt for procreation needs to be explained by procreationists. Indeed, to many the naturalness of this "natural family planning method" is not fully clear. (One thinks here of the late Gerald Vann's wry comment that in this regard the Church forbids contrivances but permits contrivance.) Also in need of explanation is

the claim that, *per se*, nature intends procreation and yet sponta-
neously aborts or allows to die *in utero* an estimated two thirds of
all conceptions; similarly, why nature allows so much "waste" in
terms of sloughed-off ova and a superabundance of spermatozoa.
Hence, it can be argued that coitus as such for human beings is
not directed primarily to procreation or at least is coequally apt
for many things. The traditional argument, in a word, is a *petitio
principii*. And those who subscribe to it should also reconcile the
assertions that arguments from reason alone are not cogent
enough to show the intrinsic evil of contraception, that the essential order of human nature can be grasped by reason, and that the
present teaching is reformable.[45]

St. Thomas understands natural law in different ways; in the
context of sexuality natural law is "most strictly speaking, that
which nature has taught all animals."[46] It is a question, therefore,
of sexual congress between a male and female, a relationship
which as such between human beings is not specifically human.
Moreover, although Aquinas recognizes that human participation
in the eternal law is through man's intellect and reason and hence
in this sense all sins are unnatural, nonetheless only certain sins
are called unnatural, namely those transgressive of the sexual order; and this very order is prior to and more stable than the
(superadded) order of right reason.[47] In other words, it is reason's
job to discern this sexual order which (the Author of) nature
has established. A different understanding of natural law, one
more in line with contemporary personalist thinking, was that of
Alexander of Hales and of Aquinas' mentor, Albert the Great. For
them natural law is the natural dictate of reason, that which is
specifically human in man.[48] With this approach it is reasonable
to see the plan of God not as a blueprint the details of which
have all been worked out but as something open to man's creative
imagination. A probing of this by the *Human Sexuality* authors
would have provided them with a more substantial foundation
for the guidelines which they articulate.

It is true that the blueprint approach has been traditionally
taught by the Church but the scriptural understanding, as the
same traditional teaching makes clear, has not presented human
sexuality as a special participation by man in the plan of divine
providence. The blessing of fertility was the "justification" for sex-

ual intercourse. Even the authors of the minority position of the Papal Birth Control Commission hold this view: "for conjugal love is above all spiritual (if the love is genuine) and it requires no specific carnal gesture, much less its repetition in some determined frequency."[49] Sexual expression is not necessary where genuine conjugal love exists; it is necessary only for procreation. Morally, the blueprint model leaves no room, for all practical purposes, for light matter,[50] makes the virtue of chastity more virtuous yet by idealizing virginal chastity that is positively motivated (the "angelic" virtue—cf. Mt. 22:30), and provokes an examination of conscience so detailed that scrupulosity is unavoidable. Canonically, the whole understanding of acts *per se* apt for generation (the ability to perform which is requisite for a valid marriage contract) is so mired in biologism that male and female impotence have been judged differently, and the most recent area of vulnerability is the view that marriage by a vasectomized male is not to be impeded since, canonically at least, he is able to perform an act *per se* apt for generation![51] That all of this is the plan of the Creator, because it is the operative theological understanding of natural law as this relates to sex, is somehow not convincing in the tradition. Repetition is no substitute for rational analysis.

## Personalist Considerations: the Natural Law Reclaimed

With their emphasis on "the nature of the human person and his acts" and "creative growth toward integration" the authors of *Human Sexuality* dramatize a personalist approach. (At the same time, though, they are diplomatically gentle and generous in their appraisal of the December 1975 Vatican declaration on sexual ethics. That, on the practical level, this document "follows the tradition closely in its treatment of specific sexual questions in the simple objective-subjective framework" is true. But that "it modifies this approach considerably by calling for greater attention to the subjective elements in pastoral judgments" is misleading.[52] Once the rhetoric is set aside, the approach is exactly the same as the objectively-grave-evil/subjectively-non-imputable framework in the standard manuals of moral theology. "[G]reater attention to the subjective elements" is no modification, much

less a "considerable" one; it is a simple recalling of the traditional
and sensitive awareness of excusing causes or extenuating circumstances.

Fr. Bernard Lonergan provides some insights that can corroborate this emphasis on personal creative growth and shed considerable light on the current sexuality debate. Contrasting the classicist with the historical world view, he writes:

> Now the common meanings constitutive of community and
> of the lives of individuals in community are not some stock of
> ideal forms subsistent in some Platonic heaven. They are the
> hard-won fruit of man's advancing knowledge of nature, of the
> gradual evolution of social forms and of his cultural achieve-
> ments. There is such a thing as historical process, but it is to be
> known only by the difficult art of acquiring historical perspec-
> tive, of coming to understand how the patterns of living, the in-
> stitutions, the common meanings of one place and time differ
> from those of another.[53]

After noting that every modern era "means the desertion, if not
the repudiation, of the old models and methods, and the exercise
of freedom, initiative, creativity," he argues:

> One can apprehend man abstractly through a definition that
> applies *omni et soli* and through properties verifiable in every
> man. In this fashion one knows man as such; and man as such,
> precisely because he is an abstraction, also is unchanging. It fol-
> lows, in the first place, that on this view one is never going to
> arrive at any exigence for changing forms, structures, methods,
> for all change occurs in the concrete, and on this view the con-
> crete is always omitted. But it also follows, in the second place,
> that this exclusion of changing forms, structures, methods, is
> not theological; it is grounded simply upon a certain conception
> of scientific or philosophic method; that conception is no longer
> the only conception or the commonly received conception; and
> I think our Scripture scholars would agree that its abstractness,
> and the omissions due to abstraction, have no foundation in the
> revealed word of God.
> On the other hand, one can apprehend mankind as a con-

crete aggregate developing over time where the locus of development and, so to speak, the synthetic bond is the emergence, expansion, differentiation, dialectic of meaning and of meaningful performance. On this view intentionality, meaning, is a constitutive component of human living; moreover, this component is not fixed, static, immutable, but shifting, developing, going astray, capable of redemption; on this view there is in the historicity, which results from human nature, an exigence for changing forms, structures, methods; and it is on this level and through this medium of changing meaning that divine revelation has entered the world and that the Church's witness is given to it.[54]

The cutting edge of any theory is its concrete application. To my reading, the *Human Sexuality* authors sufficiently flesh out Lonergan's understanding of modern man, and they apply their theory consistently, although often enough guardedly, to particular questions. It seems to me that since casuistry is a rich part of our tradition they could have with profit approached matters in that vein, at least in part, in order to strengthen their approach. Casuistic moralists tend to be in immediate contact with problem situations which very practically historicize the concept of human nature. And in this sense they are, I think, the ultimate personalists. A casuistic consideration now of a few of the topics considered in *Human Sexuality* may highlight this. Traditional moral judgments of sexual conduct have a twofold base: the order of desire for sexual pleasure, and the sexual order itself (this latter as discussed above). Both are proper to the virtue of chastity. Disordered sexual activity reflects an inordinate desire for sexual pleasure. Which is more proper?

A parallel may show the importance of this question. The scholastics defined sin as an aversion from God and a conversion to something finite. As such all sins are formally the same; they differ according to the matter involved. Murder and theft are the same inasmuch as they are aversions from God, but they are obviously two different manifestations of aversion. Accordingly, the specification of sins is based on the matter and on this basis judgments can be made regarding objective gravity. And in this way even within the various species degrees of gravity can be determined. For example, there are degrees of theft; to steal a large sum of gold is not a new species of theft because of the amount stolen but the gravity of the offense will be greater or lesser depending on other circumstances. The formality of sin, therefore, looks to disposition (in the case of theft, the disordered desire for someone else's property), the specification and degree of gravity to material content or the thing done. The obvious parallel is that all sins of unchastity are concrete manifestations of the disordered desire for pleasure. This emphasis on species is the act-centered approach to morality (*actus specificatur ab objecto*). A person-centered approach must highlight disposition or motive without excluding the activity itself.[55]

Contemporarily, this emphasis on person, without prejudice to man's acts (*actiones sunt suppositorum*), is reflected in the biblical view of sin and the moral appreciation of fundamental option. With a growing and dynamic awareness that all of created reality, including sexuality, is subject to man's domination, certain official proscriptions are at most untenable, at least questionable.

Recalling, then, that disposition is better emphasized than act, artificial insemination is easily justified since it is not motivated by an inordinate desire for sexual pleasure on anyone's part whether the insemination be homologous (AIH) or heterologous (AID) or a combination (AIHD). The procreative intent of the sexual order is realized through the inventive use of modern technology. Conception in this way should be as morally acceptable as the use of technology in effecting safe deliveries; a Cesarean section is not nature's way but is not considered unnatural either. With regard to AIH the method of obtaining semen should pose no moral problem not only because masturbation "is no longer regarded by most moralists as a serious obstacle to this procedure"[56] but because the tradition itself can provide a certain amount of support. The manualist authors commonly regard as licit post-coital stimulation by a wife in order for her to achieve orgasm, provided her husband has already climaxed, since her orgasm is in the designs of nature an aid to *foecundatio*. Hence, it is not a question of masturbation for her. The same reasoning is applied with regard to immediate pre-coital orgasm by a wife who knows that her husband intends to complete the act. However, they deny this to a husband who fails to reach orgasm during intercourse and whose wife, having already climaxed, is now indisposed for further lovemaking. For him it would be masturbatory. The detail is intimate and the inconsistency is clear; nature intends complete venereal pleasure for the integrity of the act *qua* act but morally this is to be realized differently. In other words, it would be an act of masturbation for him but not for her. Since the tradition is concerned about the unity of the act (*una caro*), a Christian tradition which preaches equality of male and female before God can hardly maintain a double standard in sexual ethics. In the wife's regard at least the approach is very humane. This same reasoning will apply also to the morality of masturbation for a sperm count or for AI purposes, which, although not in the actual physical context of marital coitus, in another and real (moral) sense is in the context of coitus with procreation intended as the earlier and stricter opinions required.[57] Nor, it may be noted explicitly, is masturbation in these circumstances motivated by a (disordered) desire for pleasure.

Heterologous insemination—which accounts for an estimated ten thousand to twenty thousand conceptions annually in the United States—carries with it the morally questionable (and legally ambiguous) notion of adultery and a restrictedly biological understanding of parenthood. Here again, it seems to me, the traditional reasons against adultery can provide a certain amount of support in favor of AID. In addition to its being prompted by the inordinate desire for sexual pleasure, adultery was condemned because it violated the promise of mutual fidelity and could occasion uncertainty of paternity and hence an injustice to the husband who would unknowingly and (presumably) unwillingly be supporting someone else's child, and the child himself would be an illegitimate heir to the detriment of the couple's own children. In the case of AID none of these reasons applies; there is no injustice and the only uncertainty is the identity of the donor, who remains anonymous. As for the understanding of parenthood, if the essence is primarily the ability to beget instead of to nurture, then adoptive parents are not truly parents. One would have a difficult time convincing such parents and their adopted children of this. And the same is true of a couple who become parents through AID. If it be urged casuistically that procreation and education together constitute the essence of parenthood, then adoptive parents are not fully parents[58]—and the same difficulty obtains. From a theological standpoint, however, an understanding of the parental-filial covenant is not and cannot be grounded in the proper functioning of the genitalia.

The *Human Sexuality* authors do not explicitly consider natural insemination by a donor. (Their reference to *in vitro* fertilization now has a new dimension; the celebrated case of Baby Louise Brown was headlined around the world in August of 1978.[59]) It is not a current question, it is true, doubtless because it is commonly regarded as adulterous—and, in legal fact, is adultery—and affectively is a more intense factor to be considered. Yet, as intercourse in the usual way it removes the danger that is attendant on the transfer process in artificial insemination and the interpersonal element is quite in evidence. But does it constitute adultery? I think not. Adultery cannot mean sexual exclusivity on a one-to-one basis for otherwise polygamy could not have been accepted in the tradition nor could retrospective approval have been given to concubinage in the Old Testament. Albert the Great, for example, held that a concubine was not really a wife but was accorded wifely affection in the sense that her purpose was to provide progeny, not to satisfy lust.[60] "Husbandly affection" could also be urged in the case of natural insemination by a donor. Other scholastic theologians argued, in the controversial situation of Hosea, that the basis of the Decalogue is justice which cannot change but particular applications in certain circumstances do change by losing their prohibitory force; hence, intercourse with someone other than one's own spouse is not adultery.[61] It seems to me that the concept of adultery must be societally and circumstantially determinable. A simple reference to the Sixth Commandment tells us only that adultery is prohibited, not what adultery is. The same is true of the other Commandments which need explication and this is, in part, the work of applied ethics. (Someone has suggested that if God had spelled out everything for Moses in detail, either there would not have been enough stone on Mount Sinai for all the tablets that would be needed or else Moses would have been so loaded down he never would have made it down the mountain!) St. Augustine recounts the instance of a wife who prostituted herself at her husband's behest in order to purchase his freedom from captivity and death. According to D. Prümmer's paraphrase, Augustine "does not dare to define that these spouses sinned, and he permits everyone to think what he will since these spouses 'in no way judged that in these circumstances that act was adultery.' "[62] By way of parallel, in recent years in discussions of situation ethics it has been popular to debate the case of a married woman imprisoned in a concentration camp who can be freed if she becomes a liability either through illness requiring hospitalization or pregnancy. She becomes pregnant by a guard, is released from the camp, and rejoins her husband and family amid great rejoicing; her husband is happy to accept the child as his own. It is instinctively easy to approve of her action, and I think the justification is the common and connatural realization of good, all things considered.[63] (We would have no problem in approving of the use of forged documents or physical violence to obtain her release.) A more pertinent parallel, perhaps, regarding the concept of adultery might be the situation of persons divorced and remarried and now living conjugally ("in sin"). According to Roman Catholic teaching that is adultery. But Roman Catholic teaching, according to Article 16 of Vatican II's *Decree on Ecumenism,* wants the spiritual heritage of the Eastern Orthodox to be venerated and preserved. Since that heritage tolerates divorce with the right to remarry and since Christian teaching does not condone adultery, our teaching on divorce must be disciplinary rather than doctrinal and the moral understanding of adultery other than is presently thought. In a word, the emphasis on marital fidelity cannot exclude activity which itself helps to realize what the prohibition of adultery would protect, namely the covenant of love between spouses. One type of such activity may be, for some couples, natural insemination by a donor.

A more practical issue relating to the traditional concept of adultery is comarital situations which the *Human Sexuality* authors cautiously, and only very briefly, allude to.[64] Nothing in traditional casuistry can support comarital sexual relations except, perhaps, the much disputed question among the scholastics of Old Testament concubinage. "Comarital," at least theoretically, places the third partner on an equal basis. The difficulty, of course, in applying the earlier dispute (recall Albert the Great's explanation) is that today's emphasis is on mutual love and companionship, not on offspring. Concerning the elderly, whom the authors of *Human Sexuality* mention only in passing, natural sterility is often enough already the case. In their regard we need to pay more attention to their sexual needs if only by urging the legal recognition of polygamy for senior citizens who might wish this arrangement.[65] With regard to comarital arrangements properly so called, the *Human Sexuality* authors should have noted and answered the common objection to monogamous sexual exclusivity, namely the intense possessiveness and insane jealousy which it so often engenders. Why may everything else be shared except sexual affection? As some ask, why is love of neighbor commanded but making love prohibited? There is much grandiose theorizing in current literature about comarital relations but, for that matter, the same kind of theorizing about the grandeur of traditional monogamy is to be found too. In all the preceding regards a reasonable criterion for what is moral is that with which couples, after joint and prayerful consideration, can be psychically comfortable. They can live with it and die with it in peace of conscience.

Traditional casuistry can easily be invoked to endorse the *Human Sexuality* views on masturbation and premarital sex. A comparison or two will show this. According to the metaphysical mind-set every voluntary seminal ejaculation must be in the context of (non-contraceptive) marital intercourse. Insistence on this leads to some logical but unreasonable conclusions. Since unnatural acts contravene both the order of reason and the sexual order itself, as noted earlier, such acts are more gravely sinful than are "natural" ones; in context, masturbation is worse than incestuous rape which results in pregnancy. Common estimation both abhors this example of rape and rejects this reasoning. Common sense prompts casuistic moralists to do the same. Some parallel examples will demonstrate this.

These moralists ask whether one who has begun sexual intercourse in circumstances of fornication is morally bound to interrupt it or to complete it. To interrupt it is unnatural—the grave sin of onanism—while to complete it is natural but less gravely sinful. Although some are consistent enough to argue for the necessity of completing the act, the more common opinion holds not only that the act must be terminated before completion but also that coitus interruptus in this case is not sinful; "for on the

one hand to continue it is evil, while on the other the pollution
which follows is not intended nor is it regarded as sinful since it is
tolerated for a just cause."[66] The assertion that "the pollution
(*sic*) which follows is not intended" is not in line with the metaphysical approach according to which *nature* intends the seminal
ejaculation. (Those who favor interrupting the act might have
strengthened their case by recalling that nature intends a seminal
ejaculation in the context of a bonded union, which fornication is
not. But then they would have had difficulty justifying inter-
ruption by spouses in circumstances of intrusion, to be considered
in a moment.) Similarly, coitus reservatus is judged to be moral
even if orgasm should follow since, according to these authors,
any ejaculation subsequent to withdrawal is only "accidental."
Here again the natural intrinsic unity of penetration-ejaculation,
insisted on in theory, is denied in practice. Otherwise, to argue
that here this unity is not intrinsic is to make a distinction too
subtle to be intelligible; it is to argue, for example, that it is the
*extravaginal* aspect that is unintended, not that orgasm is unintended. The same holds true of the moralists' approval of withdrawal in the event that a husband and wife are intruded upon
during marital relations or some other unforeseen circumstance
arises.[67] In these instances a reasonable cause justifies extravaginal ejaculation. In effect, therefore, casuistic moralists—
approved authors all—are forced by their own casuistry to abandon logic for what is reasonable or personalistic and in so doing
they show a connatural awareness of what natural law is all about.
(In an effort to preserve logic they argue that in these instances
the ejaculation is involuntary or indirectly voluntary. But, as
noted above, this is unintelligible.) They manifest this same
awareness too when they argue, often enough and always understandably, that the peace of mind of persons is not to be dis-
turbed lest material "sins" become formal ones; in fact, in the
context of pre- and post-coital stimulation confessors are urged
not to ask too many questions "since these are not only useless
but possibly scandalous as well." And they show thereby that the
traditional distinction between natural and unnatural sins is no
longer meaningful. What is unnatural from a personalist/biblical
standpoint is to be unloving, to be unconcerned about integrative
growth.

With regard to masturbation as this is commonly understood (the above instances are all, at root, traditionally masturbatory), there are, coequally, certainly reasons to argue for sinlessness, the pastoral approach taken by the authors of *Human Sexuality*.[68] However, they are too concerned with subjective non-imputability, not with sinlessness itself. But at the same time their concern is more realistically grounded in contrast to that of traditional moralists. These latter ask whether it is licit to desire a natural seminal emission, one that is spontaneous and unprovoked. It depends: to desire it just for the sake of pleasure is immoral; to desire it for some honorable reason, such as relief from sexual tension, is moral.[69] In effect they are saying that the desire for sexual pleasure needs some other justification. In requiring the integrity of the sexual act they are consistent in condemning masturbation—but inconsistent compared to their justification of coitus interruptus in certain circumstances and coitus reservatus, as well as their approval of self-stimulation by a wife pre- or post-coitally as discussed above. For their part, the authors of *Human Sexuality*, by emphasizing the integrity of the person, are consistent in applying the principles which they articulate.

Since masturbation is such a common occurrence it would be helpful, I think, for moralists to recall Cardinal Cajetan's rhetorical question in the context of passionate premarital affection (to be considered in a moment): "Does God delight in multiplying mortal sins?"[70] (One might also recall St. Alphonsus Liguori's down-to-earth reference to mortal sin: "If an elephant comes in, you notice it at once."[71]) Unless voluntarism is to reign, this looks to objective morality, not subjective imputability. Moreover, since in the view of *Human Sexuality* serious sin can be imputed only in restricted instances which prudent confessors will recognize, it seems reasonable to assert that the sin-conscious anxiety of mind on the part of striving Christians can be removed here and now by stressing the non-sinfulness or neutrality of masturbation. That is, if by a *post factum* judgment a confessor would tell an individual not to worry about it, he ought also find it moral to assure the same individual that given the same circumstances sin will not be involved in the future either.

The consideration of premarital sex in *Human Sexuality* is both sensitive and sensible and more than adequately reflects sound

moral thinking.[72] But additional considerations, both traditional
and contemporary, can serve to bolster the judgments therein
with particular regard to those who are engaged. If a given society
recognized engagement as a permanent commitment, the marriage ceremony itself being regarded as a legal and public formality, Catholic moral teaching could easily approve of sexual relations between persons engaged to be married, persons therefore
already married in intent or in conscience.[73]

In our society, however, a betrothal is not a marriage and
"infidelity" during that time is not adultery, not even *ad instar*.
The mutual promise to marry is not of its nature a permanently
binding commitment, as experience commonly testifies; stated
positively, the promise to marry is *per se* revocable. In the tradition it is only the marriage bond which is permanent *per se*. And
since moral judgments are to be made according to what is *per se*
(as in the metaphysical understanding of procreativity), engagement as *per se* revocable makes premarital intercourse sinful. But
one could also argue from the premise that moral judgments are
to be made according as things ordinarily happen ("ex communiter contingentibus").[74] And, since it ordinarily happens that
persons who marry are engaged beforehand, their mutual promise
to marry can reasonably be considered permanent and therefore
sexual relations should be moral during this time. Serious persons
will know when permanence is a realistically intended dimension
of their relationship and when sexual lovemaking is appropriate.
To acknowledge the obvious objection that a promise is either *per
se* permanent or it is not, I would simply draw a comparison (to
be enlarged on in a moment): in traditional canonico-moral treatises the marriage bond is said to be permanent by its very nature;
at the same time, however, this traditional teaching maintains
that only a consummated marriage between Christians is by both
natural and divine-positive law *absolutely* permanent. I am saying,
therefore, that engagement can commonly be regarded as permanent even though not absolutely so and, in consequence, that intercourse can be moral. Otherwise, we must convincingly explain
that intercourse by an engaged couple is sinful on Friday night
but chaste on Saturday night after the public ceremony. In addition, the usual natural law arguments adduced in Catholic teaching for the permanence of marriage—the threefold good of the

spouses, the children, and society—cannot be urged since even in Catholic teaching marriages which are sacramental but non-consummated and those which are consummated but non-sacramental are dissoluble. And, as everyone knows, in recent years "annulments" in Catholic practice have considerably refashioned the notion of permanence; the practice of granting annulments has become a back-door approach to a dynamic understanding of the natural law of human relationships, the traditional notion of a metaphysical bond notwithstanding.[75] Moreover, while complete premarital abstinence may be preached as an ideal, there is no compelling reason to require it *sub gravi* (or even *sub levi*); the state of original justice is not required in other areas of life. Affection apart from intercourse, but of its nature conducive to intercourse which (affection) in traditional casuistry is reductively the sin itself, was often enough realistically considered.[76] Finally, in an ecumenical era when official recognition is given to the fact that other Christians have valid insights, when "the ecumenical dialogue could start with discussions concerning the application of the gospel to moral questions,"[77] the stance taken by the authors of *Human Sexuality* is further seen to involve sound theologizing. These authors could have highlighted this more forcefully in the contemporary context of the ongoing tradition.

These are a few of the instances which could have been argued for in the framework of traditional casuistry. Casuistic moral teaching is geared to confessional or pastoral practice, and the longest chapter in *Human Sexuality* is the one devoted to "Pastoral Guidelines." Hence, an explication of this practice in the chapter on "Christian Tradition" (which is more narrowly Catholic than Christian) and an application in the one on pastoral guidelines could have been made with profit. By contrast, the authors reduce the "Early Modern Period (15th to 19th Century)" to a page and a half and overemphasize the sexual negativism of the era. But it is casuistic moralists who, at least to my reading, manifest a better understanding of human nature since they have to test the theory in actual flesh-and-blood situations. And it is only *in concreto* that human nature can be dealt with. Their appreciation of excusing causes and their insights into the weight of evidence and the nature of moral certainty as shown in the controversies over probabilism force a reconsideration of the static view of nature which they inherited. Even Augustine had to admit that certain aspects of his theory on what constitutes sinless intercourse clashed with reality,[78] and Abelard remarked that rigorists were allowing only a kind of marital sexuality that could never be lived.[79] On the other hand, with masterful understatement, *Humanae Vitae* observes: "It can be foreseen that this teaching will perhaps not be easily received by all."[80]

There are those who maintain that the traditional natural law understanding of sexuality is still valid; it needs only to be purified of Augustinian pessimism and infused with a balanced understanding of Aquinas' views on marriage, conjugal intercourse, and marital friendship. This approach sees the completed act of intercourse as morally and immutably normative, and in this it resembles the commercial of a few years ago for a certain dog food which was "so complete all you need add is love." But Aquinas would not be helpful in the present context (except as I have suggested earlier regarding his teaching on pleasure). It is true that he and many others articulated beautiful analyses of human love but as men socially conditioned by their times and theologically loyal to Augustine conjugal love sexually expressed was tainted.[81] With reason then the authors of *Human Sexuality* suggest "new directions" based on the "nature of the human person and his acts" as this nature is understood today in our own society.

These directions were already forged by men like Doms, Krempel, and von Hildebrand, who receive only passing mention in the *Human Sexuality* treatment of the "Contemporary Period." This is a most unfortunate omission by Fr. Kosnik and his co-authors. Had they examined and pursued the reasoning of H. Doms, for example, as do A. Auer and J. Noonan,[82] their own personalist approach would have been considerably buttressed. In 1944 the (then) Holy Office found time, while the Holocaust was raging, to condemn the view (of Doms and others) that love was on a par with procreation as an end of marriage.[83] But this decision, intended for canonists and misunderstood by moralists (who took— or mistook—it as a theology of marriage), at least affirmed indirectly that love is *an* end of marriage. This was new in official teaching. The *Human Sexuality* authors might also have recalled, by way of enunciating their appreciation of natural law understood dynamically, some contrasting statements of Popes Pius XI and John XXIII. The former, echoing an earlier approach, condemned the view "that the rights of husband and wife are equal" since to him this stressed "unnatural equality with the husband"; they enjoyed equal rights regarding the marriage contract, but "in other things there must be a certain inequality and due accommodation." Pope John, alert to the signs of the times, urged complete equality: "Since women are becoming ever more conscious of their human dignity, they will not tolerate being treated as inanimate objects or mere instruments, but claim, both in domestic and public life, the rights and duties that befit a human person."[84] And it was Pope John, it will be recalled, who commissioned a reexamination of the teaching on contraceptive birth control.

In sum, the moral teaching of the past cannot support the approach taken in *Human Sexuality*. History, however, does make that teaching "comprehensible"—to recall Teilhard. Faulty exegesis, an inadequate understanding of reproductive biology, an overall aura of sexual pessimism, and a veneration for theological giants are all interwoven in the traditional emphasis on procreativity as normative of sexual conduct. To stay with this is to fossilize that tradition. Seen dynamically, on the other hand, in the sense that insights change and that cultural conditioning is part of the human scene and can be recognized as such in historical perspective, that same tradition can be supportive of much that is said by the authors of *Human Sexuality*. A personalist understanding of natural law, one that emerges in part from casuistic considerations and which is biblical, makes signposts to the future more readable.

Chesterton once remarked that if a fence has been erected around something, one should know the reasons why before taking it down. Cardinal Cajetan said it earlier: a judgment is badly arrived at without first discussing the reasons for the judgment. The fence around sexual activity is marriage. Through the centuries all approaches have become moral mine fields. Even within the enclosure itself one had to tread lightly. Contrary to many critics, *Human Sexuality* is not the Catholic Theological Society's commissioned rendition of "Don't Fence Me In"! The work of the authors of that Report, and of many other theologians, has been to concentrate on persons, to chart a path in terms of ideals instead of pitfalls leading to eternal death (mortal sin). Their perspective is to view human sexuality as God's invitation to individuals to share in the work of creation and redemption, to see procreation as one "life-serving" aspect of this mystery. In proceeding this way the "new directions" which they intend can guide us here and now and on to the colonization of other worlds —whence, perhaps, we originated—a venture that may well require modes of reproduction not encompassed by the traditionally approved marital embrace. Tradition lives. History is not something just to be studied. History is meant to be made.

# NOTES

1. H. Jone, *Moral Theology* (Westminster, Md.: The Newman Bookshop, 1945), n. 607: "A necessary proximate occasion of sin is, e.g., company keeping with the prospect of an early marriage." Cf. ibid., n. 204.

2. Aertnys-Damen, *Theologiae Moralis* (Romae: Marietti, 1950), II, n. 913: "Mutual acts . . . even shameful ones (impudici) . . . in direct conjunction with sexual intercourse are without doubt permitted to the spouses." (The qualifier "impudici" is omitted in the 1958 ed.) The respected authors Noldin-Schmitt refer to certain acts attendant on conjugal lovemaking as enormously obscene and filthy; cf. *Summa Theologiae Moralis* (Oeniponte/Lipsiae: Pustet, 1940), n. 94. 1. b.

3. Address to Italian Midwives, AAS 43 (1951), 835–60, at 845, 851. In his encyclical *Sacra Virginitas* Pius XII urges the abstinence from the use of marriage of the Old Testament priests, lest they be unclean, as example for the perfect chastity of the New Testament ministers of the Eucharistic sacrifice. The note then refers to Lev. 15:16f. and 22:4, both texts referring to uncleanness deriving from emission of seed, and to Siricius; cf. AAS 46 (1954), 161–91, at 169f. For a discussion of Siricius, see P. Sherwood, "Tertullian and Reasons for Clerical Celibacy," *Resonance* 3 (Fall 1966), 41–44. The prescription that following a nocturnal emission Mass should ordinarily not be celebrated and that Communion should be abstained from was retained until very recently in the *Ordo Servandus*; cf. "De defectibus in celebratione Missae occurrentibus," IX, n. 5.

4. *Gaudium et Spes*, Art. 49.

5. *The Future of Man* (New York: Harper & Row, 1966), p. 12.

6. This hope may not be entirely well founded. The popular press reported the results of a World Health Organization study drawn up by twenty-three specialists from fifteen countries. According to this study which deals with sex education with a view toward healthy sexual relationships: "Another major barrier to sex education is the attitude that sex is sinful unless it is meant for procreation—a common teaching and one that can create feelings of guilt about the use of contraceptive methods. . . . Every person has a right to receive sexual information and to consider accepting a sexual relationship for pleasure as well as for procreation." See the Milwaukee *Journal*, Jan. 22, 1976.

7. Sidney Cornelia Callahan, writing in *The Critic* (Winter 1977), 73.

8. Francis T. Hurley, writing in *The Inside Passage* (July 29, 1977), 2.

9. Ibid. The archbishop notes that the debate which the book has occasioned "is to the good, even if it does cause us bishops to squirm a bit." And he concludes: "Personally, I welcome the report. I commend the authors for grappling with the almost impossible task of trying to develop in writing and for public review what is more easily and safely done in the one-to-one privacy of the counseling situation. Indeed, if nothing else they should force us to wonder just what guidelines are in effect in the teaching and counseling situation."

10. P. Browe, *Beiträge zur Sexualethik des Mittelalters* (Breslau, 1932); D. Lindner, *Der Usus Matrimonii. Eine Untersuchung über seine sittliche Bewertung in der katholischen Moraltheologie alter und neuer Zeit* (München, 1929); P. M. Abellán, *El Fin y la Significación Sacramental del Matrimonio Desde S. Anselmo Hasta Guillermo de Auxerre* (Granada, 1939); J. Fuchs, *Die Sexualethik des hl. Thomas v. Aquin* (Köln, 1949); A. Adam, *Der Primat der Liebe. Eine Untersuchung über die Einordnung der Sexualmoral in das Sittengesetz* (Kevelaer, 1954)—or, in Eng. trans.: *The Primacy of Love. A study of the place of sexual morality in the moral code*. Trans. E. C. Noonan (Westminster, Md., 1958); M. Müller, *Die Lehre des hl. Augustinus von der Paradiesesehe und Ihre Auswirkung in der Sexualethik des 12. und 13. Jahrhunderts bis Thomas von Aquin. Eine moralgeschichtliche Untersuchung* (Regensburg, 1954); L. Brandl, *Die Sexualethik des Heiligen Albertus Magnus* (Regensburg, 1955); J. G. Ziegler, *Die Ehelehre der Pönitentialsummen von 1200–1350* (Regensburg, 1956); J. Kerns, *The Theology of Marriage: The Historical Development of Christian Attitudes Toward Sex and Sanctity in Marriage* (New York, 1964); J. T. Noonan, Jr., *Contraception: A History of Its Treatment by the Catholic Theologians and Canonists* (Cambridge, 1965); D. Doherty, *The Sexual Doctrine of Cardinal Cajetan* (Regensburg, 1966); T. N. Tentler, *Sin and Confession on the Eve of the Reformation* (Princeton, N.J., 1977). For whatever

reason, most of these works (Tentler's understandably, in view of its publication date) do not appear in any of the *Human Sexuality* bibliographies. And on specific issues historically considered there is an abundance of periodical literature available.

11. Cf. Noonan, op. cit., pp. 490f.

12. Cf. Lindner, op. cit., pp. 81–145; Müller, op. cit., pp. 295–314; Abellán, op. cit., pp. 182–90; and Doherty, op. cit., pp. 269–303.

13. *Summa Theol.* I, 98, 1 and 2.

14. Müller, op. cit., pp. 19–41; and Brandl, op. cit., pp. 17–25.

15. Cf. *Opus imperf.*, *PL* 45, 1493; *Contra Jul.*, *PL* 44, 857. Concerning the controversy regarding Augustine's view on the relationship of concupiscence to original sin, see Ziegler, op. cit., p. 165, n. 1. The authors of *Human Sexuality* are guilty of an oversight in their assertion that "Although sexuality of itself was recognized as good because of its procreative function, the pleasure attached to sex was viewed as a consequence of original sin" (p. 37). Pleasure itself was not so viewed; rather, the *disordered desire* for pleasure was regarded as such a consequence. Cf. n. 33 below.

16. Noonan, op. cit., p. 42, n. 14, explains: "The Greek word for *debitum* is *opheile*. The term is used by Paul elsewhere to indicate what is owed to governmental authority (Rom. 13:7). The substantive is also used in Mt. 18:32 to designate what is due a creditor in the parable of the stern master."

17. John Chrysostom understood 1 Cor. 7:2 to mean that the primary purpose of marriage is not to procreate but to extinguish the fire of lust; in his writings he repeats this more than twenty times. Cf., e.g., his commentary on 1 Cor. 7, *PG* 51, 213. In our own era this would be translated into personalist terms. In this regard Noonan's suggestion regarding Chrysostom is not fully intelligible. Asking whether the doctrine on contraception might have been different if Chrysostom's views had prevailed, Noonan says, op. cit., p. 139: "Suppose the doctrine had been adopted that marriage was no longer for procreation since the Resurrection had defeated death, that love was a value which the union of husband and wife incorporated and symbolized, that original sin and concupiscence had no special association with sexuality. . . . It can scarcely be denied, however, that if Chrysostom's ideas had become the leading ones in theological development in the West, a different theological tone, a different way of looking at marriage might have led to different results in the active rethinking of theology, which, after the period of preservation of Augustine from 500 to 1100, was to take place on Augustinian terms." But it is the same Chrysostom who saw marriage to be necessitated by the Fall and therefore a condition of death and slavery and "the only port in the sexual storm following the Fall." Cf. *De Virg.*, *PG* 48, 543–47; and *In Gen. Hom.*, *PG* 53, 149, 153.

18. In the curious comparison of Gregory the Great, *Moralia, PL* 76, 659f., when a person is surrounded by a wall he goes over the lowest part. We are surrounded by a wall of illicit pleasure so we go over the lowest part—viz., where there is the least sin, namely, into marriage.

19. Cf. Müller, op. cit., p. 254, n. 67.

20. Ziegler, op. cit., p. 218.

21. Ibid., p. 269. According to a report in *Time* magazine, Dec. 19, 1969, p. 37, as he was preparing for his wedding on the Johnny Carson show, "Tiny Tim announced that his honeymoon would begin with 'a three-day fast from S-E-X. . . . If only more people followed the ways of St. Paul and King David.'" His reference to Scripture is more than slightly off but his heart is in the right place in attempting to recall the Tobias Night before being married on "The Tonight Show"!

22. For the origin of this saying, see Noonan, op. cit., pp. 47, 80.

23. Ziegler, op. cit., p. 250f.

24. Müller, op. cit., p. 69: "Mit dieser Abstellung auf die Gottesliebe als das Prinzip des sittlichen Lebens hat Abaelard unser Problem auf eine höhere Ebene gestellt wie alle seine Vorgänger. . . . Gottesliebe ist darum auch das richtige Motiv zum Abschluss der Ehe wie zum Vollzug des ehelichen Aktes. . . . Mit dieser Darstellung hat Abaelard dem vieldeutigen Ausdruck 'zur Vermeidung von Unzucht' einen eindeutig sittlich wertvollen Sinn gegeben." Noonan's exposition of Abelard's views is misleading; cf. op. cit., p. 194.

25. Müller, op. cit., pp. 226–27. Huguccio, on the other hand, understood venial sin to mean "not too big a mortal sin" ("quod veniale dicitur esse peccatum, non quia non sit mortale, sed quia non tantum mortale. . . ."); cited by Müller, loc. cit., n. 125. Since this theological consideration is psychologically important, see, also by Müller, *Ethik und Recht in der Lehre von der Verantwortlichkeit* (Regensburg, 1932), Sachregister, under "Bussdisziplin—Pädagogische Absicht und Abschreckungstendenz" and under "Sünde—Unterscheidung von peccata nach allg. menschlicher Sprechweise." Cf. n. 50 below.

26. Müller, *Die Lehre des hl. Augustinus*, pp. 158f., 311f.

27. *De Civ. Dei*, L. 14, cc. 19–25, esp. 21 and 24, *PL* 41, 427–33; and ibid., c. 26, 434: "eo voluntatis nutu moverentur illa membra quo caetera. . . . Neque enim quia experientia probari non potest, ideo credendum non est." There may be an isolated instance of such experience. An actor in the pornographic film industry is reportedly in demand for his "ability to perform virtually tirelessly and on command"; see R. Blumenthal, "Porno Chic," New York *Times Magazine* (Jan. 21, 1973), 28–34, at p. 30.

28. *De Civ. Dei*, L. 14, c. 15, *PL* 41, 423; cf. cc. 17, 20, ibid., 425, 428.

29. *Summa Theol.* I–II, 17, 9 ad 3: the sexual organ "est quasi quod-
dam animal separatum, inquantum est principium vitae, principium
autem est virtute totum . . . et ex membro genitali virtus exit semi-
nalis, quae est virtute totum animal."

30. *De Civ. Dei*, L. 14, c. 22, *PL* 41, 429.

31. For a good summary, see S. MacDonald, "Theological Development of Marriage as a Sacrament," *Resonance* 4 (Spring 1967),
87–117. Cf. n. 81 below.

32. *In IV Sent.*, dist. 2, q. 1, a. 1; ef. *Suppl.* 42, 3 and *Summa Contra
Gentiles* IV, 78.

33. *Summa Theol.* I, 98, 2 ad 3; cf. *De Civ. Dei*, L. 14, c. 26, *PL* 41,
434.

34. *Summa Theol.* I–II, 2, 6 c.

35. Ibid., ad 1.

36. Ibid., 31, 1 c.

37. Ibid., 33, 4 c. and ad 2; cf. II–II, 151, 3 c: "Delectationes autem
proportionantur operationibus, quarum sunt perfectiones."

38. *Suppl.* 49, 6 c.

39. *Summa Theol.* I–II, 25, 2 c: "Delectatio enim est fruitio boni,
quae quodammodo est finis, sicut et ipsum bonum." Cf. ibid. 11, 3 ad
3; and 33, 4 ad 2.

40. *Comment. in Summam Theol.* I–II, 4, 2, nn. II, IV; or see my
own work (cited above, n. 10), pp. 57–60. Cf. J. B. Becher, "Die
moralische Beurtheilung des Handelns aus Lust," *Zeitschrift für kath.
Theol.* 26 (1902), 448–65, 673–700.

41. Cf. *Summa Theol.* I–II, 34, 1 ad 2; II–II, 153, 2 ad 2; *Suppl.* 49,
4 ad 3.

42. Cf. Cajetan, op. cit., I–II, 34, 2, n. II: "Bonum autem et morale
constituitur ex consonantia et dissonantia ad rationem, et non ad ap-
petitum."

43. *Summa Theol.* I–II, 141, 6.

44. Ibid., 153, 2 ad 2; cf. *Suppl.* 49, 1 c. Bonaventure, among others,
rejected this parallel between sensual and sexual pleasure; see J. Fuchs,
op. cit., pp. 126f., 225ff. For St. Thomas' view, see *Summa Theol.*
II–II, 154, 2 ad 6.

45. Cf. "The State of the Question," the Minority Report of the
Papal Birth Control Commission, in *The Birth Control Debate*, ed.,
R. Hoyt (Kansas City, Mo.: The National Catholic Reporter Publishing Co., 1968), p. 34: "If we could bring forward arguments which
are clear and cogent based on reason alone, it would not be necessary
for our commission to exist." A few pages later, however, p. 51: "The
essential distinction between mutations which are dependent on extrinsic conditions and the stability of principles deduced by right

reason is ignored." The discrepancy notwithstanding, the question may be asked: whose right reason? And, from the *Declaration on Certain Questions Concerning Sexual Ethics*, nn. 3, 4: "These fundamental principles, which can be grasped by reason, are contained in 'the divine law—eternal, objective and universal . . . a plan conceived in wisdom and love.' . . . This divine law is accessible to our minds. . . . divine Revelation, and in its own proper order, philosophical wisdom, emphasize the authentic exigencies of human nature. They thereby necessarily manifest the existence of immutable laws inscribed in the constitutive elements of human nature and which are revealed to be identical in all beings endowed with reason." Finally, Msgr. F. Lambruschini, a spokesman for Pope Paul, was widely quoted as saying *Humanae Vitae* is "not irreformable"—as the *Human Sexuality* authors note on p. 48.

46. *Suppl.* 65, 1 ad 4. Cf. *Summa Theol.* I–II, 94, 2 c. And O. Lottin, "Le droit naturel chez saint Thomas et ses prédécesseurs," *Ephemerides Theol. Lovan.* 1 (1924), 369–88; 2 (1925), 32–53, 345–66; 3 (1926), 155–76.

47. *Summa Theol.* I–II, 91, 2 ad 3; 94, 3 ad 2. Cf. II–II, 154, 11 and 12.

48. Cf. Lottin, art. cit. 2 (1925), 37–40, 43–51.

49. Loc. cit., pp. 54f. *Humanae Vitae* considerably tempered this strange assertion: "This love is first of all fully human, that is to say, of the senses and of the spirit at the same time" (n. 9); AAS 60 (1968), 481–503, at p. 486.

50. Cf. Chap. 6 of A. Adam's *The Primacy of Love*, pp. 137–57, "The Teaching of *Parvitas Materiae* and the Singling Out of the Sixth Commandment." Traditional teaching holds that sins against the Sixth Commandment are mortal either *ex genere suo* or *ex toto genere suo*; the former admit at times of parvity of matter, the latter do not. In both instances venial sin is possible. This is sufficiently detailed in the decalogic approach of the moral manuals. But it may be of interest to note, by way of adding to Adam's account, that canonists and moralists supply more precision when they discuss the obligation of a penitent to denounce a priest guilty of the sin of solicitation (seduction in relation to confession). Since the penalty is so severe (and since "odiosa sunt restringenda"), the sin in question must be *grave* and *certain;* the inference is interesting. Some authors hold that a priest is to be denounced no matter what precisely because the matter is always grave. But the more common opinion distinguishes "inter res stricte venereas, in quibus revera non datur parvitas materiae, et actus vel dicta minus honesta vel etiam indifferentia, quorum malitia et gravitas ex circumstantiis sunt conicienda (cfr. Tom. III, n. 246). Ita e.g. si verba aliqua quae saperent sollicitationis *ex levitate* tantum dicta evidenter apparent, non videtur urgenda denuntiatio; deest culpa gravis. Aliud certo dicendum, si quamvis actio in se sit

levis, ex adiunctis prava intentio confessarii ulterius progredendi evidenter appareat." Cf. L. J. Fanfani, *Manuale Theorico-Practicum Theologiae Moralis*, Tom. IV (Romae: Libraria "Ferrari," 1951), n. 446; the reference in Tom. III deals primarily with suggestive speech and "dirty" jokes. The above distinction does not explain what a *res stricte venera* is, but the important thing is the role of intention or disposition, not gravity or parvity of matter; cf. n. 55 below. Perhaps the most incisive statement in the whole manualist analysis of sin is one tucked into a discussion of blasphemy (itself gravely sinful *ex toto genere suo*): "the general rule is that to condemn any action as gravely sinful its grave malice must be obvious. Therefore, to affirm that some action is not gravely sinful, the probability that it is not grave suffices." (In dubio utrum aliqua locutio sit necne blasphema, blasphema non est iudicanda; quia regula generalis est quod ad actionem aliquam certo damnandam de gravi peccato de eius gravi malitia constare debet. Ideo ad affirmandum actionem aliquam culpa gravi carere, sufficit quod probabile est non esse gravem. Eadem ratione ad statuendum locutionem aliquam blasphemam esse, de blasphemia constare debet.) Cf. Aertnys-Damen, op. cit. (n. 2 above), I, n. 458, III.[20] Although traditional teaching regarding the Sixth Commandment leaves virtually no room for probable opinions, there is merit, I think, in rejecting that stance; see Chapter Six below, nn. 17, 26.

51. *AAS* 69 (1977), 426.

52. *Human Sexuality*, p. 52.

53. "The Transition from a Classicist World View to Historical Mindedness," ed., J. F. Biechler, *Law for Liberty: The Role of Law in the Church Today* (Baltimore: Helicon Press, Inc., 1967), pp. 126–33, at pp. 128f.

54. Ibid., pp. 129f.

55. See Doherty, *The Sexual Doctrine of Cardinal Cajetan*, pp. 95–104, 111–13. The parallel is not perfect, however, since the aversion involved in sin is only a secondary consideration; it is consequent upon the intention of the sinner which is not to turn away from God but to enjoy the created good. One who fornicates, to recall St. Thomas' own illustration, does not intend to turn away from God but to enjoy venereal pleasure; cf. *Summa Theol.* II–II, 20, 1 ad 1. In the *Summa*—II–II, 154—Aquinas emphasizes the sexual order, in *De Malo*, q. 15, the order of desire. This preference for the sexual order is reflected also in the *Summa* designation of certain sins as unnatural even though it is man's nature to be reasonable and all sins are therefore unnatural; cf. I–II, 94, 3 ad 2.

56. *Human Sexuality*, p. 138.

57. See my article "Sexual Morality: Absolute or Situational?" in *Continuum* 5 (Summer 1967), 235–53, at pp. 242f.

58. Cf. *Summa Theol.* III, 29, 2 regarding the completeness of the union of Mary and Joseph.

59. One of the reasons why the *Human Sexuality* authors advise against *in vitro* fertilization is the unanswered question: "How can this be reconciled with our Christian understanding that the child is to be the product of mutual parental love?" Yet in approving of AI they say on the page immediately preceding, p. 138: "The principal moral concern that 'the child should be the fruit of love' does not seem to be threatened in any way by the biological modification in the process of insemination." The Christian understanding regarding the child and mutual parental love should be equally clear in both instances.

60. In a short (unedited) treatise on marrying by St. Albert, cited by G. LeBras, "Mariage," *Dict. Théol. Cath.* IX, 2176: "Dicimus quod non fuerunt plures uxores sed uxorio affectu cognitae. Si autem quaeritur quid sit uxorarius affectus, dico quod mulieris affectus spe pietatis in prole et non intentione libidinis dicitur uxorarius affectus."

61. Cf. *Summa Theol.* I–II, 100, 8, esp. ad 3.

62. This is cited in the context of the possibility of invincible ignorance of the natural law; cf. D. Prümmer, *Manuale Theologiae Moralis* (Friburgi Brisgoviae: Herder and Co., 1935), 1, 111, 1. And Augustine, *De Sermone Dom. in Monte*, PL 34, 1254.

63. A detailed justification can be found in D. Maguire, *The Moral Choice* (Garden City, N.Y.: Doubleday, 1978), pp. 241f.

64. Pp. 148f.

65. For some details in this regard see my *Divorce and Remarriage: Resolving a Catholic Dilemma* (St. Meinrad, Ind.: Abbey Press, 1974), pp. 141–49.

66. Aertnys-Damen, op. cit. (n. 2 above), I, n. 603. Consistently enough, they argue that there must be no danger of consent to the pleasure; cf. ibid., 619, III, 19. According to all authors, direct voluntary masturbation can never be justified, whether to avoid fornication or even to save one's life. But fornication, once begun, is something else, it seems. More precisely, the question is "an fornicarius copulam semel incoeptam abrumpere teneatur." What about the moral obligation of a woman in the same circumstance? Does the same reasoning apply? Well, maybe (or, as the manualists would say, "controvertitur"). On the one hand, it should apply because in the context of masturbation it is argued: "Etiam pollutio in feminis, ad intra vel ad extra, est peccatum mortale et quidem eiusdem speciei ac in masculis, non PROPRIE quidem, sed AEQUIVALENTER." (The moral difference between "proprie" and "aequivalenter" is not clear!) The argumentation with its emphasis on nature is telling: "Ratio . . . est quia etiam haec pollutio frustrat finem a natura intentum sc. generationem quam natura ex omni actu venereo et emissione seminis, tam feminae quam masculi, intendit." Cf. loc. cit., II. On the other hand, however, the common approval of pre- and post-coital stimulation by a wife to the point of orgasm, as detailed earlier, would seem

to indicate a double standard which Christian morality cannot tolerate. In any event, the question is not important in itself. It may be of
interest to recall some of the "natural or hygienic remedies" for masturbation recommended by moralists; among others, according to Noldin-Schmitt: physical exercise to the point of exhaustion (or at least
moderate fatigue—Prümmer), sleeping on one's right side (with
hands folded over one's breast—Prümmer), in the morning bathing
the genital area with ice water mixed with vinegar, etc. Of more interest is the much disputed question of prostitution; moralists commonly
but very qualifiedly concur that this evil may be tolerated by civil authority in order to avoid greater evils and that a prostitute is morally
entitled to keep her immorally acquired earnings; in fact, she even has
the moral right to demand payment. None of this is an approval of
prostitution but a recognition of reality even though prostitution occasions many evil including "unnatural" sins.

67. Aertnys-Damen, op. cit., II, n. 895, 40: "Onanismus cum fortuita
et necessaria copulae abruptione confundi non debet; coniuges enim
possunt copulam interrumpere v.g. ad evitandum scandalum . . . ;
tunc quippe copulam abrumpunt, non iam ut semen extra effundant,
sed ex alio fine, unde illa seminis effusio praeter intentionem eveniens
pollutioni involuntariae aequiparatur."

68. Pp. 225–29.

69. Aertnys-Damen, op. cit., I, n, 243, 2⁰.

70. "Numquid gaudet Deus in multiplicandis peccatis mortalibus?"
Cf. *Comment. in Summam Theol.* II–II, 152, 2, n. XIII.

71. Cited in *A New Catechism: Catholic Faith for Adults* (New
York: Herder and Herder, 1967), p. 453.

72. Pp. 152–75.

73. Cf. *Suppl.* 46, 2 c.: ". . . quantum ad forum conscientiae . . .
carnalis copula non habet quod perficiat matrimonium cuius sponsalia
praecesserunt per verba de futuro, si consensus interior desit." And
ibid., ad 1: "ille qui carnaliter commiscetur, facto consentit in carnalem copulam secundum rei veritatem: sed in matrimonium non consentit ex hoc ipso nisi secundum interpretationem iuris." In the case
of persons solemnly engaged, the question is asked whether fornication with someone else has the added malice of injustice. There is a
triple probable opinion: the first affirms it, the second denies it, the
third affirms it with a distinction (obviously cultural)—namely, a
grave injustice for a woman who is engaged, a light injustice for a
man.

74. In establishing the immorality of fornication despite the fact that
any child conceived might be provided for, St. Thomas concludes,
*Summa Theol.* II–II, 154, 2 c. :"id quod cadit sub legis determinatione, iudicatur secundum id quod communiter accidit, et non
secundum id quod in aliquo casu potest accidere." The whole Catho-

lic tradition rejects—unreasonably, I judge—the application which I am making of this principle.

75. See. D. Doherty, "Marriage Annulments: Some Theological Implications," *The Jurist* 38 (1978), 180–89.

76. Cf. n. 70 above, and ibid., 154, 4, n. X: "Sed de sponsis de futuro obstat quod adhuc possunt dissolvi. Videtur autem quod, sicut sponsalitium inchoatio quaedam est coniugii, ita huiusmodi actus inchaotio quaedam est carnalis copulae. Et quemadmodum concessum est ut inter sponsalia suspirent se invicem . . . ita concessa videntur huiusmodi oscula inter eosdem; secundum indulgentiam tamen, quavenialia conceduntur (1 Cor. 7:6) . . . Et nisi ut huiusmodi inchoationes permissae venialiter in ordine ad promissas nuptias excusentur, nescio excusare sponsorum de futuro, propter delectationem, etc., oscula, amplexus, etc." Even for husband and wife, it may be noted, sexual affection apart from coitus was commonly regarded as venially sinful (because superfluous) just as was intercourse itself unless properly motivated, as discussed earlier. Cf. also *Summa Theol.* II–II, 154, 2 ad 6.

More generally, some earlier authors showed great agility—in reality, human concern—in minimizing the gravity of physical affection. After a comparative analysis of opinions relating to the nature and gravity of the *actus imperfecti*, especially on the part of the young, Chrysostomus Javelli wrote in 1537: "Hos autem [namely, "amatores" adolescentes] damnare de peccato mortali, durum est, et totam adolescentiam maxime in sexu muliebri illaqueare . . . Declino igitur ad hanc viam: et ratio opinionis oppositae non concludit; concesso enim, quod operans haec consentiat in delectationem tactus, nego quod regulariter consensus in tali delectatione sit consensus in delectationem fornicationis. . . . quum istae duae delectationes, licet videantur assimilari, non tamen sunt eiusdem rationis. Nam altera est sicut via ad terminum malum, altera autem sistit in se; et ut in se sistit, non habet unde possit de mortali damnari." The *actus imperfecti* are those which are tendential to completion or climax. See his *Christiana Philosophia* (Lugduni, 1580), *Opera Omnia* II, IIa Pars, tract 7, de temperantia, p. 471.

77. *Unitatis Redintegratio*, Art. 23.

78. Cf. *De Bono Conj.*, PL 40, 384: "Quod tam magnum est, ut multi hodie facilius se tota vita ab omni concubitu abstineant, quam modum teneant non coeundi, nisi prolis causa, si matrimonio copulentur." Also n. 27 above.

79. Recalled by Müller, op. cit., p. 64.

80. N. 18; AAS 60 (1968), 481–503, at p. 494.

81. In their booklet *On Understanding Human Sexuality* (Chicago: Franciscan Herald Press, 1977), p. 44, W. E. May (contributor to the present volume) and J. F. Harvey impute to the *Human Sexuality*

authors "a very unbalanced view of Thomas' teaching on marriage, the male-female relationship in marriage, and the relationship between marital intercourse and the ends or goods of marriage." But they fail to recall that Aquinas taught that only for childbearing does a man need a woman "since for any other work man is more conveniently helped by another man than by a woman" and that "a woman is naturally subject to a man since in a man the discretion of reason is more in abundance" (*Summa Theol.* I, 92, 1); that "in sexual intercourse man becomes like a brute animal" (ibid., 98, 2); that "the use of sex keeps the soul back from that perfect intention of tending toward God" (ibid., II–II, 186, 4); that—and this directly from Augustine (*Soliloq.*, PL 32, 878)—"there is nothing which perverts a man's mind more than the caresses of a woman and that bodily contact without which a wife cannot be had" (ibid., and *passim*).

Further, in his commentary on 1. Cor. 7:1 St. Thomas cites this same passage as the first reason, "for the sake of the soul," why man should not touch woman. "Secondly, for the sake of the body, which a man subjects to the power of his wife by marrying, freely making himself her slave. And this servitude is bitter in comparison to all other kinds. . . . Thirdly, for the sake of external things" with which a husband must necessarily be concerned. Cf. *S. Thomae Aquinatis, Super Epistolas S. Pauli Lectura* (Romae: Marietti, 1953) I, lect. i, n. 314. That St. Thomas says, *Summa Theol.* II–II, 26, 11 ad 4: "For a man loves his wife principally on account of carnal union" is to be understood in the same sense that generation is postulated as the principal or primary end of marriage, namely as fundamental by reason of origin, not principal by way of emphasis; cf. Brandl, op. cit., p. 204.

In view of the above, it is curious to read in Noonan, op. cit., p. 501, after he reviews the teaching of J. Fuchs on love as an objective end of intercourse: "At last the neglected thought of St. Thomas that fidelity (*fides*) was an objective end of intercourse was revived, with 'love' substituted for fidelity." This thought deserves to be neglected. Far more insightful is a statement by Cajetan who nonetheless, out of allegiance to Aquinas, could not jettison Augustine's pessimism. Rejecting the view of those who taught that sexual pleasure must be abhorred, which Cajetan branded as stupid, he emphasizes the complete sinlessness of conjugal intercourse properly motivated—"puta propter prolem, etc."—and calls delight therein a "donum Dei . . . Unde non debet persona de huiusmodi delectatione percepta dolere, sed potius Deo gratias agere." Cf. *Comment. in Summam Theol.* II–II, 153, 2.

82. A. Auer, *Open to the World*, trans. D. Doherty and C. Callaghan (Dublin: Gill & Son, 1966), pp. 236–45; and Noonan, op. cit., pp. 496–501.

83. *AAS* 36 (1944), 103.

84. *Casti Connubii, AAS* 22 (1930), 539–92, at p. 568; *Pacem in Terris, AAS* 55 (1963), 257–304, at pp. 267f.

*Chapter Four*

✢

# SEXUALITY AND CRITICAL ENLIGHTENMENT

GREGORY BAUM

The Report, *Human Sexuality*, wants to summarize in a systematic way contemporary Catholic thought on sexual morality and spell out its implications for counseling and spiritual guidance. The Report, if I understand it correctly, does not understand itself as an original contribution to the field of moral theology. Its purpose is more modest. It simply wishes to report to the reader what Catholic moral theologians have been teaching over the last decade, how this relates to the Church's official statements, and above all what all this means to the priest in the exercise of his pastoral ministry.

This limited objective is both the strength and the weakness of the Report. Because it does not defend a new and original theological position but simply records the development that has taken place in Catholic thought, the Report is a testimony of what the Catholic community actually believes about the meaning of sexuality in God's world. The Report cannot be passed off as the views of a few private individuals. It documents an evolution taking place in the Catholic Church. Even if the Church's official teaching has not yet caught up with the new approach, it is likely that, after a period of resistance and hesitation, the ecclesiastical magisterium will acknowledge the evolution that has taken place. We recall that in the area of political morality—religious liberty and civil rights—the evolution of Catholic theology outstripped the Church's official position, and that after long decades of discord, the ecclesiastical magisterium eventually changed its mind. Here too, we note, the controversy had to do with the degree to which people can be trusted to define themselves and assume responsibility for their lives.

At the same time, the limited purpose of the Report is also its weakness. For as a summary of contemporary Catholic thought on sexual morality, it cannot possibly offer a complete and coherent theology of human sexuality. The theological sources upon which the Report draws are partial and tentative: they are mere signposts indicating a new direction of Catholic theology. The authors of the Report cannot be blamed for the lack of originality: they have simply executed the limited task assigned to them. In this chapter I wish to point to aspects of theology that have not been sufficiently explored in the Report.

## Enlightenment and Biblical Method

At the outset, let me say a few words about the method of reading the biblical message. The Report, as I understand it, clearly affirms a fundamental hermeneutical principle, namely that the arrival of enlightenment thought makes a significant difference for the understanding of the revealed message. For Christian theology it is not simply a question of what a biblical teaching meant when it was first preached: it is above all a question of what this teaching means today. Let me illustrate the power of this principle by referring to a non-controversial issue: Jesus was a healer of the sick, and he asked his followers to be healers likewise. What did this call mean to the early Church? It commissioned Christians to take care of the sick and help them recover, and to pray to God to send them health. Thanks to the enlightenment, we have discovered that diseases have causes, analyzable causes. Germs produce illnesses, and certain social conditions such as inadequate diet or lack of hygiene foster sickness. Jesus knew nothing about germs. Jesus shared with his age a very rudimentary knowledge of how illnesses are related to social conditions. After the enlightenment, therefore, the Christian community is bound to read Christ's message to become healers in a new manner. The gospel message includes the call to promote research in the health sciences and to struggle for the creation of more healthful living conditions. When we examine the national budgets to see how much money is spent on health research and how much on armament and aggression, we realize how closely related are the illnesses from which a people suffer to the manner in which they spend their resources. These are new perspectives. It follows from this that the Christian community would be disobedient to Christ's call to become healer if, after the enlightenment, it simply followed the practice of the early Church.

In the contemporary Church, a parallel argument is made for the Gospel call to solidarity with the poor. At one time, this call of Christ summoned Christians to give alms to the poor, to see in them brothers and sisters deserving respect, to love them, and to learn from the insecurity and simplicity forced upon them to become more reliant upon God. In some instances, Christians took upon themselves a life of poverty in order to become more wholly reliant upon God's daily mercy. It was again thanks to the enlightenment that Christians discovered that poverty has causes, analyzable causes. It is possible to examine the processes of production and distribution and isolate the reasons for the shortage of food and the maldistribution of the earth's resources. Since poverty has analyzable causes, it is man's collective responsibility to remove them. To follow Christ's love of the poor today, therefore, demands much more than giving alms and praying on their behalf. If we simply followed the practice of the early Church today, we would be sinful. What is demanded of us—this has been repeatedly emphasized in recent theology as well as in episcopal documents—is to discern the causes of poverty and to collaborate with others in an effort to overcome them. Since this new reading of the biblical message implies a criticism of the dominant economic system, many Christians are upset by the Church's contemporary social teaching. What was right and good at one time is right and good no longer. This complaint is true enough: the Church seeking fidelity to the gospel in the present age has changed its moral teaching. The enlightenment has a profound effect on the Church's reading of the Scriptures.

What do I mean by enlightenment? I am referring here to two

interrelated modern intellectual trends, namely "science" and "critique." The early French and English enlightenment explored the rational structure of the universe and developed scientific categories for the explanation of the world and its history. This trend became more and more identified with the empirical sciences. The only true knowledge, it was argued, was scientific knowledge. And the success of this approach to the exploration of nature persuaded many thinkers that it could also be applied to the study of human existence. Social sciences were generated that saw themselves as the extension of the natural sciences to the field of human life and history: they applied the scientific method of demonstration to the new object, man.

Some people understand the term "enlightenment" as referring mainly to this rationalistic and specific phase, and hence do not regard it as a turning point for the philosophical and theological understanding of human life. While they appreciate of course the enormous contribution made by the sciences to the understanding and control of the powers of nature, they look upon its impact on philosophical thought as an impoverishment.

There is, however, a second phase of enlightenment, often referred to as "late enlightenment," which can be characterized by the term "critique." This was on the whole a reaction against rationalism. Hegel, Marx, Nietzsche, Freud, and many others discovered the ambiguity of consciousness. Consciousness is grounded in social life, it reflects a cultural tradition, it is constituted by personal history. Reason itself is historically constituted and hence shares in this ambiguity. Demonstration is no guarantee of truth since the application of formal reason may be nothing but an exercise in false consciousness. What are required, therefore, are critical principles, in the light of which thinkers examine the intellectual tradition they have inherited as well as their own exercise of research and reflection. The second phase of the enlightenment recognizes the need for an ongoing critique of knowledge and brings out the limits of the scientific method. It is this second phase that has had a profound influence on philosophical and theological thought since, thanks to these "critiques," the researchers are able to assess the limitation and the power of their own conclusions. While there is an enormous divergence among the critical thinkers of the nineteenth and twentieth centuries, they all in one way or another regard knowledge, including scientific knowledge, as part of man's making of man.

This reading of the enlightenment in two phases, early and late, where the late phase critically transcends the first, would demand careful argument and documentation. While this seems to me the reading common in German scholarship, Troeltsch, Scheler, Mannheim, Tillich, and the Frankfurt School, it is not the common interpretation in Anglo-American scholarship, which easily reads the nineteenth-century critics in line with the rational enlightenment. It is of course possible to understand Marx and Freud simply as rationalists and scientists. These brief reflections on the Report on human sexuality are not the place to engage in this discussion. I prefer to read the great sociological and psychological literature as sources of critique, as the delivery of principles that help us to come to a new self-understanding, both collectively as culture and personally as people. The late phase of the enlightenment convinces us that the surface deceives, that truth is hidden in the depth, and that to be in touch with it, we have to change, our own consciousness has to undergo transformation. How can the truth claims of these critics be demonstrated? They have to be defended rationally, of course; they have to be supported by evidence; but ultimately they cannot be demonstrated by the scientific method because their power is precisely to initiate us to a new consciousness and a correspondingly new perspective on the world. Even if the great critics exaggerate and look upon reality in a one-sided manner, and hence may be proven "wrong," I would defend the view that they represent a threshold of consciousness and hence demand of us that we apply their principles, in whatever nuanced and modified form, to the contemporary understanding of self and world. I offer the following pages as types of reflections on human sexuality that have become necessary today, even if the arguments I propose, based on particular psychological and sociological theories, turn out not to be the most useful.

The Report is conscious of the impact of the enlightenment on the understanding of the biblical message, but it spends more time on the scientific than the critical phase. An entire chapter deals with the anthropological findings of sexual life among the cultures of the world and with zoological research on the sexual

activity of the higher mammals. The usefulness of this chapter is
rather limited. We learn that a great variety of sexual behavior
has been approved in human history, that the sexual taboos have
shifted from one society to the next, and that even the sexual behavior of animals does not betray any clearly definable natural
law. The chapter tries to overthrow various untested assumptions
about sexuality that are often operative in the thought of traditional Catholic theologians. What is regrettable is that psychology is here simply classified as an empirical science and hence that
psychology's contribution to the understanding of human life appears mainly under the rubric of demonstrable knowledge. What
the chapter (and the Report on the whole) tends to neglect is the
critical phase of the enlightenment. There are some references to
critique, but they are never explored. We read, for instance, that
"Pre-reflective subjectivity can never be totally bracketed when rational analysis is undertaken" (p. 54). Such a radical acknowl-
edgement would have deserved the greatest attention, especially
when dealing with sexual morality. It is here that the great critics
of modern times help us to reveal the factors operative in the formation of human consciousness.

The Report listens to the empirical sciences, but it does not
give in to any form of scientific reductionism. Implicit in its synthetic understanding of human sexuality is faith in the person, understood along the lines of modern personalism. The dignity of
the human person and man's quest for self-realization and self-
transcendence in community constitute the principal elements of
the anthropology adopted by the Report. This personalism is the
theoretical context in which the results of the empirical sciences
are inserted and offer their truth beyond all temptations of reductionism. The Report favors the view that modern personalism is
in profound accord with the biblical understanding of man. Man
created by dialogue, man constantly growing and moving forward,
man freed from subservience to the law by a power beyond his
reach, man rooted in matter alive by the spirit. This philosophical
personalism, produced in a particular period of Western culture,
reveals itself as liberal and optimistic: the guidelines for man's
sexual education are creativity and integration. In the foreground
is not man's personal woundedness nor the brokenness inflicted
upon him by society, but his destiny toward freedom and whole-

ness. In the Report, this trust is ultimately not a philosophical conviction but an exercise of Christian faith in the divine promises.

In all of this the critical phase of the enlightenment is somewhat neglected. In the following pages I wish to make a few remarks on the contribution which critical thought can make to the understanding of sexuality and its role in the self-constitution of man. It is this contemporary view of sexuality that forms the horizon in which the Scriptures should be read and in which they reveal their power.

## Depth Psychology and Enlightenment

Let me begin with a few reflections on the discoveries of depth psychology. Here human sexuality is seen in a new light. It appears as part of the dynamic process by which people constitute their character and personality. From the very beginning the infant participates in a drama of overpowering dimensions, out of which issues forth, at the time of adolescence, adult sexuality. So overpowering are aspects of this drama, so overwhelmed is the child by feelings of attachment, dependency, competition, and hostility, that the turmoil of the early years is very largely repressed from memory and forgotten. But when adult sexuality eventually emerges, it carries with it links to all kinds of other drives. The growing person experiences sexuality as confusing. The early stirring of adolescent sexuality, the youthful crushes and sexual exploration have the purpose of bringing to light this confusion. Growing up is to be therapeutic: it is meant to enable young people to leave behind the childhood memories, to overcome the fusion of sexuality with other drives, and to make sexuality an organ of communication and affection, freed from its compulsions and the desire to hurt others. In a certain sense, human sexuality never wholly leaves behind its ambiguous character. The demon of sexuality, that is to say the destructive potential associated with sex, cannot simply be described in terms of selfishness, as we do in moral theology, nor simply as lack of integration, as is done in personalist philosophy. The demon is related to the drama of leaving the womb, of defining oneself in relation to mother, father, and the rest of the family, of passing through the powerful urges and yearnings of infancy to possess and to be possessed, and of struggling in competition with others. And since sexual energies generated in this drama affect the direction of life, however freely lived, the unresolved conflicts of infancy affect every aspect of personal life including one's relationship to others and one's personal creativity. For this reason, sexuality remains ambiguous and is in need of transformation.

Related to this ambiguity is the discovery of depth psychology that sexuality cannot be rationally controlled. There may indeed be an appropriate way of educating the emotions, but the traditional ascetical rules do not achieve the desired effect since they are based on an outmoded understanding of sexuality. If, for fear of punishment, we follow the rules imposed upon our search for sexual self-expression from without, we easily do violence to ourselves, negate aspects of our vitality, and since these energies remain alive in us albeit in a hidden way, we become vulnerable to wholly unpredictable, irrational manifestations of these energies in disguised form. Repression always distorts. This does not mean of course that discipline is harmful and that it is impossible to translate libidinal energies into culture power—we recall here Freud's famous little book on Leonardo da Vinci—but the existence of healthful discipline and cultural sublimation cannot be used as an argument against the distorting effect of repression. The violent exclusion from consciousness of the libidinal substance of human life is dangerous. The manner in which we are related to our own sexuality, then, plays a great part in the self-constitution of our lives. From this it follows that sexual morality has to do not with sexual conduct but with the way in which we relate ourselves to our sexual energies. Since repression has harmful effects on oneself and one's community, it is part of the quest for holiness to transcend the self-inflicted distortions, to be in touch with one's sexual energies, to affirm them, despite their ambiguity, in the forward movement of life. The positive attitude toward exploration and discovery does not imply a rejection of discipline, of boundaries and fidelity. What people long for is the expression of their sexuality within the bounds of reason and love in a non-repressive context. It is, I suppose, to such an evolution of sexual self-possession that the Report refers as creativity and integration. What the Report does not sufficiently examine is the ambiguity and the infantilism from which such a transformation proceeds.

The recognition of the ambiguity of sexuality and the mechanism of repression has profound consequences for moral theology. There are situations where "following the rules" is not an expression of holiness, but a re-enforcement of sexual repression accompanied by anxieties and displacement phenomena. People follow the traditional moral rules governing sexual life for a variety of conscious and unconscious motives, and hence a moral theology that looks simply at the sexual conduct is not able to provide sound guidelines for action. The compulsive obedience to rules, which was at one time demanded by Christian education, reveals itself as highly problematic. Because of the ambiguity of sexuality what people look for is not obedience but transformation and redemption. While the Report recognizes that people yearn for the transfiguration of their sexuality, it does not fully acknowledge the brokenness into which we are born or the turmoil that may accompany the entry into sexual creativity and integration.

Christian theologians often reject the Freudian insights into sexuality because in Freud himself and in many of his followers these insights are part of a deterministic framework and promote a one-sided, dangerous, and reductionist understanding of man. It is true that the great critics of the late enlightenment were heirs of the scientific tradition of the earlier phase and that they carried forward this scientific rationalism in their own theories, even though—and this is their remarkable achievement—the critiques they offered transcended their own presuppositions. Freud transcended positivism by positivism. His quest for scientific truth led him to raise questions about the formation of consciousness and hence make problematic, beyond scientific confidence, the pursuit of pure rationality. Contemporary theologians will not be uncritical followers of the Freudian system of thought, but they will want to assimilate his discoveries as part of the horizon, in which they are addressed by God's word in the Scriptures.

What follows from these remarks is that all men and women, especially in contemporary culture, have to deal with their sexuality in a creative way and that this ongoing endeavor is part and parcel of their life project. This endeavor affects the manner in which people situate themselves in the world and the way in which they look upon the human reality. For this reason, then, the scholarly approach to the topic of human sexuality is never a wholly neutral procedure: despite its scientific detachment, it remains part of the life project. I am not suggesting that scientific, philosophical, or theological explorations of human sexuality are simply rationalizations of personal problems or justifications of the life one has chosen for oneself. I defend the view that scholarship reaches out for objectivity, that it proposes rational arguments to defend its conclusions and seek validation of its insights that has universal appeal. Still, while guarding the quest for rationality, the light in which scholars examine human sexuality, the approach that they take, and the selection of data they look at all reflect in some way or other the role of sexuality in their own life struggle. Studying and theorizing about sexuality is a way of dealing with one's life project. Understanding sexuality is never a purely scientific task: it is a vital issue and hence includes an existential dimension. Again this view does not condemn scientists, philosophers, and theologians to inevitable relativism: still, it does claim that the scholarly quest of understanding sexuality is related to the scholar's own self-understanding and hence is in some sense dependent on personal life options.

I would be willing to argue that the same holds true for the scholarly research into other central dimensions of human existence, such as religion and work. The perception of religion (or work), which enters into a scientific study and rational investigation of religion (or work), is related in one way or another to one's own life project. Since the object that is being studied is not altogether outside of the scientist but operative from within, the research raises inevitably vital questions about one's own self-definition and is guided by the orientation of one's own commitment.

The critique derived from depth psychology is something a theology of human sexuality cannot overlook. It reveals the ambiguity of sexual life and its need of redemption. It also reveals that the Church's moral teaching must be evaluated in terms of its effect on the attitudes and the consciousness of the people. Sexual teachings must be therapeutic: they must serve the personal quest for creativity and integration. In this context it must be said quite honestly that a view of sexuality, worked out by a group of males dedicated to sexual continence, will correspond to a particular life situation and hence suffer from one-sidedness.

## Enlightenment and Sociological Reflection

Let me now turn to another area of critique that cannot be omitted in any discussion of sexuality. Sociological studies have revealed that sexuality is not only a personal phenomenon, shaped by the events and decisions of one's personal history, it is also a social phenomenon, formed by the requirements of the social organization. Sociologists have shown, for instance, that the "Puritanism" of the Victorian age was closely linked to the expanding capitalism of the period and the need for hard work, dedication, and the sacrifice of pleasure on the part of workers in the factory, clerks in the office, and even the owners in their position as entrepreneurs and managers. The capitalism of the age was wholly geared toward production, and it was the demand of the economic organization that called forth a public morality ready to avoid leisure, pleasure, and expansive sexuality. Of course, the hypocrisy of the Victorian age is also well documented. It was important in that age to defend the strict norms of sexual morality, even if one did not follow them oneself, since without the seriousness of the work ethic society could not pursue its aim.

It is of interest to note that this dedicated Puritanism did not affect the Catholic cultures on the European continent. They were still largely pre-industrial societies defined by aristocratic tradition and peasant culture. Here the public attitude toward leisure, pleasure, and sexuality differed greatly from the ethos of capitalism. Even though the Church's teaching provided strict norms, the manner in which these teachings were assimilated and lived out revealed an affirmation of bodily joy. Baroque art reveals a Christian spirituality that rejoices in man's bodily being and delights in swelling breasts, muscular legs, vibrant flesh, and the erotic dimension of the human personality. Protestants thought that Catholics were lazy, that they had far too many feast days, that they lacked seriousness in their worship, that the line between the sacred and the profane was not carefully enough drawn, and that therefore bodily sensuality could pass for religious enthusiasm.

The Victorian age, associated with the early phase of industrial capitalism, has long been left behind. We have mastered the problem of production. A sophisticated technology has removed large-scale drudgery from the factory and the office, and even on the management level rational planning has taken the place of risk-taking and adventure. The present problem of the economy, it has been argued, is consumption. Since capitalism demands the continual expansion of production, we find ourselves with a superabundance of products and society must make a great effort to expand the market and sell the goods. To do this we need markets overseas and armies or political power to protect them. More than that we have to become consumers ourselves. We have here the origin of what sociologists call "consumerism"—the culturally created attitude that makes people yearn for a higher standard of living, for comfort, for an ever changing variety of goods to be enjoyed. Karl Marx called the endless desire produced by the later stages of capitalism "the fetishism of commodities." In the present age public culture turns us into spenders. While it is still necessary to be efficient and dedicated from nine to five in the factory and the office—here the old work ethic still holds—at night and over the weekend we must become swingers, spend money, and consume products. Our culture has created a new kind of hedonism, a hedonism the satisfaction of which costs money and devours products.

We note in passing that this expensive hedonism is quite different from the search for pleasure that characterized the youth movement in the sixties and the unconventional freedom found in various liberation movements. There pleasure was not bought but shared. There pleasure was a gesture of protest against a forbidding society and an anticipation of the freedom that liberation was to bring. The evaluation of such pleasure will depend on how sound and useful one judges the impatient protest of the youth movement against the dominant ethos produced by imperialism abroad, racism at home, and the calculating outlook characteristic of capitalism.

The expensive hedonism of late capitalist society is, in any case, quite different. Here sexuality becomes merchandise. Sex is used in advertising to promote the sale of commodities, and itself becomes a product in the vast entertainment industry. The purpose of sexuality is to transform people into spenders and swingers. Some critics of the present economic system even suggest that late capitalism wants people to trivialize their free time and recreation lest they study the issues of the day, engage in discussion of serious things, and become critics of the established order. Today the impact of the industrialized societies on the less developed nations is followed by the same artificial sexualization with devastating effects on the pre-industrial cultures. By contrast, the Communist countries whose main problem is still the production of goods advocate sexual norms and public morals that correspond to our own Victorian age.

The sociology of sexual mores is of great importance to moral theology. While at one time the Church's official teaching exhibited distrust of sexual expressions unless they were related to married life (even though the typical Catholic cultures never followed this), contemporary Catholic theologians, under the impact of personalist thought, have come to a more trusting, more affirmative, more generous approach to sexuality. This trend is clearly represented in the Report. It represents a long-needed liberation from the overly biological understanding of sexuality. At the same time, the ambiguity of this turn to liberalism must not be overlooked. We live in a culture that is excessively sexualized by the needs of the economic system and pushes people into a disconnected and unreflective search for pleasure that often damages their lives. Catholic moral teaching must deal with this. As so often in history, Christian theology must wrestle simultaneously on two different fronts: theology must defend the right to personal growth and the freedom of sexuality within the bounds of reason and love against the old, legalistic morality; and at the same time theology must defend reflection, discipline, and fidelity in sexual life seeing that these are undermined by the onslaught of the artificial hedonism characteristic of late capitalist society. The Church's teaching on sexual morality ought to raise the consciousness of people in regard to the power society holds over them.

Sociological reflection provides another, related critical perspective. It has been argued that sexuality is a metaphor of politics. Already Plato drew a close parallel between the self-understanding of persons and the perception of society. To well-ordered personal

life where reason holds sway over the lower faculties corresponds
the well-ordered republic in which the rule of wise government
guides and controls the subordinate classes of society. A hierarchical self-understanding where reason exercises its authority over the
emotion and sexuality is reflected in a hierarchical ordering of
society where the government is lord over the activities of the
people. Plato's love of rational order was so great that he sought
to banish the poet and the dreamer from his republic.

The Platonic intuition is vindicated by contemporary sociological research on the authoritarian personality, that is to say
men and women who favor authoritarian government. In these
cases, the vertical perception of society, people ruled by a just
ruler, corresponds to a psychological self-understanding that is
equally vertical, the instincts ruled by the disciplined self. The
authoritarian personality thinks of himself as deeply divided between rational head and disordered, unruly, and seething desires,
and he regards it as his central human task to submit his lower
drives to the dictates of his higher consciousness. In this context,
the rigid control of sexual feelings and impulses comes to symbolize the ordered society with the lower classes in subjection to their
rulers, while an unconventional and expansive sexuality comes to
stand for civil disobedience, criticism, and revolt. Man's relationship to his own sexuality comes to be a metaphor of his politics.

This line of investigation sheds light on a variety of political
and ecclesiastical developments. It shows the close connection between obedience and chastity in the Christian Platonic tradition.
There is good reason to think that the ecclesiastical insistence on
a celibate clergy is related to the high value placed by the Church
on obedience and submission of the will. The same line of
thought explains why the groups in society that see themselves as
the guardians of sexual morality and campaign against sexual license and pornography are usually defenders of right-wing politics.
Here the demand for sexual control becomes an expression of
"law and order." The same principle also makes plausible the observation that radical movements, socialist or anarchist, at odds
with the established powers, often symbolize their resistance by a
special indifference to the commonly accepted sexual mores. At
least, the defenders of the tradition accuse the radicals of under-

mining the family and engaging in shocking sexual practices. The churches themselves tended to accuse heretical movements of encouraging sexual immorality, from the Apocalypse which suspected heretical groups of condoning fornication to the Catholics during the Reformation who made Luther into a man of the flesh. Friedrich Engels noticed this ecclesiastical practice and compared it to the anti-socialist propaganda of his day accusing all socialists of practicing free love.

It can be argued that if people opt for a more cooperative understanding of society and engage themselves in the struggle to change the existing order, they also acquire—unbeknownst to themselves—a more cooperative understanding of themselves. They see themselves as people who define their life project through a conversion in which intelligence, feelings, and sexuality take an active part. As the ideal society is one which is constituted by the participation of all sections, so the integrated personality is one in which all the inner voices can express themselves and even the passions have their say. There is then a political dimension to sexual ethics. The manner in which we relate ourselves to our own sexuality (whether in an authoritarian or a dialogical way) is linked to our political vision of society and the authority exercised in the Church and state to which we belong. This is an aspect, it seems to me, which moral theology cannot overlook. The Church's sexual teaching must be both therapeutically and politically responsible.

There is a political dimension even in the defense of such time-honored values as the institution of marriage and the interdict of abortion. Émile Durkheim claimed that if anyone offered him a detailed description of family life he would be able to construct in detail the society to which this family belonged. The regulation of authority and sexuality in the family is a parable of society at large. Christian theologians must be willing to turn to sociological research to discover the political convictions that motivate movements which on the surface deal mainly with traditional morality. In Latin America, right-wing groups often organize around the defense of tradition, family, and property. Conservatives are more sensitive to the stability, loyalty, and cohesion of the family while critics are more aware of the patterns of subservience in the family and their projection upon the social order. Even the evaluation of the various anti-abortion movements demands a political analysis. If anti-abortion groups persuade people to make this single issue the key to their political loyalties, one must examine who is in fact being helped by this policy. In some contexts people look upon abortion as an extreme expression of capitalism: from claiming full control over one's property pro-abortionists defend full control over one's body. In other contexts, the pro-life movement is tied to the desire for greater control over sexuality and fosters law-and-order politics coupled with free enterprise ideals. The Catholic theologian will have to look at homosexuality from the same point of view. Today the political forces in North America that stand against the emancipation of gay citizens often represent the political right wing, for whom homosexuals are the only minority left that it is still respectable to hate. The exclusion of homosexuals from human nature, in which Church and society have cooperated, has produced an age-old story of cruelty and hatred the proportions of which are just beginning to emerge. To formulate norms of sexual behavior as if this political dimension did not exist has, after the enlightenment, become irresponsible.

These elements of critique are not treated in the Report. Since they have hardly been explored by Catholic theologians, we cannot blame the Report for leaving out this critical perspective. Still, since the present volume represents an evaluation of the Report's achievement, it must be pointed out that in its acknowledgment of the enlightenment only the scientific phase is respected, while the critical phase remains almost wholly undeveloped. Christians seeking fidelity to the gospel today cannot simply repeat what was said in previous centuries: they must listen to God's word in a new context, a context defined by enlightenment culture. They will hear a message that the ancients did not and could not hear. This does not mean that theologians want to water down the gospel in an attempt to assimilate it to the world. The preceding remarks have shown that the contrary is true: dialogue with the critical tradition enables us to draw from the revealed teaching a judgment on the world and a promise for liberation that are at odds with the structures and the cultural ideals of the wicked world.

## Chapter Five

❧

# AN INTEGRIST UNDERSTANDING

### WILLIAM E. MAY

Elsewhere I have offered criticisms of the book *Human Sexuality: New Directions in American Catholic Thought*. The most extensive critique, co-authored with John Harvey, O.S.F.S., focused on five areas of the work:

1. its understanding of human sexuality and its purpose;
2. the moral methodology that it employed;
3. its use of Scripture and of the Catholic tradition, in particular its use of the documents of Vatican Council II;
4. its employment of empirical data; and
5. its treatment of the specific issue of homosexuality.[1]

The editor of this volume, Professor Dennis Doherty, has commented already on this previous critique,[2] claiming that it was "a hastily written misunderstanding" and that the criticisms it offered were hardly "devastating," as Harvey and I had contended.[3] Readers are encouraged to consult this previous critique and Doherty's review of it so that they can judge for themselves whether or not it presented evidence and arguments sufficient to show that the authors of *Human Sexuality* "have done a disservice to truth and to the Catholic community."[4]

Here I intend to set forth as clearly as I can the reasons why there is a sharp disagreement between the authors of *Human Sexuality* and persons like myself on questions of sexual morality. Disagreements over the rightness or wrongness of specific sorts of sexual behavior (e.g., contraception, premarital sex, adultery) are rooted, I hope to show, in more fundamental disagreements over the nature of human sexuality, the meaning of the human person, and the moral meaning of human acts. There is operative in the authors of *Human Sexuality* and in those writers upon whom they rely and to whom they appeal an understanding of human sexuality, of the human person, and of the moral meaning of human acts that is quite different from that operative in, for example, Pope Paul's encyclical *Humanae Vitae* and in the thought of those who believe that the genital expression of human sexuality is morally good only within the framework of a true marriage between man and woman.

Thus in the first part of this chapter I shall try to set forth the understanding of human sexuality, of the person, and of the moral meaning of human acts discernible not only in *Human Sexuality* but also in the writings of those Catholic theologians upon whom Kosnik et al. rely and to whom they appeal in the development of their positions. Although some of the theologians upon whom Kosnik et al. rely may disagree, and even disagree substantively, on specific conclusions and even with their proposal that human sexuality is to be understood as creative and integrative rather than as unitive and procreative,[5] these disagreements are in the nature of a family quarrel. They speak the same language, as I hope to show, and their language is quite different from that spoken by me and by many others.

In presenting the views of this school of thought I shall focus attention primarily on the understanding of human sexuality central to it, giving subsidiary attention to the correlative understanding of the person and of the moral meaning of human acts. My reason for centering attention on the understanding of human sexuality is simply that the sexuality in question is that of *human persons* and it is "in the nature of the human person and his acts"[6] that the authors of *Human Sexuality*, in company with other contemporary writers seeking to follow the lead of the Second Vatican Council, seek to discover the moral meaning of human acts.[7]

In the second part I shall endeavor to articulate a quite different understanding of human sexuality, the human person, and the moral meaning of human acts. This understanding, too, is developed by Catholic writers[8] who seek to discern the moral meaning of human acts "in the nature of the human person and his acts." The point is that these writers have a very different understanding of human sexuality, of the human person, and the moral meaning of human acts from that at the heart of *Human Sexuality*. These Catholic writers see their understanding at the heart of *Humanae Vitae's* teaching, a teaching which in their judgment expresses the developing Catholic tradition. In both parts of the chapter I shall take up the question of contraception as an issue that concretely and forcefully illustrates these differing understandings of human sexuality, the human person, and the moral meaning of human acts.

## The "Separatist" Understanding of Human Sexuality

The understanding of human sexuality, the person, and the moral meaning of human acts central to *Human Sexuality* will here be designated as a "separatist" understanding, and the meaning of this term will become clear as we proceed. This understanding emerged in the efforts of Catholic writers to show that contraceptive marital intercourse is morally justifiable. The principal arguments were articulated in the years immediately prior to the publication of *Humanae Vitae*, that is, from 1961 to 1967,[9] and since then have been accepted by many Catholic authors.[10] These arguments are warmly endorsed by the authors of *Human Sexuality*.[11] Since these arguments were persuasively brought together by the authors of the celebrated "Majority Report" of the Papal Commission on the Regulation of Fertility, I will first summarize the position developed in this Report[12] in order to introduce us to the understanding of human sexuality that is common to these Catholic writers.

In developing their rationale for a change in the teaching of the Church on the intrinsic malice of artificial contraception the authors of the Majority Report pointed to the changed sociological conditions of contemporary life, to our newly discovered knowledge of the process of human generation, and above all to "a changed estimation of the value and meaning of human sexuality and . . . a better grasp of the duty of man to humanize and to bring to greater perfection for the life of man what is given in nature."[13]

What did these authors mean by "a changed estimation of the value and meaning of human sexuality"? By it they meant, as Louis Janssens was later to say, that "the most profound meaning of human sexuality is that it is a relational reality, having a special significance for the person in his relationships."[14] Here we find a key notion taken over by the authors of *Human Sexuality* for in describing the meaning of human sexuality Kosnik et al. stress that it is "preeminently . . . the mode whereby an isolated subjectivity reaches out to communion with another subject," thereby "serving the development of genuine personhood by calling people to a clearer recognition of their relational nature, of their absolute need to reach out and embrace others to achieve personal fulfillment."[15]

The authors of the Majority Report recognized that there is a generative aspect of human sexuality and of sexual union; this is ordered to the procreative good of human sexuality and of marriage, namely, the conception, birth, nourishing, and education of new human beings. In addition, they held that there is a relationship between these two thrusts of human sexuality (the unitive-relational and the generative-procreative) insofar as the procreative good[16] requires that children be begotten in an act expressive of the love between parents who will provide them with the home and education they need and inasmuch as the parents, whose life is shared in marriage and in the marital act, are summoned to share their life generously with children.[17] The unitive, relational aspect of human sexuality, moreover, must be realized in every act of conjugal union, but it would be irresponsible and indeed impossible for every marital act to realize the procreative aspect of sexuality.[18] These authors thus concluded that married persons could avoid the contraceptive mentality indicative of a selfish hedonism by being generously and responsibly procreative within the whole of their married life.[19] They could, in short, use artificial contraceptives *in individual acts of marriage* in order to regulate fertility responsibly and thus serve the procreative good of living children and the good of their conjugal love and still

avoid a contraceptive mentality, that is, a hedonistic rejection of
the good of children.[20] They were further justified in doing this
because God has given man dominion over "what is given in physical nature . . . to develop it with a view to the good of the whole
person."[21] Now the biological fecundity of human sexuality pertains to that which is given by physical nature. In and of itself it
is not a *personal* value of human sexuality, as is its unitive, relational dimension; it is rather a *material given* that needs to be, as
the authors of the Report put it, "assumed into the human
sphere," that is, brought under control of human reason.[22]
(Here too we note a central teaching found in *Human Sexuality.*[23])

In sum, the great human and Christian value of human sexuality that needs to be protected and honored in the conjugal act is
its unitive, relational dimension, "its most profound meaning."
The procreative good of human sexuality is, in the concrete, the
living children who are begotten in acts of love between their parents and nourished and educated by them. The biological fecundity of human sexuality is itself a matter of man's biological, not
personal, nature, and it is to be given human and personal
significance by being ordered to responsible fertility.

The argument just summarized, one congenial to the authors of
*Human Sexuality,*[24] recapitulates the principal reasons leading
many Catholic theologians to conclude that contraceptive intercourse can, within the framework of a generously fruitful marriage,[25] be justified.

Although this argument provides us with an initial indication
of the understanding of human sexuality operative in these Catholic writers and in the authors of *Human Sexuality,* a deeper insight into their mode of thought can be gained if we reflect on the
significance that the lived experience of marriage on the part of
many sincere and devoted couples had in the development of this
position. Moreover, in examining this aspect of their thought we
shall see why these Catholic writers, including Kosnik et al.,[26]
have come to the conclusion that there is no morally significant
difference between rhythm and artificial contraception and why
they have unanimously rejected the moral methodology found in
*Humanae Vitae* and in authors who support the teaching of
*Humanae Vitae* as "physicalistic."

A principal consideration contributing to the conclusion that contraception can be morally responsible was the lived experience of many good-hearted couples who found the teaching of the Church proscribing contraception as intrinsically evil to be harsh and unrealistic.[27] These people could see little difference of moral significance between the use of artificial contraceptives and the practice of rhythm, which requires calculation.[28] If it is morally permissible to regulate conception by rhythm, why is it not morally permissible to regulate conception by artificial means? After all, God has given us the right and the responsibility to use human intelligence to subdue nature—and surely the biological and physiological processes leading to conception are part of the world of nature[29]—to serve the true good of persons.

The response of the Majority Report, one quite acceptable to the authors of *Human Sexuality*,[30] to this question is important and therefore merits close attention. In this Report we read:

The true opposition is not to be sought between some material conformity to the *physiological processes of nature* and some artificial intervention. For it is natural to man to use his skill in order to put under human control *what is given by physical nature*. The opposition is to be sought really between one way of acting which is contraceptive and opposed to a prudent and generous fruitfulness, and another way which is in an ordered relationship to responsible fruitfulness and which has a concern for education and all the essential human and Christian values.[31]

Note first that this passage confirms something already noted, namely, the belief on the part of those who justify contraception in this way that the biological fecundity of human sexuality is something "given by physical nature," consisting in "physiological processes." As such this biological fecundity or procreativity is *not* an essential human and Christian value.[32]

Note secondly that this passage claims that the use of artificial contraceptives, within the framework of a generously fruitful marital relationship, is not a truly contraceptive way of acting. I confess that I find it somewhat paradoxical, to say the least, that one can deliberately choose to practice contraception and yet not act contraceptively (something to which I shall return later), but within the framework of the understanding of human sexuality central to the argument of these authors justifying contraception this does make some sense, for in this understanding contraception is defined as the selfish, hedonistic exclusion of children from a marriage.

The third very important thing to note is how this way of thinking has led those Catholic writers upon whom the authors of *Human Sexuality* rely and the authors of *Human Sexuality* themselves to equate the practice of contraception with the practice of periodic continence. The Majority Report equated the two by asserting that each could be ordered to responsible procreation in a *non-contraceptive* way. More recent writers, for example Bernard Häring, James Burtchaell, and Kosnik et al., speak of two types of contraceptives, "artificial" and "natural."[33] Their point is that there is no morally significant difference between the regulation of conception by artificial means and by the practice of periodic continence. In fact, Kosnik et al. include complete abstinence from marital coition as a "method of contraception."[34]

*Humanae Vitae*, on the other hand, sees a significant moral difference between these ways of meeting spousal and parental obligations, judging that the one, the use of artificial contraceptives, is intrinsically a morally disordered act and that the other can be, when properly motivated, morally legitimate.[35] Catholic thinkers who justify contraception for the reasons already given find this teaching almost incredible. They believe that it is an indication of the physicalistic ethic upon which the encyclical is based, and, as Charles E. Curran has observed in an article contrasting *Humanae Vitae* and *Human Sexuality* physicalism is *the* basic flaw in the encyclical, the reason why its teaching simply cannot elicit the support of theologians and people today. Curran observes that the encyclical, while granting that the value of procreation can be intentionally excluded from a particular act, insists that its "physical structure" cannot be interfered with. He then notes that, since it is clear to human reason and in human experience that contraceptive marital relations can be an expression of love, it follows that the encyclical has placed a moral value on the biological structure of the act. But this is simply physicalism, the attachment of a moral value to the biological structure of the act.[36] The

authors of *Human Sexuality*, along with such other Catholic
writers as Daniel Maguire and Joseph Selling, are in definite
agreement with Curran in claiming that physicalism is the major
flaw in the encyclical and in the moral methodology it and authors who support its teaching employ.[87]

It is now time to reflect on the arguments we have been reviewing. I shall begin by commenting on the relevance of experience
to the question of contraception and on the claim that there is no
morally significant difference between "natural" and "artificial"
contraception. I shall then reflect on the understanding of human
sexuality, of the human person, and the moral meaning of human
acts disclosed in the thought of these Catholic authors.

There is a real obligation to take the experience of people
seriously into account in making any moral evaluation. Yet experience needs to be interpreted and understood, and there is the
difficulty that different people experience marital life in different
ways. To me it is quite relevant that a great many married couples, both Catholic and non-Catholic, refuse to use contraceptives
not because they are blindly following laws laid down by some authority extrinsic to them but precisely because they believe that
the practice of contraception entails the rejection of something
truly good and worthy of human love, namely their God-given
power to procreate new life. Such people evidently have a much
different understanding of human sexuality than do the authors of
*Human Sexuality* (and we shall look at this later). Here I simply
want to note that this experience also needs to be taken into consideration. These people appreciate deeply the agonizing problems
that all married people face in the endeavor to strengthen their
love and to exercise their procreative powers responsibly. They
simply believe that the contraceptive choice is not the morally responsible way to meet these obligations. Experience, in other
words, is a two-edged sword that cuts both ways. Of itself it neither justifies nor condemns contraception. It needs to be critically
assessed.

The contention by the Catholic authors, including Kosnik et
al., whose thought we have been reviewing, that there is no morally significant difference between contraceptive intercourse and
the practice of periodic continence (or even, in some instances, of
complete continence within a marriage for years), is simply er-

roneous. The reason is that those who practice contraception and those who regulate conception by periodic continence *are doing different sorts of human acts* and are *intending different things*, as Elizabeth Anscombe, among others, has pointed out quite clearly.[38] I grant that someone acts contraceptively and that rhythm is equivalent to contraception morally if he or she determines to prevent *this particular act* from being procreative (or this series of acts from being procreative) by any means necessary and then chooses rhythm for aesthetic or hygienic reasons. As she and others note, it is *not* the physical structure of the act that determines the morality of the deed (as those who defend contraception and consider *Humanae Vitae* and its supporters as physicalists insist that this encyclical and the arguments of its supporters must be interpreted as holding), but the *different intentionalities* involved and the *different sorts of human acts* that are being chosen and done. A couple who contracepts and a couple who practices periodic continence may well agree in their purposes (or *intentions* in this sense of the word), for both may be legitimately seeking to avoid a pregnancy here and now. But they are doing different things, that is, choosing different kinds of human acts as means to bring this purpose about. Those who practice contraception are, after all, contracepting. They choose both to have sexual relations *here and now* and to make *this act* of sexual union infertile by using a contraceptive, that is, some agency whose sole purpose is to destroy the procreative thrust of *this act*. They make their act of marital (or non-marital) union *anti*-procreative, not merely non-procreative; they make it to be the sort of act that is no longer the sort of act by which life can be given. This is the thrust, purpose, or intent of their deed insofar as it is contraceptive. This is the precise reason why they use contraceptives. Those who seek to meet parental and spousal responsibilities by the practice of periodic continence choose to do different sorts of acts. First of all, they choose to abstain from having marital relations when making love might lead irresponsibly to conception or would compel them to use contraceptives. They abstain, not because they consider the marital act something wrongful—far from it, for they regard it as inherently good. They abstain from it *here and now* because in these circumstances it would not, in their judgment, be a truly conjugal act because it would either be an irresponsible use of their procreative power or it would, by making them use contraceptives, mean a rejection of the goodness of their procreativity. They rightfully choose to have marital union when the wife's procreative power although present is in a condition when it cannot be actualized; this choice is surely justifiable, for there is no obligation that every marital act lead to the conception of a child and there is the good of conjugal love that can be expressed in and through this act.[39] They are being non-procreative, but they are not being anti-procreative. They are not engaging in contraception.

These reflections on the difference between contraceptive and non-contraceptive behavior are, in my judgment, crucial for understanding the underlying disagreements between the advocates of what I term a "separatist" understanding of human sexuality (whose thought we have been examining) and those who propose what I term an "integrist" understanding of human sexuality. Before turning to an investigation of this integrist understanding of human sexuality, of the human person, and of the moral meaning of human acts, however, it is necessary to comment on the separatist understanding of human sexuality, of the human person, and the moral meaning of human acts.

I have noted already that the authors of *Human Sexuality* and the writers whose thought charts the "directions" they pursue believe that the most profound meaning of human sexuality is its personal, relational significance, the fact that it enables persons (originally, in the development of this line of thought, married persons[40]) to share their life and love. The procreative good of human sexuality is, concretely, the living child, responsibly begotten and educated. The biological fecundity of human sexuality is ordered to these human and Christian values (interpersonal relationships and responsible procreativity), but of itself it is simply a biological process, a material given, a part of the physical world over which the human person has been given dominion. The authors of *Human Sexuality* surely entertain this understanding of human sexuality. In fact, they wish to move beyond the view that human sexuality is unitive and procreative (and they wish to do so *because* this view is too limiting[41]) to the view that it is creative and integrative.[42]

I call this a *separatist* understanding of human sexuality. By this I mean that these Catholic authors (including Kosnik et al.) have developed an understanding of human sexuality that in effect separates the unitive and procreative dimensions of human sexuality, deeming the former alone the personally and humanly significant dimension of human sexuality and the latter as, of itself, purely a functional value that can *become* personally and humanly valuable when it is assumed into consciousness and rationally controlled and ordered to the procreative good of human sexuality, namely living children.

In short, the understanding of human sexuality central to the arguments of *Catholic* authors,[43] including the authors of *Human Sexuality*, to justify contraceptive intercourse sees the most profound and humanly significant meaning of human sexuality to consist in the ability it gives to us to enter into intimate personal relationships with others and in this way to develop genuine personhood and to reach out to embrace others.[44] For these writers the biological fecundity of human sexuality is, of itself, only a material given, not a *personal* value.[45]

A notion of the person is likewise involved in this understanding of human sexuality. Many who articulate this vision understand man as an "incarnate spirit"[46] or as a free and conscious subject aware of itself as a self and capable of making choices. In Kosnik et al. the human person is, in fact, described as a "subject" or "subjectivity" that is embodied in either a male body structure or a female body structure.[47] The personality of the human subject consists in his/her ability to relate to other persons or selves, and it is for this reason that the most profound meaning of human sexuality lies in the capacity it provides to reach out and to touch others in an intimacy of shared life and love.

This view is, ultimately, a dualism in the pejorative meaning of that term, in my opinion; it places the body beneath the person, regarding it as a material substrate distinct from the person. This subject cannot be pursued more thoroughly here.[48]

Concomitant with the emergence of this understanding of human sexuality as primarily a relational reality of personal value was the development of a theory concerning the moral meaning of human acts. In fact the two—the separatist understanding of human sexuality and the normative moral theory—proceeded hand in glove, as familiarity with the efforts on the part of Peter Knauer,

William Van der Marck, and Cornelius Van der Poel during the period 1965-68 to interpret the old principle of double effect testifies.[49] Intimations of this new theory are discernible in the Majority Report,[50] and no wonder, inasmuch as one of the authors of this Report and an author who has deeply influenced Kosnik et al.,[51] Joseph Fuchs, later developed the theory in a much more comprehensive (even if somewhat ambiguous) way in an influential article in *Gregorianum*.[52] Richard McCormick has brilliantly chronicled the development of this new theory, to which he has contributed significantly himself, in his influential "Notes on Moral Theology."[53] Briefly put, this theory collapses the old principle of double effect—a principle that presupposes, as Michael B. Crowe so perceptively notes, "that there are some actions . . . that may never, in any circumstances, be directly willed"[54]—into the principle of proportionate reason or good. According to its advocates, and the authors of *Human Sexuality* clearly indicate that they are to be counted among these,[55] one can rightly intend directly the destruction of a premoral, non-moral, or ontic good (such as that of the fecundity associated with human sexuality or even life itself) so long as intending this evil is required in order to protect or enhance a higher good.[56] If one applies this principle to the issue of contraception, it follows that one can rightly intend directly the disvalue or "ontic evil" of contraception (the deprivation of a sexual act's biological fecundity) when this is necessary to enable participation in the higher good of sharing life made possible by the relational dimension of human sexuality.[57]

This understanding of the moral meaning of human acts fits in well with the understanding of human sexuality and of the person in the separatist mentality. It holds that in conflict situations one has the right to act for the "higher" good even if this means that one must deliberately, of set purpose, choose an act in which one cannot not intend the destruction of a "lower" good. The bodily goods of human life, insofar as they are, of themselves, not dependent upon consciousness and intersubjective relationships, are always of a lower order of goodness than the "personalistic" or "personal" goods of human life, i.e., goods in which we can participate only as conscious subjects.

*The "Integrist" Understanding of Human Sexuality,*
*the Human Person, and the Moral Meaning of Human Acts*

The teaching of *Humanae Vitae* that contraceptive acts are intrinsically disordered is well known.[58] According to Pope Paul it is the teaching of the Church, acting in its capacity to interpret the natural law, that "each and every marriage act must remain open to the transmission of life."[59] Since Paul himself recognized that not every marital act can result in conception and since he also taught that there is no moral obligation for spouses to have a positive procreative intent whenever they choose to express their love for one another through the marital act, it should be obvious that he was not seeking to describe the physical structure of the marital act when he said that "each and every marriage act must remain open to the transmission of life." His meaning must be different. It becomes clear when we realize that what he is saying is morally wrong is the anti-procreative choice entailed in choosing to contracept: "excluded is every action which, either in anticipation of the conjugal act or in its accomplishment, or in the development of its natural consequences aims, whether as end or means, at making procreation impossible."[60]

What is the understanding of human sexuality, the human person, and the moral meaning of human acts underlying Pope Paul's thought? I call it an *integrist* understanding. With respect to human sexuality it holds that the unitive or life-uniting dimension or power of human sexuality and the procreative or life-giving dimension or power of human sexuality are both personally and humanly good and are, moreover, inherently and indissolubly interrelated. That this understanding is central to *Humanae Vitae* is clear, for in the encyclical Pope Paul affirms that the teaching regarding the intrinsically disordered nature of contraceptive acts is "founded upon the inseparable connection—which is willed by God and which man cannot lawfully break on his own initiative—between the two *meanings* of the conjugal act: the unitive and the procreative meanings."[61] This is the key affirmation of the encyclical. Note that Paul here refers to the *meanings* of the conjugal act (and of human sexuality); he does not refer to biological functions or processes. Another central passage, of great impor-

tance in rightly understanding its message, is that in which the
Pope says:

> indeed it is justly considered that a conjugal act imposed upon
> one's partner without regard for his or her condition and lawful
> desires is not a true act of love, and therefore it goes against the
> requirements which the right moral order calls for in the rela-
> tionship between husband and wife. By the same token it must
> be acknowledged that a mutual act of love, which jeopardizes
> the possibility of transmitting life . . . goes against both the di-
> vine design of marriage, and the will of the first Author of
> life.[62]

Here Paul is teaching that what is wrong or immoral, what is contrary to right reason, are marital acts in which *either* the unitive
*or* procreative meaning of the act is repudiated. The reason must
be that he regards each of these meanings as values or goods par-
ticipating in the goodness of the human person and thus worthy
of human love. Thus the deliberate intent to reject either is not a
morally good intent, and therefore human acts expressing this intent are not the sort or kind of human acts that human persons
ought to be willing to do.

But why does Pope Paul affirm that the unitive (life-uniting)
and the procreative (life-giving) meanings of human sexuality are
*both* goods intrinsic to the human person and why does he hold
that they are indissolubly related? To answer these questions is to
understand the teaching of *Humanae Vitae* and to grasp what I
have called an integrist understanding of human sexuality.

Since the separatist understanding of human sexuality recognizes that the life-uniting or unitive meaning of sexuality is
humanly and personally valuable, it is not necessary to dwell on
this point (although I believe that this separatist understanding,
precisely by severing the personal bond between the procreative
and the unitive-relational meanings of human sexuality, actually
fails to do justice to the full richness of the unitive meaning of
our sexuality). Thus my focus here will be on the personal value
or goodness of the procreative dimension of our sexuality and on
the bond between the unitive and the procreative.

To grasp why an integrist view sees the procreative meaning of human sexuality as a good intrinsic to the person, it is first necessary to realize that for this understanding a human person is *not* a conscious subjectivity (although a human person, precisely in virtue of being a person to begin with, is capable of becoming a conscious subject). On this understanding the term *person* is properly predicated of any living member of the human species insofar as any and every member of this species is a being of moral worth, an entity of priceless and irreplaceable value. Philosophically this understanding of person can be defended on the grounds that the human species is radically different in kind from other species of our experience.[63] Religiously, it is rooted in the belief that a living human being is the flesh to which God wills to communicate his own life and love, that it is the flesh that God himself became in Jesus. This living flesh is capable of becoming a conscious, experiencing subject able to relate to other subjects; but, on this view, living human flesh does not *become* a person; it *is* a person.

On this understanding, too, to be a human person is to be a sexual person. There are no asexual members of the human species; all of us are male or female persons, two equal but differing and complementary icons or created words of the divine Persons who *are* asexual.[64] Male and female do not, of course, belong to different species: each is fully and equally human, but being male or being female is not a merely contingent happenstance, and it is not precisely because the *body* of a human person is not something other than the person but is rather constitutive of the *being* of the person. The *body* I am, the *person* I am, is a sexual person, not asexual. Sexuality is thus integral to the human person, and the sexuality of a human person is of necessity either a male sexuality or female sexuality. Human persons are thus males and females, adult men and women, boys and girls, boy babies and girl babies (both pre- and post-natally).

This is why the integrist understanding of human sexuality sees the life-giving or procreative dimension of human sexuality as something personally and humanly significant, for it is rooted in a power, sexual in nature, of the person, just as the life-uniting or unitive meaning of human sexuality is rooted in a power, sexual in nature, of the person. As human, personal, sexual powers the unitive and procreative dimensions of human sexuality participate in the dignity and sanctity of the person and are thus goods *of* the person, not goods *for* the person. Both are personal and thus real goods (*bona honesta*) and not merely useful or functional goods (*bona utilia*). The procreative dimension of human sexuality is not, therefore, on the integrist view as distinguished from the separatist, a merely biological given or function; rather it is a personal, sexual power.

The integrist understanding also sees these two personal sexual powers, the power to give life and the power to give love or unite lives, as intrinsically interrelated, meant for each other, reciprocally interpenetrating and meaning-giving. They are intrinsically interrelated both because they are powers of the one human person and because they are brought into exercise in one and the same act, the "touch" of genital coition. What is truly remarkable, furthermore, is that each of these powers is expressed differently yet complementarily by the male and the female in this uniquely significant act. This is the "sex act," the act that possesses its full meaning, the meaning that it is meant to have and ought to have, only when it is in truth the marital act, so that its meaning is debased, distorted, and abused when it is *not* the marital act. Reflections on the uniqueness of this act are necessary in order to realize why an integrist understanding of human sexuality sees the unitive and procreative meanings of human sexuality as intrinsically linked, and why this understanding insists upon the sexual differentiation of the species and the complementarity of the sexes and the significance of their complementarity for the question of contraception.

The marital act is uniquely significant, first, because it involves a way of touching that is irreducibly different yet complementary for the male and the female. The female does not have a penis and therefore cannot, in this unique act, enter the body, the person, of the male, whereas he can and does personally enter into her; on the other hand, the female is uniquely capable of receiving personally into her body, her person, the male, and her act of receiving in a giving sort of way is just as central to the meaning of this "touch" as is the male's act of giving his person to her in a receiving sort of way.[65] The male cannot, in this act, give himself to the female, unite his person with hers, i.e., exercise the unitive power of his sexuality, unless she gives herself to him by receiving him, nor can she receive him in this self-giving way by the exercise of her unitive power of sexuality unless he gives himself to her by letting himself be received by her. The "touch" has an entirely different meaning if there is not this giving in a receiving sort of way by the male and this receiving in a giving sort of way by the female.

This way of touching is unique, secondly, insofar as it is the sort or kind of act that makes it possible for the male and female to exercise their beautiful personal and sexual powers of procreation, of giving life to a new human person. It is the sort or kind of act —indeed the only sort of human act—that is "open to the transmission of life" in a procreative way.[66] The "touch" of marital coition, in other words, is an utterly unique way of touching and of being touched because in it and through it the life-uniting or unitive and life-giving or procreative sexual powers of the male and female are meant to be exercised together insofar as this act is the sort of act that is life-uniting and life-giving. This is, in my judgment, what Paul VI meant when he spoke of this act as being "open to the transmission of life." This is surely the reason why the integrist view of human sexuality sees the unitive or life-uniting and the procreative or life-giving meanings of human sexuality as indissolubly related.

Since I have already commented on the complementary way in which male and female exercise their sexual power to unite their lives in the marital act, I should now like to show how the complementary sexuality of male and female is manifested in the exercise of their sexual power to give life in this act. The male is continuously fertile and, moreover, knows that he is or at any rate ought to know that he is. This means that in choosing the marital act (or pseudo-marital acts) he necessarily chooses to actualize simultaneously both his life-uniting and life-giving sexual powers. The female, however, is not continuously fertile. That is, her sexual and personal power of giving life is cyclical, so that it is not fully actualized every time she chooses the marital act. There is surely no reason why she may not choose to touch her husband and be touched by him in the beautiful touch of marital union when her wonderful power of giving life is present but not fully actualizable by the coital touch. In choosing to unite their persons in this act, husband and wife are still choosing the sort or kind of act that is open to the transmission of life, for it is the sort of act that expresses acceptance of the goodness of the human sexual powers to unite persons and to give life. The act may not be procreative, but it is not anti-procreative.

We have now seen the understanding of human sexuality and of the person in the integrist view. A moral method or an understanding of the moral meaning of human acts is also central to this integrist view and to the teaching of *Humanae Vitae*. Central to this moral theory is the recognition that we make or break our lives in and through our choices. We give to ourselves an identity by our willingness to choose to do deeds of a specifiable sort. There is, in other words, an inherent relationship between the acts or deeds that a human person chooses to do and the moral being or identity of that person. Our acts or deeds, in fact, are like "words" that we, the living words of God, speak; and in speaking them we are saying "yes" or "no" to his offer of friendship and of life.[67]

Because the moral theory at the heart of an integrist view of human sexuality, the person, and the moral meaning of human acts affirms the living connection between acts and being, it cannot accept the "paradoxical" teaching of the separatists that a person can choose to engage in individual acts of contraception—indeed, to make it a policy to engage in contraceptive intercourse over a prolonged period of time—and not take on the identity of a contraceptor or develop a "contraceptive" mentality. Acts that we freely choose to do not only express the moral person we are, they generate the moral person we become. An isolated, individual act of adultery or contraception may not, in truth, be the expression of an adulterous or a contraceptive mind—the one acting in this way may not be truly "himself" or "herself" here and now; the act contradicts or is in conflict with his or her being. But if a person makes it a policy to choose to do deeds that are truthfully describable as deeds of adultery or contraception or killing, that person will take on, as part of his or her moral identity, the identity of an adulterer, a contraceptor, a killer, even if he or she refuses to admit this identity to himself or herself. Actions speak louder than words. The "paradox" of the separatists on this matter—namely, that one can make it a policy to engage in acts of contraceptive intercourse and still not take on a contraceptive "mentality"—is simply a good example of the way we can fool ourselves and hide from ourselves the reality that is ourselves.[68]

The integrist understanding of the moral meaning of human acts holds that we ought not to be willing to choose or intend evil of deliberate purpose, even for the sake of a higher good.[69] We are not to do evil so that good may come about (cf. Rom. 3:8). In an integrist understanding, we are to pursue good and avoid evil. The good we are to pursue includes the whole range of truly human goods, "noble goods" (*bona honesta*), goods such as life itself, including bodily life and the goods of human sexuality, peace, justice, friendship, truth. These are real goods of human persons, and as such worthy of human choice. None of these goods is the Absolute Good or the *Summum Bonum,* for God alone is the Absolute Good. Yet all of these real goods (*bona honesta*) are true goods of human persons, and as such gifts from this *Summum Bonum* for which we should be grateful.[70] These goods correspond to needs rooted in our being; we hunger for these goods even if we do not consciously know them; and, as consciously grasped in knowledge, these goods serve as starting points or principles for moral deliberation.[71]

According to an integrist understanding of the moral meaning of human acts, the moral goodness or badness of our acts depends on the attitude of the person toward these goods as disclosed in the acts one chooses to do. Far from being a physicalistic ethic, determining the moral meaning of human acts from their physical structure, the integrist understanding sharply distinguishes between the "natural" or "physical" species of an act (e.g., inserting a hypodermic needle into human flesh, sexual union) from the moral species of an act (e.g., giving insulin to a diabetic or killing someone by a lethal injection, marital union between spouses or fornication, even of the "tender, loving kind" variety).[72] In our acts, according to an integrist understanding, we are to be open to the true goods of human persons, affirming them and joyously accepting them. Thus intentionality plays a crucial role in the determination of the moral meaning (the rightness or wrongness) of human acts. If, in a given act, we must of necessity directly intend evil (i.e., the deprivation of a true good), then this is the sort or kind of act that we ought not to be willing to choose to do, for we are choosing an evil means in order to secure some good. An act in which we must, of necessity, intend that evil be is not the sort or kind of act that we ought to choose to do and is therefore an immoral act because, in an integrist understanding, in choosing this sort of act we are choosing evil. But it is good that we are to do and pursue and evil that we are to avoid.[73]

This integrist understanding of the moral meaning of human acts, so different from the separatist understanding (which holds, as we have seen, that one can rightfully directly intend evil provided there is a "proportionate reason" or "good" to justify the direct intention of evil), is rooted in the biblical teaching that we are to be of clean heart, that is, open to all that is good. It is, moreover, rooted in the thought of Aquinas, and I should like *briefly* now to show the Thomistic basis for this understanding of the moral meaning of human acts.

For Aquinas the first precept of practical reason, that is, of human intelligence as deliberating about what is to be brought into being through human acts,[74] is that *good is to be done and pursued and evil is to be avoided*. The good in question is by no means limited to what authors of the separatist school term the "moral" good as distinguished from "ontic" good. Rather it includes the whole range of real human goods, the *bona honesta* or "noble goods" of human persons.[75]

St. Thomas likewise stressed that moral goodness enters in when we speak of the attitude or disposition of the human agent to these real goods of human persons. He taught a teleology of virtue: by this I mean that he taught that a human act is truly good and truly the work of the virtue of prudence only when the agent is properly disposed to all ends or goods of the human person.[76]

In Aquinas' understanding of conflict situations, that is, those tragic instances in which our actions are ambiguous in the sense that no matter what is done or undone some evil will come about, *intention* plays a key role. He holds that it is morally legitimate, for instance, to defend oneself even if one foresees that by doing so he will bring about the death of the assailant *if, and only if,* one's intent is to pursue the good of self-defense and not to kill the assailant.[77] This understanding, namely, that in effecting evil in the pursuit of good one's intent must be directly on the good that the deed does and in which it actually participates, became a pivotal element in the development of the principle or rule of double effect,[78] and there can be no doubt that for Aquinas the deed could not morally be chosen if in choosing it one must directly intend the evil it causes.[79]. As Crowe has shown, this presupposes that there are some sorts or kinds of deeds that one cannot rightly choose no matter what the circumstances may be or what greater good may come about.[80] Yet this is precisely what the authors of *Human Sexuality* and those Catholic authors whose directions they pursue claim, for they deny that there are any sorts of acts that are intrinsically evil in a moral sense.[81]

In this presentation I have sought to express the principal characteristics of two quite different understandings of human sexuality, the human person, and the moral meaning of human acts: the separatist and the integrist understandings. The separatist understanding not only finds it relatively easy to justify contraception but also holds that other forms of sexual behavior previously regarded in the Catholic tradition to be immoral can, at times, be justified. In other words, the separatist does not hold that the genital expression of one's sexuality be governed by a norm that such expressions be within the covenant of marriage. Marital coition, in other words, is an ideal toward which we should strive, but it is not normative of human coital activity.[82]

The integrist, on the other hand, holds that marital coition is *normative* for the genital expression of human sexuality, and that therefore non-marital modes of coition are modes of acting contrary to the "nature of the person and his acts."

I believe that the separatist understanding we find in much recent Catholic thought and articulated in *Human Sexuality* is erroneous. I believe that it arose from a misplaced compassion. The integrist view set forth in the second part of this chapter is, in my opinion, the understanding central to the still developing Catholic tradition, and it is an understanding quite crucial if we are to build a community in which every member of the human species is recognized as a being of moral worth, where every human being will be wanted and loved.

# NOTES

1. "On Understanding *Human Sexuality*: A Critique of the C.T.S.A. Study," *Communio* 4 (1977), 195–225.
2. This critique was published in a somewhat more extensive form as a booklet in the Franciscan Herald Press "Synthesis Series" under the title *On Understanding "Human Sexuality"* (Chicago: Franciscan Herald Press, 1977).
3. Dennis Doherty, review of *On Understanding "Human Sexuality,"* *The Linacre Quarterly* 45 (1978), 310–16.
4. In my own obviously biased view, Doherty's review is a hastily written misunderstanding of the critique given by Father Harvey and me. For instance, our principal point in referring to the writings of Edward Schillebeeckx and Pierre Grelot on the teaching of the Old Testament was to show that these scholars, along with many others (e.g., John L. McKenzie), insist that the "creation accounts" in both Genesis 1 and 2 are the story of the creation not only of Man as a species sexually differentiated into male and female but also of marriage. They explicitly relate these creation accounts to marriage. This the authors of *Human Sexuality* do not do. There is no need here to comment further on Doherty's review. Let readers read and judge. (Cf. Chapter Three above, n. 81.)
5. For example, Richard A. McBrien does not believe that the shift from procreative-unitive to creative-integrative is justified. Still he is quite sympathetic to the document (cf. his review of the work in *Church World* July 14, 1977). It is most instructive to note that Philip S. Keane praises the work for its "sound sexual anthropology" and believes that its moral methodology is rooted in the thought going on in Catholic circles today, although it is not as rigidly and systematically developed and applied as he believes necessary. The point is that Keane, who here typifies a general consensus on the part of Catholic thinkers upon whose work Kosnik et al. draw, is basically sympathetic to the general approach taken and, in particular, to its sexual anthropology. See Keane, *Sexual Morality: A Catholic Perspective* (New York: Paulist Press, 1977), p. 228.
6. *Gaudium et Spes,* 51.
7. Here it is instructive to note that Charles E. Curran has recently stressed that different understandings of human sexuality give rise to different evaluations of specific sorts of sexual behavior. Curran is

making much the same point that I am seeking to make. See his "After *Humanae Vitae* A Decade of Lively Debate," *Hospital Progress* 59 (1978), 84–89.

8. In specifying Catholic writers I by no means wish to exclude scholars from other Christian traditions. For instance, the integrist understanding that I seek to develop in the second part of this chapter is found in the writings of Paul Ramsey, the noted Methodist ethicist at Princeton University (despite his acceptance of contraception; on this see note 43 below), Siegfried Ernst (in his *Man: The Greatest of Miracles* [Collegeville, Minn.: Liturgical Press, 1975]), and in others.

9. For a history of the development of the argument for contraception see Ambrogio Valsecchi, *Contraception: The Birth Control Debate 1958–1968* (Washington: Corpus Books, 1968).

10. The literature here is abundant. See, for instance, the essays in *The Catholic Case for Contraception*, ed. Daniel Callahan (New York: Macmillan, 1969); Bernard Häring, "The Inseparability of the Unitive-Procreative Functions of the Marital Act," in *Contraception: Authority and Dissent*, ed. Charles E. Curran (New York: Herder and Herder, 1969), pp. 176–92; Louis Janssens, "Considerations on *Humanae Vitae*," *Louvain Studies* 2 (1969), 231–53; Keane, op. cit., pp. 121–28; etc.

11. See *Human Sexuality*, pp. 114–26.

12. The so-called "Majority Report" was written by the majority members of the Papal Commission on the Regulation of Fertility between June 4 and 9, 1966. It was made public in 1967, undoubtedly to put public pressure on Pope Paul VI to change the traditional teaching. Two documents were included in this Report, namely the *Documentum Syntheticum de Moralitate Regulationis Nativitatis* and *Schema Documenti de Responsabili Paternitate*. Both were published in the April 19, 1967, issue of *National Catholic Reporter* and both were reprinted in *The Birth Control Debate*, ed., Robert Hoyt (Kansas City: National Catholic Reporter, 1969), with the *Documentum* called "The Question Is Not Closed" and the *Schema* entitled "On Responsible Parenthood." Callahan, op. cit., reprints "On Responsible Parenthood."

13. "On Responsible Parenthood," Chapter 3; in Callahan, op. cit., p. 161.

14. Janssens, op. cit., 249.

15. *Human Sexuality*, pp. 83, 85.

16. This, at any rate, was the thought expressed in the Majority Report (cf. "On Responsible Parenthood," Chapter 3). Today some Catholic authors who accept the line of reasoning in the Report will justify the generation of children outside of acts expressing the love of their parents. In other words, today some authors hold that artificial

insemination by a donor and other modes of generating new life outside the coital embrace are justifiable. Kosnik et al., p. 139, argue for
the acceptability of artificial insemination by a donor.

17. Majority Report, "On Responsible Parenthood," Chapter 3, pp.
160–61; cf. Janssens, art. cit., 249–50.

18. Janssens, art. cit., 250. On this also see the essay by Michael
Novak, "Toward a Positive Theology of Sex," in *What Modern Catholics Think About Birth Control*, ed. William Birmingham (New
York: Signet Books, 1964), pp. 109–28. Novak distinguished between
the "biological imperative" of sexuality (i.e., procreation), an imperative easily fulfilled, and its "psychological imperative" (i.e., union).
The second is by far the more human and urgent.

19. Majority Report, "On Responsible Parenthood," Chapter 3, pp.
159–63.

20. *Ibid.*; cf. Janssens, art. cit. 245–50.

21. Majority Report, "On Responsible Parenthood," Chapter 2,
p. 158.

22. Majority Report, "The Question Is Not Closed," Chapter 2,
nn. 3–4, in Hoyt, op. cit., pp. 70–71.

23. *Human Sexuality*, pp. 114–26.

24. Ibid., pp. 114–26.

25. It is necessary to stress that the authors of the Majority Report
insisted that they were seeking only to justify one sort of sexual behavior, namely contraceptive intercourse for married couples. At the time
of the Report many others argued that, if contraception could be morally justified for the married, many other sorts of sexual activities
previously considered inherently immoral might also be justifiable.
Charles Curran has recently observed, and quite correctly, that the
concerns of those opposed to the reasoning in the Majority Report
were quite just, for today many Catholic writers use the reasoning employed by the Majority Report to justify marital contraception in
order to justify certain kinds of premarital sexual relationships, homosexual acts between homosexually oriented persons within a relatively
stable relationship, etc. See Curran, *Ongoing Revision* (Notre Dame,
Ind.: Fides, 1975), pp. 77–78.

26. See *Human Sexuality*, pp. 118 and 122, where Kosnik et al. indicate their agreement with those theologians who consider the argument in *Humanae Vitae* "physicalistic." By this they mean that it sees
"non-interference with the biological processes" as the crucial point in
the condemnation of artificial contraception as immoral by the encyclical. On pp. 114, 293, and 295 they include not only "rhythm"
but abstinence as "methods of contraception."

27. As Robert Hoyt put it: "the single most important *kind* of testimony influencing the papal commission's eventual recommendation

for change was that dealing with the existential realities of sexual togetherness in marriage." In Hoyt, op. cit., p. 19.

28. Here the words of James Burtchaell are instructive. He wrote: "Of all these methods [of regulating conception] I should be tempted to think of rhythm as the most unnatural of all, since it inhibits not only conception, but the expression of affection." See his "'Human Life' and Human Love." *Commonweal* (November 15, 1968), reprinted in *Moral Issues and Christian Response*, eds., Paul Jersild and Dale Johnson (New York: Harper & Row, 1971), pp. 139–40.

29. On this it is instructive to cite Daniel Maguire: "Birth control was . . . impeded by the physicalistic ethic that left moral man at the mercy of his biology. He had no choice but to conform to the rhythms of his physical nature and to accept its determinations obediently. Only gradually did technological man discover that he was morally free to intervene creatively and to achieve birth control by choice." "The Freedom to Die," *Commonweal* (August 11, 1972), 423–24.

30. *Human Sexuality*, pp. 114–26.

31. Majority Report, "On Responsible Parenthood," Chapter 3; in Callahan, op. cit., p. 162.

32. The authors of *Human Sexuality* seem to agree with the authors of the Majority Report on this point. They consistently speak of the procreative dimension of human sexuality as a biological "given," and they refer favorably to the position that human beings are called upon to transcend the limits imposed upon them by "biochemical and anatomical givens"; see pp. 62f., 84.

33. Burtchaell, loc. cit.; Bernard Häring, *The Ethics of Manipulation* (New York: Seabury, 1975), pp. 92–96; *Human Sexuality*, pp. 114, 293, 295.

34. *Human Sexuality*, p. 293.

35. *Humanae Vitae*, n. 16.

36. Charles E. Curran, art. cit., 84–89; pp. 84–87 are concerned with the "physicalism" of the encyclical.

37. On Maguire's views, note the text cited in note 29 above; see Joseph Selling, "Moral Teaching, Traditional Teaching, and *Humanae Vitae*," *Louvain Studies* 7 (1978), 24–43. Selling's article is a summary of a doctoral dissertation from Louvain University under the direction of Louis Janssens.

38. Elizabeth Anscombe, *Contraception and Chastity* (London: Catholic Truth Society, 1974), pp. 17–21. See also James O'Reilly, *The Moral Problem of Contraception* (Chicago: Franciscan Herald Press, 1975); William E. May, "Contraception, Abstinence, and Responsible Parenthood," *Faith and Reason* 3 (1977), 34–52.

39. Here I want to note that many medieval theologians, among

them Thomas Aquinas, held that marital intercourse without procreative intent can be a very good deed insofar as it serves the good of
*fides.* See Thomas Aquinas, *In IV Sententiarum,* d. 31, q. 2, a. 1.
Good commentaries on Aquinas' thought are provided by Fabian Par-
misano in an article critical of Noonan's interpretation of medieval
writers, "Love and Marriage in the Middle Ages," *New Blackfriars* 50
(1969), 599–608, 649–60; and by Germain Grisez, "Marriage:
Reflections Based on St. Thomas and Vatican Council II," *Catholic
Mind* 64 (1965), 4–19.

40. As already indicated, the authors of the Majority Report intended
that their argument to justify contraception be an argument to justify
contraception for *married* persons. Since then, beginning with Michael Valente in his significant book *Sex: The Radical View of a
Catholic Theologian* (New York: Bruce Publishing Company, 1970),
Catholic authors have used the notion of human sexuality and the understanding of the moral meaning of human acts found in the Majority Report to justify non-marital sexual relations and to justify contraception for the unmarried.

41. *Human Sexuality,* p. 86: "We believe that this formulation ["creative growth toward integration"] while being essentially rooted in the
traditional expressions of the procreative and unitive purposes of sexuality *moves beyond the limitations inherent in this formula*" (emphasis added).

42. Ibid., pp. 83–86.

43. I wish to stress that this separatist notion of human sexuality is
the notion central to the major arguments developed by Roman Catholic writers in an effort to justify contraception. One Protestant
thinker, Paul Ramsey, definitely holds that human sexuality is to be
understood in an integrist manner. He is truly remarkable for his insistence on the inherently interconnected meaning of the unitive and
procreative aspects of human sexuality. He does justify contraception,
but solely on the grounds of the distinction between a lifetime of
procreative openness vs. individual acts of contraception. See his
*Fabricated Man* (New Haven: Yale University Press, 1971), pp.
30–33. I personally believe that Ramsey's argument to justify contraception is not consistent with his own moral theory. In private correspondence he has told me that his understanding of human sexuality
is certainly integrist and thus closer to the view set forth in the second
part of this chapter than to the view of human sexuality entertained
by Catholic advocates of contraception and by the authors of *Human
Sexuality.*

44. This view of human sexuality, incidentally, is surely shared by
many important humanists and writers whose thought has deeply
influenced American society. See, for instance, Ashley Montagu, *Sex,
Man, and Society* (New York: G. Putnam, 1971), Chapter 1; Robert

and Anna Francoeur, eds., *The Future of Sexual Relations* (Englewood Cliffs, N.J.: Prentice-Hall, 1975).

45. See above, nn. 21, 22, 31.

46. E.g., Janssens, art. cit., p. 249: "Personalism considers man as incarnate spirit."

47. *Human Sexuality*, pp. 83–84.

48. There is a spectrum of anthropologies discernible in the writings of the separatists. It is instructive, I believe, that theologians with this understanding of the human person are very reluctant to use the term *person* to designate the unborn child, and many, (e.g., Daniel Callahan, Daniel Maguire) explicitly indicate that they do not believe the unborn child to be a person. For Callahan, see his *Abortion: Law, Choice, and Morality* (New York: Macmillan, 1970); for Maguire, see his *Death by Choice* (New York: Doubleday, 1974), p. 80, where he speaks of fetal life as "expanding toward infant and personal life."

49. These efforts are summarized by Richard McCormick in his *Ambiguity in Moral Choice* (Milwaukee: Marquette University Theology Department, 1973). Peter Knauer's article was "The Hermeneutic Function of the Principle of Double Effect," *Natural Law Forum* 12 (1967), 132–62; William Van der Marck developed his version both in *Love and Fertility* (New York: Sheed and Ward, 1965), pp. 45–63, and in *Toward a Christian Ethics* (New York; Newman, 1967), pp. 61–67; Cornelius Van der Poel set forth his views in "The Principle of Double Effect," in *Absolutes in Moral Theology?*, ed., Charles E. Curran (Washington: Corpus Books, 1968), pp. 199–208.

50. On this see my *Sex, Love, and Procreation* (Chicago: Franciscan Herald Press Synthesis Series, 1976).

51. For Fuchs's influence on Kosnik et al., see *Human Sexuality*, pp. 89ff. and note 18 to Chapter 4.

52. Joseph Fuchs, "The Absoluteness of Moral Terms," *Gregorianum* 52 (1971), 415–58.

53. See McCormick's "Notes on Moral Theology," in the March 1972, March 1975, and March 1978 issues of *Theological Studies*.

54. Michael B. Crowe, *The Changing Profile of the Natural Law* (The Hague: Martinus Nijhoff, 1977), pp. 285–86.

55. *Human Sexuality*, pp. 89ff.

56. The way in which McCormick sums up this theory is instructive, for he says that we can intend the evil *in se sed non propter se* or that we can intend evil *in se in ordine ad finem proportionatum.* See, for example, his "Notes on Moral Theology," *Theological Studies* 33 (1972), 74–75.

57. This is precisely the argument in the Majority Report. A more recent version is given by Philip S. Keane, op. cit., pp. 123–25.

58. *Humanae Vitae*, n. 14.

59. Ibid., n. 12.

60. Ibid., n. 14.

61. Ibid., n. 12.

62. Ibid., n. 13.

63. On this see Mortimer Alder, *The Difference of Man and the Difference It Makes* (New York: Meridian, 1968). See my "What Makes a Human Being to Be a Being of Moral Worth?" in *The Thomist* 40 (1976), 416–44.

64. That God is *not* a sexed being but is rather beyond sex is the teaching of contemporary biblical scholars in their interpretation of the creation narratives in Genesis 1 and 2. On this see John L. McKenzie, *The Two-Edged Sword: An Interpretation of the Old Testament* (New York: Doubleday Image Book, 1968), pp. 113–32.

65. Here I wish to express gratitude to Robert Joyce for his insights into this subject. He develops the idea here expressed in his forthcoming study, *The Human Ecology of Sex*.

66. This is true even today when it is possible to reproduce human life in the laboratory. Such reproductive acts are not truly sexual procreation. For a brief discussion of this subject, with references to pertinent literature, see my *Human Existence, Medicine, and Ethics: Reflections on Human Life* (Chicago: Franciscan Herald Press, 1977), Chapter 3.

67. On human acts as "words" that we speak see Herbert McCabe, *What Is Ethics All About?* (Washington: Corpus Books, 1969).

68. This is a criticism that I develop more at length in my *Sex, Love, and Procreation* (Chicago: Franciscan Herald Press, 1976).

69. *Humanae Vitae*, n. 14.

70. The ideas developed here are set forth at much greater length in Germain Grisez, *Contraception and the Natural Law* (Milwaukee: Bruce Publishing Company, 1964), Chapter 3; by the same author in his *Abortion: The Myths, the Realities, and the Arguments* (New York: Corpus, 1970), Chapter 6; and in an article of mine, "Ethics and Human Identity: The Challenge of the New Biology," *Horizons* 3 (1975), 17–38.

71. This aspect of the integrist position, namely that real goods of human persons serve, when consciously known, as starting points of moral deliberation, is confirmed by the investigations of developmental psychologists such as Lawrence Kohlberg. I have attempted to show this at some length in an essay, "The Natural Law, Conscience, and Developmental Psychology," *Communio* 2 (1975), 3–31.

72. On the distinction between the natural or physical species of an act and its moral species see Thomas Aquinas, *Summa Theol.* I–II, q. 1, a. 3, ad 3.

73. For a further development of this see Germain Grisez, "The First

Principle of Natural Law: A Commentary on *Summa Theologiae* 1–2, Q. 94, A. 2," *Natural Law Forum* 10 (1965), 168–201; and John Finnis, "Natural Law and Unnatural Acts," *The Heythrop Journal* 11 (1970), 361–69; see also my own "The Nature and Meaning of the Natural Law in Aquinas," *American Journal of Jurisprudence* 22 (1977), 168–89.

74. On the significance of Aquinas' notion of reason as ordered to action (the practical intellect) as functionally (not really) distinct from reason as ordered to speculation (the speculative intellect), see John Naus, *The Notion of the Practical Intellect According to St. Thomas Aquinas* (Rome: Gregorian University, 1959).

75. *Summa Theol.* I–II, q. 94, a. 2. In this article Thomas argues that there are many *first* principles or precepts of practical reason. *Good is to be done and pursued and evil is to be avoided* is one among many, precisely because the good to which the human person is ordered is pluriform, corresponding to the "natural inclinations" of the human person. On this subject see not only the articles mentioned above in note 73 but also Thomas Gilby, Appendices 2 and 3 ("The Background to Moral Good" and "Placing Moral Good") in St. Thomas Aquinas, *Summa Theologiae*, Vol. 18, *Principles of Morality* (1a2ae. 18–21), Latin text, English translation, Introduction, Notes, Appendices & Glossary by Thomas Gilby (New York: McGraw-Hill, 1966), pp. 131–39. See also R. H. Armstrong, *Primary and Secondary Precepts on Thomistic Natural Law Teaching* (The Hague: Martinus Nijhoff, 1966).

76. On this see *Summa Theol.* I–II, q. 56, a. 3, where Aquinas stresses that one can act prudently only if one has rectified his desires for the goods or ends of human life. On this also see Frederick S. Carney, "McCormick on Teleology," *The Journal of Religious Ethics* 6 (1978), 81–107. In this article Carney contrasts Aquinas' teleology of virtue with McCormick's consequentialistic teleology.

77. *Summa Theol.* I–II, q. 64 a. 7. Here it is helpful to read Grisez, "Toward a Consistent Natural-Law Ethics of Killing," *American Journal of Jurisprudence* 15 (1970), 64–96, in particular those sections in which he criticizes the interpretations of this passage by Peter Knauer and William Van der Marck.

78. On this see Joseph T. Mangan, "An Historical Analysis of the Principle of Double Effect," *Theological Studies* 10 (1949), 40–61; and J. Ghoos, "L'Acte à Double Effet: Étude de Théologie Positive," *Ephemerides Theologicae Lovanienses* 27 (1951), 30–52. Although Mangan and Ghoos disagree over the role of Aquinas in the development of this principle, they both show that intentionality is central to it.

79. See *Summa Theol.* I–II, q. 64, a. 7.

80. Crowe, loc. cit. (n. 54, above).

81. On this see *Human Sexuality,* p. 89. Here it would be instructive to read McCormick's "Notes on Moral Theology" in *Theological Studies* 39 (1978) and compare this essay with my own, "The Moral Meaning of Human Acts," *Homiletic and Pastoral Review* 79 (1978), 10–21.

82. On this see Charles F. Curran's survey of recent Catholic thought in "Sexual Ethics: A Reaction and A Critique," *The Linacre Quarterly* 43 (1976), 147–64.

## Chapter Six

꙳

# OF SEX AND ETHICAL
# METHODOLOGY

### DANIEL C. MAGUIRE

David Hume lamented that his *A Treatise of Human Nature* "fell dead-born from the press, without reaching such distinction as even to excite a murmur among the zealots." He grieved further when his *An Enquiry Concerning the Principles of Morals* "came unnoticed and unobserved into the world." The authors of *Human Sexuality*, though they have legitimate complaints, cannot join in Hume's lament. No American Catholic study in our time has won more scrutiny or elicited more response.

Though the book *Human Sexuality* is significant and interesting, the reaction to it is theologically and also psychologically more intriguing. It is almost more than a little schizoid. Indeed, if some future worldwide apocalypse were to come upon us destroying every single copy of *Human Sexuality* but sparing all the reactions to it, future scholarship would definitely arrive at a two-source theory. It would simply be inconceivable that such contradictory reactions could have been stimulated by a single literary source.

This source has changed the *status quaestionis* for sexual ethics in this and in many countries. One cannot address sexual ethics in a Catholic context and ignore this Report: a fatuous or inept study could not have achieved this. Part of the strength of the Report is its honesty. It has called to an end a period of evasion and pretense by professing openly "that there is a growing gap between what the Catholic Church officially teaches in matters sexual and what the faithful have come to believe and practice" (p. 78).

I am not saying that the Report ushers in a new orthodoxy. It is painstakingly tentative in tone and probing in character. The response it merits is respectful dialogical criticism. It is the beginning of a new process which has already borne some wholesome theological fruit, and it does not pretend to be any more than a beginning.

It should be noted that any significant work in ethics is a contribution to theory or it may justly be considered a piece of reportage which might, perhaps, be fascinating and useful in its own way, but is not ethics. The indispensable work of ethics is theory and method. Ethics, even in addressing particular subjects, illumines how it is that we sensitively know and evaluate in the moral realm, or it fails as ethics. *Human Sexuality* does not fail in this fashion, for it did not evade the methodological challenges.

In fact, it should be noted too that one of the major services of this Report is that it brought to the surface some of the methodological agenda that have long gone abegging in Catholic moral theology. The authors of the Report addressed these neglected areas, sensing accurately that sexual ethics could not be fruitfully reappraised in any other way. The authors are not to be indicted for not finishing the work in these areas. They are to be praised for making new beginnings and showing where followup work has to be done. My own methodological analysis and conclusions follow.

## Theological Critique

1. *Unitive and Procreative.* The Report, while not rejecting the unitive and procreative purposes of sexuality, offers creative and integrative as more broadly regulative of sexual behavior. This suggestion must be seen as unfinished business. It also must be seen in its historical context. It comes out of a history where *procreative* was seen as primary and *unitive* as secondary. This was altered when the rhythm birth control method was seen as legitimate even to render a marriage permanently childless, and later

when Vatican II with very deliberate care taught that the other ends of marriage were not to be considered as of lesser account than the procreative end.[1]

Vatican II's formulation and *Human Sexuality*'s treatment, however, are incomplete and call for further distinctions. The mistake in the older teaching and in Vatican II was in proceeding in an ordinal fashion as though the ends of sexuality were competitively related and in need of ranking as higher, lower, or equal. Unless we are to turn to cloning on a planetary scale, sex is obviously the physical medium of reproduction. From the viewpoint of species needs, it might even be argued ordinally that reproduction is the prime purpose of sex. I would not so argue since I feel that even here the ordinal ranking of sexual purposes would be specious and unhelpful. It might, for example, also be argued that the unitive and socializing purpose of sexual encounters is equally primary for society, etc.

At any rate, the fact that sex is the physical means of reproduction does not mean that sexual exchange should *semper et pro semper* be reproductively oriented. Indeed, social justice and other virtues might require that it not be reproductive. Unitive, however, is another matter. Sex, I will argue, is unitive by orientation for all who participate in it. Sex is not ecstasy without a mission. It is a sacrament of intimacy leading to self-revelation, trust, and friendship. It is unitive. But unitive and procreative are not conjoined in every sexual union. *The confusion here has been between individual realizations of sexuality and the needs of the species—and these are separable.*

The Report need not have exposed itself to charges of a dichotomy between unitive and procreative on the one hand and creative and integrative on the other. All four purposes should be maintained. There is no need to downplay the sex-specific purposes of unitive and procreative. What is needed is to distinguish between species and individual needs. In so saying, I am not introducing a novelty. Celibacy would be immoral if chosen by the whole human race, but we have not taught that the species-need for reproduction was a moral argument against voluntary celibacy.

In point of fact, it should be noted that the Report did not abandon the unitive rubric but actually includes it in a number of ways. The Report need only distinguish between species need and individual obligation to treat reproductive purpose properly. The unitive dimension of sex is very present throughout the Report. It is in the Report's description of sexuality, in its theological use of the symbol of the union between Christ and the Church, and in its stress on the integrative aspect of sex, in the need for fidelity, and elsewhere.

It is sometimes carelessly said that the unitive and procreative purposes of sex are inseparably conjoined. That statement is an enigma. That sex is unitive and procreative may be readily affirmed. That these two aspects of sex are inseparably conjoined is quite another matter. Let us concede again that sex is the physical means of reproduction, since few truths are as evident as that. However, it should not be surprising that this *physical* function does not exhaust the full *personal* meaning of sex. Sex for persons is not just instinctual and reproductive; it is also liturgical and symbolic. To explain sex as a complex natural liturgy and thus provide a better understanding of the unitive and procreative aspects of sex, let me turn illustratively to another natural liturgy, the meal. The comparison of the two liturgies is important.

The table is not a trough and a meal for persons is not just feed time. People who dine together are not just consuming proteins and carbohydrates. We do not normally invite people to dinner because they are notoriously hungry. A guest list is not predicated on malnutrition. There are two things that show a meal to be a natural liturgy: it is intrinsically social and socializing, and it is heavy with symbol. It is by its nature a friendship event, which, like a sacrament, both symbolizes and effects friendship. (It is not surprising that the Christian religion and other religions favored the meal as a symbolic matrix.) Hence the exquisite attention to elegant detail that goes into a meal. We are not just feeding our friends when we invite them; we are expressing our love. The way the food is presented, the setting, the silver, the crystal, all suggest the seriousness of a symbolic event.

Not all meals are fully symbolic, but the social urgency is always there. The busy housewife or househusband who has gotten the children off to school, and sits for a bit of breakfast, reaches for the phone or the television or a magazine to ward off the aloneness that offends a meal. And if all this stress on sociality, love, and respect as essential ingredients of a meal seems too lyrical, think of what happens when you are forced to eat with someone whom you seriously dislike. The consequent indigestion will bear witness to the fact that mere foodstuffs and a table do not a meal make. If you ate beside a stranger every day at a diner counter, it would be very difficult to ward off the intimations of communication and conviviality that go with personal eating. You would have to become friends of a sort.

What happens in a natural liturgy like a meal is that there is a material substratum and a large symbolic superstructure. Food and nutrition go with a meal but these could be received intravenously and you would not call it a meal. The symbolism, therefore, is as intrinsic as the nutrition.

The same is true for sexual exchange. Sex does meet physical needs such as distraction, relaxation, and nervous release. Sometimes when the personal dimensions are minimal, as when sex is commercialized, there may be little more to it than this. But there is symbolic power in sex which, given due chance, will assert itself. Sex has a power to engender and express endearing emotions and intense personal expectations. It is an intense form of sharing that invites more sharing. In the sexual encounter, the parties are not just physically enveloping and interpenetrating one another; there is psychological envelopment and penetration as well. One is personally as well as physically naked in shared orgasmic experience. The event is truly a *revelatio*. The usual cosmetic defenses with which we gird ourselves about do not easily survive such liturgy. The force of the encounter is unitive. The lover may remain only an experience, but she tends to become a way of life. The lovers have shared a secret together. They have shared a powerful symbolic event that both signifies and effects friendship. "Getting involved" is a corollary of "having sex" if it is not the prelude.

This is not to say that the symbolic aspects of sex cannot be repressed or almost extinguished in certain cauterized personalities or at lower stages of personality development. But without some manifestation of cherishing and affection, the sexual meeting is not even going to be a sensual success. And if depersonalized sex is repeated, the personal and unitive dimensions are likely to emerge. It is ironic to note that the romantic sexual encounter which is certainly a high form of fun has such a lugubrious legacy in terms of songs of broken hearts, the blues, and literary tragedies. Its unitive potential explains this to some degree. The unitive potential is felt by one of the parties and not the other or circumstances prevent the union that is so commandingly required by the relationship. "A pity beyond all telling is hid in the heart of love," wrote the poet Yeats, and many persons who move into a sexual encounter learn the poignant adaptations that the poet's words can have.

Morton Hunt, in his 1974 study *Sexual Behavior in the 1970's* offers this conclusion:

> . . . sexual liberation has not dismantled the romantic-passionate concept of sex and replaced it with the recreational one . . . while most Americans—especially the young—now feel far freer than formerly to be sensation-oriented at times, for the great majority of them sex remains intimately allied to their deepest emotions and inextricably interwoven with their conceptions of loyalty, love and marriage. The web of meaning and social structure surrounding sex has been stretched and reshaped, but not torn asunder.[2]

In no culture does sex remain purely frivolous and merely physical, although rather depersonalized modalities of sexual exchange can be found. There is abundant witness to the unitive thrust of sex. To my mind this points to enduring grounds for asserting the marital orientation of sexual exchange.

Marriage I would define as *the ultimate form of friendship achievable by sexually attracted persons.* Friendship is the dominant reality and sex is the specifying mode. This means sex in the genital sense and in the myriad other forms that sexual attraction may take.

If it is clear, then, how sex is unitive, what is the moral import of its reproductive purpose and how does this conjoin with the unitive? It does not conjoin in the sense that the species need for reproduction can be translated into an absolute moral obligation binding every act of sexual exchange or every marriage. This would be neither physically possible nor morally responsible. It would depersonalize sex, reducing women to brood mares and men to studs. And no one actually defends the proposition that sex is only permitted when fertilization is possible and likely.

The unitive and the reproductive do conjoin in one way: reproduction can be the most unifying and maritalizing experience of a
relationship. The ecstatic sharing both in the miracle of birth and
in the sacramental joys of childhood may be the most bonding of
experiences for parents. It explains, I think it reasonable to opine,
why the family is such a remarkably stable phenomenon in
human societies. As anthropologist Ralph Linton writes:

> The ancient trinity of father, mother, and child has survived
> more vicissitudes than any other human relationship. It is the
> bedrock underlying all other family structures. Although more
> elaborate family patterns can be broken from without or may
> even collapse of their own weight, the rock remains. In the
> Götterdämmerung which otherwise science and overfoolish
> statesmanship are preparing for us, the last man will spend his
> last hours searching for his wife and child.[3]

Reproduction, however, is not necessary or feasible for every
union and thus it is not essential to every marriage. It is also not
the grounds for ruling that every homosexual union is dehumanizing and immoral. The definition that I gave of marriage above
does not require heterosexual orientation. Homosexual marriages
and childless heterosexual marriages should also exemplify the unitive fidelity of love and thus be personally and socially fruitful in
their own way.

Though the sexual ethic I propose here gives marriage a para-
mount position, I do not accept the simplism that you can draw a
perpendicular line, call it the ceremony of marriage, and say that
every consciously sexual thought, word, or deed to the left of that
line is immoral and dehumanizing. Such simplicity would be
unique in the whole of ethics. And sexuality is so mysterious and
in many ways so varied in its manifestations, as anthropology
testifies, that it would seem a most unlikely candidate for such
tidy and convenient divisions. What I do say is that the sexual
encounter, allowing for cultural and developmental psychological
factors, is unitive and hence serious. It is a kind of binding pleasure and intimacy-making concelebration. It engenders potent
emotions. Herein lies its moral seriousness. The Report, I believe,
takes great pains to point out this seriousness.

The Report also repeatedly stresses the social significance of sex. As Abraham and May Edel write, "sex is nearly everywhere highly charged morally, for in addition to its high emotional potential, it is part of the most central nexus of human social interrelationships."[4] The sexual encounter mirrors one's social attitudes. Sexism and racism reveal themselves in patterns of sexual behavior. The ancients said that in play morals reveal themselves (*inter ludendum, mores se detegunt*). This is certainly so for sexual play. Add to all of this the unitive, symbolic, and liturgical power of sexual expression, and the Report is even more obviously correct in standing for the ultimate seriousness of sexual behavior.

There is, however, a tendency toward mysticalization of sex that is rather broadly present today and is also visible in the Report. In the past we seemed to be locked into the contradictory position of saying. "Sex is dirty; save it for someone you love!" In rediscovering the goodness of sex, we must again beware of the pendular reaction. I am uneasy when I read in the Report: "Sexual intercourse is an expression of a person's whole being, the deepest core of one's personality" (p. 167).[5] Even in a good marriage sexual intercourse will not always be all of that. I am also uneasy when I read: "Sex is seen as a force that permeates, influences, and affects every act of a person's being at every moment of existence. It is not operative in one restricted area of life but is rather at the core and center of our total life-response" (p. 81). I would prefer to say not that sex permeates personality, but that personality permeates sex in persons, and that this is precisely why it is difficult to limit sex to its recreational dimensions. It is for this reason that merely sexual interest is disruptive since sex between persons means more than sex. Sex in humans is permeated by personality, with all of personality's manifold and insistent needs.

Strangely enough, a lot of the criticism of the Report regarding reproduction relates to homosexuality. As is apparent in some of the criticisms of the Report, one of the ethical chores of the reproductive rubric is to foreclose on homosexual relations. The methodological abstractionism here is neat. You define moral sex in such a way as to include some and exclude others. You establish moral sex as *heterosexual-marital*, thus leaving all homosexuals with no moral mode of sexual expression. For them it is either celibacy or sin. For the heterosexual it is better to marry than to burn; for the homosexual, there is only burning. The Report, quite properly, rejects this sweeping and cruel abstractionism. The Report accepts the view "that meaningful and wholesome sexuality need not always be evaluated in terms of its relationship to procreation" (p. 204). The Report is, in my view, correct in this, since, as I have argued, the species-need for reproduction is not inseparably conjoined as a moral condition to sexual exchange.

The Report even goes on to say that a particular homosexual relationship may be counseled "not simply as a lesser of two evils but as a positive good" (p. 215). And it concludes "that where there is sincere affection, responsibility, and the germ of authentic human relationship—in other words, where there is love—God is surely present (p. 218)." I find this better ethical theory than is represented by those who say, even while justifying homosexual sex, that it is always ontically evil, not human expression at full term, falling short of the full meaning of human sexuality, the result of the infecting power of sin, etc.[6] This puts the homosexual couple into the position of having to say of their relationship —which may be an ideal and heroic realization of Christian love, reconciling power, and hope—that it is ontically evil but morally sound. The problem arises from saying that heterosexual marital relations remain the ideal. What does it mean to a permanently homosexual person to say that heterosexuality is the ideal for him? Clearly it would not be ideal for the human race if everyone were homosexual. Clearly it is ideal that historically most have been heterosexual, else in harsh times the species may not have survived. But it is a large leap from this blunt fact to say to a particular homosexual couple that their union is not ideal for them *because of the species' already well-met needs for ample heterosexuality.*

Heterosexuals discussing homosexuality suffer from abstractness. Let me be concrete. I know two homosexual women who consider themselves married. Both are degreed in special education and plan, as legally single women, to adopt several retarded and emotionally handicapped children who would otherwise be raised in public institutions. The homosexuality of these two women is and, by their intention, will remain private. They know the infinite demands of children, healthy and normal or otherwise, and they want to meet those demands for these children in a way that no institutional care could provide. If ethical theory puts the procreative element of sex in its distinguished place, there is no need to tell these women that their union is ontically evil in a way that heterosexual unions are not. Thomas Aquinas tells us that human actions are good or bad according to their circumstances.[7] Given all the circumstances of these two women, I would describe their union as ideal *for them*. The unitive power of sexuality hopefully will help sustain them in the generous direction that their marital friendship has taken them.

Catholic moral theology has some outstanding debts to homosexual persons since we are to some degree responsible for the afflictions they experience. We impose a normative ethical ideal which for them is neither normative, nor ideal, nor feasible. Such an approach sacrifices the concrete reality of irreversibly homosexual persons to an imperfect and incomplete conceptualization of the human sexual situation. Homosexuality is and remains a mystery for us and even for the experts who have tried to fathom it and discern its etiology. Many societies simply have seen it as a variant, not as an abnormality. Our society views it with morbid horror and puts a heavy socio-cultural stigma on it. This stigma certainly impinges upon the relationships of homosexual persons and then when the effects of this stigmatizing become known to us in terms of negative data on homosexual relationships, we facilely conclude that we were right all along. It is not yet clear that we have done any more than prove that, in significant ways, we get back what we project.

2. *Teleology vs. Deontology*. Reflected in the Report are the effects of the debate, which I submit is misconceived, between teleology and deontology in ethics. In fact, the Report involves both teleology and deontology and this is as inevitable as it is proper. Marital fidelity until death and the heroic love required by parenting will never be evaluated in purely teleological terms. An exclusively teleological ethics misses the affective, mystical import of normal moral experience. A narrowly teleological understanding of marriage or of childrearing will be, of necessity, jejune and pale.

Rationalistic ethics does not blend teleology and deontology; it concentrates on one or the other and achieves a practical divorce of the two. If you accept, however, that ethics involves not just principles and reasoning and the calculation and weighing of effects but that it also involves mystical and affective *appreciations*, then the clumsy category of deontology might truly describe some of the evaluational experience.

In adjudicating something like group sex or "swinging," we do not have to limit ourselves to projecting the effects of such activity or await word from the social scientists on how such sexual behavior tests out in their studies. The *humanum* we explore is a *mysterium tremendum et fascinosum* and some of our deepest appreciations of it are at the mystical, precordial depths of contemplation. It is for this reason that I stress the role of *Gemüt*, or affectivity, and creative imagination in ethics. A rationalistic ethic downplays the need for these faculties and constricts ethics to the realms of speculative reason, principles, and language. It is fair to say that the social sciences, though a valuable tool for criticism, are not always critical. They may at times merely reflect the dominant myths of a society and give those myths prestige by dressing them in the snobbish and chic apparel of elitist *Wissenschaft*. Hence, they are limited in what they can do for ethics. We need a judicious reliance on the social sciences, for otherwise we will be prone to what Sartre called the greatest evil possible—treating as abstract that which is concrete. Nor do we come embarrassed to our partnership with the social scientists; they have a lot to learn from us. Neither do we come, however, to enlist them as the latest recruits in our stable of *ancillae*. Rather, we come together with modesty; to recall St. Paul's masterful epistemological insight, each of us knows "in part." Such sexual activity as group sex or swinging, therefore, might stimulate our *sense of profanation;*[8] it might jar our evaluative *Gemüt* even before all the measurable data are in on what happens when folks do this sort of thing.

Such affective appreciations are not infallible, neither are they negligible in doing ethics. If this involves one in a degree of deontology, so be it. Such deontological appreciations should be supplemented by teleological analysis, not as though one were going from a lower to a higher court, but simply in the name of exercising all of our evaluative capacities. Evaluation in which either deontological or teleological aspects are omitted is truncated.

Thus in the Report itself, the somewhat diffident judgment against swinging ("While remaining open to the results of further research, we find that, given the qualities of wholesome sexuality discussed above, swinging seems destructive and alienating and therefore generally dehumanizing."—p. 149) could be more firmly negative without lapsing into the intuitionism of an older moral theology. I would be inclined to put such things in the category of *the unimaginable exception.*[9]

The teleology-deontology debate is mistaken and a lot of mischief can be avoided by correcting the mistake. Teleology teaches that actions are right or wrong according to the *telos*, end, or goal to which they lead. Consequentialism and utilitarianism are teleological theories. Deontology affirms that certain things are wrong regardless of the consequences. For example, promise-keeping might be defended teleologically in view of the disruptive effects on society if confidence in promises perished. An exclusively teleological approach, therefore, would say that promise-keeping is good *because* it promotes a milieu of confidence. The question is, however, is that judgment complete?

W. D. Ross helps us here with his case of the promise made to a dying man. After the death of the promisee, if no one knows about the promise, why must it be kept? How would the general welfare or other social consequences be impinged on if this promise were ignored? As Ross puts it: "We need not doubt that a system by which promises are made and kept is one that has great advantages for the general well-being. *But that is not the whole truth.*"[10] There is the nub. As William Frankena says, the deontologists "assert that there are, at least, other considerations which may make an action or rule right or obligatory beside the goodness or badness of its consequences."[11] This position does not deny moral significance to the consequence. The consequences are morally significant, but in W. D. Ross's phrase, "that is not the whole truth." Hence, given the nature of the sexual encounter, as described in number 1 above, I would feel confident in denying the moral status of good to swinging and to open marriage. That judgment proceeds from my pluriform moral consciousness—from my practical reason, from historical experience, from creative imagination, from affective appreciation, from judicious reliance on religious and other cultural authorities, etc. In other words, I have a lot going for me in making that judgment even if some empirical studies are still pending. Those pending studies will really have to be quite something to overwhelm what I already know about the precious yet fragile tenderness of human sexual relationships and marriage. Might I be surprised by pending research? As David Ben Gurion says, there are no experts on the future. There are such surprises in history. But with as much firmness as we can bring to many moral judgments, I can pronounce my negative moral judgment with vigorous firmness.

In so doing, I have, of course, not joined those Catholic intuitionists who with Prichardian simplicity can intuit the intrinsic finality of human sexuality so clearly and metaphysically that they know unwaveringly that sexual thoughts, words, or deed, are either marital or immoral, yesterday, today, or tomorrow anywhere in the world. I have also not joined the alleged conspiracy of those who purvey an insidious novelty known as "the principle of ethical proportionalism." The term *proportionality* in ethics may not be the best of terms because of the mathematical and physical biases it may introduce, but some term like it is inevitable in ethics. Proportionality symbolizes the necessary comparative weighing that the "balancing art" of ethics must perform. Only intuitionists whose motto must be *fiat intuitio, pereat mundus* could dream of dispensing themselves from the weighing and balancing and comparing work of moral evaluation.[12]

What I have done here is assert that the current rush to teleology in Roman Catholic ethics is an overreaction to the deontological excesses of our past. Having sinned by excluding teleological considerations in the past (as the term *teleology* is used in current debate), there is now an ensuing disposition to sin by excluding deontological aspects from ethical method. This reaction is abetted by the love of tidiness to which our ethical tradition has long been unduly prone. And, of course, it must be conceded that when one admits affective considerations into their rightful place within ethical method, tidiness departs. Paradox, enigma, and the discrete defensibility of logically contradictory options become our portion.

3. *Contextualized Moral Principles*. The Report raises the issue of how *contextualized* moral principles should be. The Report has been criticized widely for using creative and integrative and its septad of middle axioms to regulate sexual behavior. The charge is that these criteria are not sex-specific; they could apply to any form of human activity from the practice of medicine to the playing of cribbage.

My reaction here is mixed. On the one hand, the Report on this point relates well to older theological teaching on the connection of the virtues. A person cannot be sexually responsible if he is bad in every other way. The rapacious, aggressive person will not be likely to blossom edifyingly in the sexual encounter. There are, therefore, good reasons to bring in the kinds of more generic, non-sex-specific principles as the Report does.

On the other hand, I find interesting the resolute insistence on specifically sexual principles to judge sexual behavior. It is interesting because the same insistence is not found elsewhere. For example, in treating violence as a means for social change we have regularly used principles such as proportionality and discrimination (or the limitation of harm) which could also be used in business ethics and in marriage and anywhere where power operates *violently or not*. These principles are violence-specific and that has not bothered us. I think it should.

The methodological point I would urge here is this: we should look for principles that derive from *what* we are treating. Other more generic principles should also be employed for the reasons just mentioned, but our analysis is less likely to go astray if we seek to derive our basic generalizations from the particular and specific behavioral zone we are studying. This would help us to avoid the pitfalls between an abstract essentialism and a nominalistic particularism. In other words, we are not looking for an entelechy that can be intuitively perceived and which encapsulates the quintessential moral meaning of one form of behavior for all times and cultures. Neither would we indulge in a Sartrian actualism which would give to a situation only the meaning the participants bring to it. The quest for contextualized principles is a hedge against both extremes.

Strange as it may seem, then, I believe our ethics of violence can profit from this debate on *Human Sexuality*—and I am not imposing a sick joke. If the kind of insistence on sex-specific principles found in this sexual debate were applied to violence, we would come up with principles that would make violence more difficult to justify. If we noted that *by its nature* violence makes post-violence community-building more difficult, that it is addictive, that it minimizes the conditions for rationality and creative imagination, that it is inherently escalatory, and tends to bypass the needs for social and cultural restructuring, that it unleashes primitive vindictive instincts, etc., some principles will occur to us that would make the usual just war principles seem bland and permissive.[13]

4. *Neo-Probabilism.* I would appeal on the occasion of *Human Sexuality* for a return to probabilism, or rather neo-probabilism, since I believe the reaction to the book has evoked a wide wave of what could be called neo-mitigated-tutiorism. It has also provoked explicit attacks on the achievements of the debate on the moral systems and of probabilism in particular. For example, one writer in this debate has disparagingly referred to probabilism as "that extrinsic legalistic probabilism of the 17th and 18th centuries when authors were counted to affirm that some activity was safe in practice."[14]

Probabilism, like all good things, was abused, but the theological achievement that it represents was significant and until we see how it relates to the charismatic theology of Paul and John and the concept of the moral inspiration of the Holy Spirit in Augustine and Thomas Aquinas, it has not been given its theological due. Another reason for bringing probabilism down from the Catholic attic is that after Vatican II's recognition of the truly ecclesial quality of Protestant Christian churches, neo-probabilism could be the test of ecumenism. Is our ecumenism merely ceremonial or can we really begin to take Protestant moral views into account in discussing liceity in doubtful matters? The older probabilism did not even face such a question.

With all the calls for a return to the Catholic tradition that were leveled by critics of the Report, it is ironic that no one congratulated the authors for bringing probabilism back into Catholic ethical discourse. The triumph of probabilism in the Church was an achievement of many of our long-suffering theological forebears and we do well to hearken back to their work. Let me briefly repeat what probabilism is all about. Probabilism arose, and finally gained prominence over competing systems, as a way of solving practical doubt about the liceity of some kind of behavior. In practice, it confronted a situation in which a rigorous consensus claiming the immorality of certain behavior was challenged. The question was: at what point does the liberty-favoring opinion attain such respectability in the forum of conscience that a person could follow it in good faith? Those who said that even frivolous reasons would justify departure from rigorous orthodoxy were condemned as laxists by Popes Innocent XI and Alexander VII. At the other extreme were the absolute tutiorists who taught that one could never follow the liberal opinion unless it was strictly certain. Even being most probable (*probabilissima*) was not enough. In graph form the situation was this:

---

A             /B

---

A represents the dominant rigorous opinion claiming that certain activity could never be moral. B represents the liberal dissent. Laxism claimed that the most tenuous B would override A. Absolute tutiorism claimed that until B replaced A and was beyond challenge, it could not be followed. The Jansenists found absolute tutiorism attractive, but Alexander VIII did not, and he condemned it on December 7, 1690. Thus between the two banned extremes of laxism and absolute tutiorism, the Catholic debate raged with probabilism gradually becoming dominant.

Probabilism proceeded from the twin insights that a doubtful obligation does not bind as though it were certain, and that where there is doubt there is freedom. It held that a solidly probable opinion could be followed even though more probable opinions existed. To be solidly probable, a liberal opinion had to rest upon cogent though not conclusive reasons (intrinsic probability) or upon reliable authority (extrinsic probability). As Tanquerey puts it in his manual of moral theology, to be probable, an opinion could not be opposed to a "definition of the Church" or to certain reason and should retain its probability when compared with opposing arguments.[15] Since there is no "definition of the Church" regarding the issues disputed in *Human Sexuality*, and since furthermore it is clear that the Church does not have the competence to define such issues infallibly,[16] that condition cannot stand in the way of using probabilism.

Intrinsic probability, where one followed one's own lights to a solidly probable opinion, was not stressed in the history of probabilism, but it was presented as a possibility. Stress fell upon extrinsic probability where one found "five or six" moralists known for their "authority, learning, and prudence." Even one extraordinarily pre-eminent teacher alone could constitute probability. What this meant is that minority B on our graph became solidly probable through private insight or through the insight of five or six learned experts even though the enormous majority of theologians disagreed. Note well that the basis of probabilism is insight—one's own or that of reliable experts. Insight is an achievement of moral intelligence. It cannot be forbidden; neither does it await permission to appear.

Note also that probabilism does not require a consensus or absolute certitude. As Father Henry Davis writes: "when I act on the strength of a probable opinion, I am always conscious that though I am morally right in so acting, since I act prudently, nevertheless, the opinion of others who do not agree with me may be the true view of the case."[17] Obviously, the perennial debate will be between those who argue that the defenders of probability in a particular case are actually crypto-laxists and those who argue that the deniers of probability are disguised absolute tutiorists.

Probabilism was a remarkable development and represents a high point in Catholic moral thought. It recognized that the apparent safety of absolute tutiorism was only apparent. The acceptance of such a rigorous position, as Father Tanquerey explained, would impose an impossible burden on the faithful contrary to the mind of the gospel, which promises that the yoke will be sweet and the burden light; it would thus increase sins, generate despair, and drive many from the practice of religion.[18] Those reasons and probabilism itself are still relevant today.

To dismiss probabilism as the legalistic bickerings of the sixteenth and seventeenth centuries is theologically shortsighted. In the heyday of the debate, extravagant claims were made. Caramuel, who became known as the "prince of the laxists," taught that Adam and Eve used probabilism successfully to excuse themselves from many sins, until their wits and their probabilism failed them and they did fall. Vigorous efforts were made to trace the formal doctrine of probabilism to Augustine, Jerome, Ambrose, Gregory Nazianzen, Basil, and Thomas Aquinas. One need not become party to such adventures to insist on and argue how compatible probabilism is with deep Christian traditions. The early Church was remarkably sanguine about the presence of the illumining Spirit in the hearts of the faithful. As Vatican II says:

> The Spirit dwells in the Church and in the hearts of the faithful as in a temple (cf. 1 Cor. 3:16; 6:19). In them He prays and bears witness to the fact that they are adopted sons (cf. Gal. 4:6; Rom. 8:15–16 and 26). The Spirit guides the Church into the fullness of truth (cf. Jn. 16:13) and gives her a unity of fellowship and service. He furnishes and directs her with various gifts, both hierarchical and charismatic, and adorns her with the fruits of His Grace (cf. Eph. 4:11–12; 1 Cor. 12:4; Gal. 5:22).[19]

The Church has shared the confidence of St. Paul when he said that the spiritual man "is able to judge the value of everything" (1 Cor. 2:15). Augustine and Thomas manifest in strong theological language this exuberant confidence in the presence in all Christians of the illumining Spirit of God. Augustine asked: "What are the laws of God written by God in our hearts but the very presence of the Holy Spirit?"[20] And Thomas Aquinas, arguing that the new law is not anything written (including the New Testament), cites Jeremiah's promise that in the future testament God will put his law into the minds of his people and inscribe it on their hearts. In its primary meaning, then, the new law for Thomas is not the writings of biblical authors, church officers, or theologians, all of which are secondary, but the instructive grace of the Holy Spirit.[21]

This, admittedly, is a heady doctrine which called for and did historically elicit a theology of the discernment of the Spirit. One must test one's claimed inspiration against all the witnesses to truth within the community. And yet this heady doctrine, with all of its perils, is not a private preference of the current charismatic movement in the Church, but is rather *bona fide* mainstream

Catholic thought. It is also, I believe, eminently congenial with the spirit of the debate that led to the championing of probabilism. The debate on probabilism in many ways seems a curious and stilted period piece, but it would be ungrateful and unconservative of us to reject this achievement of the Catholic tradition. And reject it, in effect, we did. Of course, it maintained its presence in the manuals but in practice it was rendered nugatory. This was done by simply ignoring the genuine possibility of intrinsic probability and by controlling the theological enterprise in such wise that any theologian favoring a liberal opinion that did not square with the contemporary Vatican view was quickly deemed neither learned nor prudent. Thus did extrinsic probability pass. And thus were the doors thrown open to a juridical positivism based on the hierarchical magisterium.

The neo-probabilism for which I call would have to be extended to include Protestant witnesses to moral truth. Vatican II said of Protestant Christians that "in some real way they are joined with us in the Holy Spirit, for to them also He gives His gifts and graces, and is thereby operative among them with His sanctifying power."[22] It becomes unthinkable, therefore, if these words mean anything that we accept, that solid probability could not also be achieved through the witness of Protestant Christians who are also subjects of the "gifts and graces" of our God. I submit that if that thought is unpalatable, our ecumenism is superficial and insincere.

Two things have emerged in the debate on *Human Sexuality*; one is a kind of new-style mitigated tutiorism and the other is age-old magisteriological fundamentalism that is a lingering Catholic nemesis. The new tutiorism emerges subtly enough in that criticism of the Report which stresses defensively that this Report and its conclusions do not represent a consensus or a majority opinion of the Catholic Theological Society of America or of Catholic theologians in general. In old language this seems to say that the opinions are not *probabilissimae* and are therefore irrelevant. It may even imply that the opinions are not *stricte certae* and are therefore of no import—but this would be the absolute tutiorism condemned by Alexander VIII. What this indicated to me is that the categories of the moral systems debate of the sixteenth and seventeenth centuries are reductively perennial and are not out-dated tools of a localized and passé conflict.

Regarding the magisteriological fundamentalism which would bypass moral inquiry by appeal to the hierarchical magisterium and the notion of official truth, much has been said, and the problems here will not be met by what I can say in this brief format. I would only point out that by definition and not by permission, non-infallible teaching admits of dissent. As the Belgian bishops said in their statement on *Humanae Vitae*: "Someone . . . who is competent in the matter under consideration and capable of forming a personal and well-founded judgment—which necessarily presupposes sufficient information—may, after a serious examination before God, come to other conclusions on certain points. In such a case he has the right to follow his conviction, provided that he remains sincerely disposed to continue his inquiry."[23] This merely reflects the common teaching of the manuals that a Catholic could have good reasons to withhold assent to the teachings of the ordinary magisterium.[24] It also reflects the tradition of probabilism. I might add too that in response to the Report some bishops have finally called for greater collaboration with theologians. A few bishops now seem to see that moral theology is pastoral by its nature. But history prompts me to wonder whether the call for collaboration is simply a wish for control over liberal positions (or at least their publication). To tell moralists, as some are doing, to theologize but keep out of the pastoral domain is to tell them to think but reach no conclusions (at least no published conclusions). This is absurd. Moral theology is no longer a clerical preserve. Moral theologians are no longer writing *Penitential Books* to be mediated through a semiliterate clergy to an illiterate laity. An articulate laity knows what moral theology is up to and joins or follows in the work.

As to the notion of official truth which is implied in the idea of "official teaching," there are some staggering problems here. The idea of official truth involves a contradiction of symbols. It is like speaking of a valid kiss or an orderly ecstasy or a circular trapezoid. Truth cannot be official; neither can teaching. This confuses the juridical and the epistemological orders. There can be a core of central beliefs that give meaning to a particular religious communion and I have argued elsewhere that there is such a thing as a Christian moral credo and even a specifically Catholic ethic.[25] But the particular issues of *Human Sexuality* are not the specifying themes of Christian or Catholic existence. God has not given us an inflexible *code* by which to neatly measure our sexual orthodoxy. The discernment of orthodoxy and of moral truth is considerably more complex than that. The quest for an official ethics in sensitively disputed areas where serious and committed Christians differ is illusory and factionalizing. Revelation cannot be conceived as a substitute for moral discernment. Yet many of the laments about the abandonment of the traditional and official teaching of the Church imply nothing less.

Also I would say that appeals to the official teaching of the Church issued to end debate on these disputed issues of sexual ethics are at odds with contemporary ecumenical theology. What they are saying is that Protestant Christians (along with dissenting Catholics) do not represent the voice of the illumining Spirit if they dissent from the non-infallible teaching of the hierarchical magisterium. I would have to ask those who say this how they know that, or, what is the deeper question, how they could know that.

As a final word on this I would say magisteriological fundamentalism undermines probabilism and common sense. In support I quote again Father Davis:

> In its ultimate analysis, probabilism is common sense; it is a system used in practical doubt by the majority of mankind. People rightly say: I am not going to debate all day before acting in doubtful matters; there must be some very obvious way of making up my mind. At all events, if I cannot make up my mind for myself, I will act as some good people act, though many other good people might disapprove. That practical solution of doubt is common sense, and it is probabilism.[26]

In conclusion, I judge *Human Sexuality* to be a serious and courageous work. The authors chose not just to offer theoretical vignettes and platitudes, but to touch upon the specific issues. Had they chosen to stay general and edifying their work would have created no stir but merely been filed away as another theologically harmless and unhelpful statement. But they dared to face issues which most Catholic moralists have not faced with candor. In so doing, they have smoked us all out and have guaranteed a more substantive and helpful discussion of human sexuality than we have had in years. Because of their work the debate they have stimulated also promises to be an event in theory. What committee of the Catholic Theological Society of America has ever done more?

# NOTES

1. See *AAS* 43 (1951), 835–54, 845–46, 859 on the "very wide" set of reasons that could justify the permanent prevention of children in a marriage. This was more revolutionary than was generally perceived at the time. If procreative openness was to be the kingpin of sexual finality and if a marriage could be deliberately rendered non-procreative even by birth.control, it was not easy to say how much marriages fulfilled the procreative rubric at all. Contorted efforts to turn to the subjunctive to salvage the linkage between procreative and unitive are not helpful. Thus, to say that procreative purpose is maintained by the couple's saying that if they were to reproduce it would be through and with the other does not speak to a situation where the couple for good reasons are determined not to reproduce or cannot reproduce. On the productive end in marriage in Vatican II, see *Gaudium et Spes*, Art. 50 and n. 168. The key phrase in Latin is "non posthabitis ceteris matrimonii finibus."

2. Morton Hunt, *Sexual Behavior in the 1970's* (Chicago: Playboy Press, 1974), p. 253.

3. Ralph Linton, "The Natural History of the Family," in *The Family: Its Function and Destiny* (New York: Harper & Brothers, 1959), p. 52.

4. May Edel and Abraham Edel, *Anthropology and Ethics* (Springfield, Ill.: Charles C. Thomas, 1959), p. 81.

5. But for a contrary emphasis, see p. 157.

6. See pp. 202–3 for a list of some authors in this vein.

7. *Summa Theol.* I–II, q. 18, a. 3.

8. On my use of the term "sense of profanation," see Daniel C. Maguire, *The Moral Choice* (Garden City: Doubleday, 1978), pp. 81–83, 290–93.

9. See ibid., p. 162.

10. W. D. Ross, *The Right and the Good* (Oxford: Clarendon Press, 1930), p. 39. Emphasis added.

11. William K. Frankena, *Ethics* (Englewood Cliffs, N.J.: Prentice-Hall, 1963), p. 14. On the misplaced debate between teleology and deontology, see my *The Moral Choice*, pp. 157–63. The term "teleological" is not univocal. In traditional Catholic moral theology the term was used to denote the intrinsic finality of an action leading to a deontological conclusion on the behavior whose finality had purportedly been discerned.

12. For a critique of the hammers of proportionalism, see Richard McCormick, "Notes on Moral Theology," *Theological Studies* 39 (March 1978), 90–97.

13. I develop these ideas in *Death by Choice* (New York: Doubleday, 1974; Schocken Books, 1975), pp. 209–16.

14. Francis X. Meehan, "Love and Sexuality in Catholic Tradition," *America* 137 (1977), 234.

15. "... ei nec definitio Ecclesiae nec certa ratio adversetur." See Ad. Tanquerey, *Theologia Moralis Fundamentalis: De Virtutibus et Praeceptis*, Tomus secundus (Parisiis: Desclée et Socii, 1955), p. 293.

16. See my "Moral Absolutes and the Magisterium," in which I argued that it is not meaningful to say that the Church is infallible in specific issues of morality, in *Absolutes in Moral Theology?*, ed., Charles E. Curran (Washington: Corpus Books, 1968), pp. 57–107.

17. Henry Davis, *Moral and Pastoral Theology* (London and New York: Sheed and Ward, 1949), Volume 1, p. 107. Some have attempted to limit the application of probabilism, especially in nervous matters such as sexuality. Again, Father Davis: "Since the system is one that has been formulated chiefly to help those who are in a state of doubt, it would be of little practical use if there were numerous exceptional circumstances in which the system could not be applied ... It is the merit of Probabilism that there are no exceptions whatever to its application." Ibid., p. 96.

18. Tanquerey, op. cit., p. 287.

19. *Lumen Gentium*, Art. 4.

20. *De Spiritu et Littera*, P.L. 44, 222.

21. "Et ideo dicendum est quod principaliter nova lex est lex indita, secundario autem est lex scripta." *Summa Theol.* I–II, q. 106, a. 1, in corp.

22. Walter M. Abbott op. cit., pp. 15, 34.

23. Statement of the Belgian Hierarchy on *Humanae Vitae*, quoted in Joseph A. Komanchak, "Ordinary Papal Magisterium and Religious Assent," in *Contraception: Authority and Dissent*, ed., Charles E. Curran (New York: Herder and Herder, 1969), p. 117. The bishops,

of course, did point out the need to avoid "questioning the very principle of authority." Probabilism does not question that principle. Neither would an ecumenically enlarged neo-probabilism.

24. See Komonchak, art. cit., ibid., 101–26; and Daniel C. Maguire, "Moral Inquiry and Religious Assent," ibid., pp. 127–48.

25. See Daniel C. Maguire, "Credal Conscience: A Question of Moral Orthodoxy," *Anglican Theological Review*, Supplementary Series 6 (1976), 37–54, and "Catholic Ethics with an American Accent," in *America in Theological Perspective*, ed., Thomas M. McFadden (New York: Seabury Press, 1976), pp. 13–36.

26. Henry Davis, op. cit., p. 93.

## Chapter Seven

❧

# A WORD FROM THE HOME FRONT: CONSCIENCE —WITH COMPASSION

### MAYO MOHS AND
### PATRICIA TURBES MOHS

We hold no special brevet or degree to merit our presence in this company of scholars—and perhaps that is just the point. We are American Roman Catholics, with all the peculiar tensions that name implies. We practice our faith (or "practice at it," as a friend frankly explains her own efforts) in the sometimes schizoid manner of the times. We have been married almost a decade, loving and quarreling along the way. We have two young children, a son who will be seven when this book appears, a daughter who will then be five. Our thoughts here turn most particularly on them, and on what kind of people we would like them to be. They seem destined to grow up in a post-Christian society, but we hope, and pray, that they will choose to be Christians all the same.

They are both in a Catholic school, as we once were. Patty, a graduate of Minnesota's College of St. Catherine (A.B. '69), never darkened the door of a public school from kindergarten on. Mayo (Xavier University of Ohio, A.B. '55, M.A. '57) spent only kindergarten and first grade in public schools, and dabbled in predoctoral courses at UCLA before irredeemably defecting to news-magazine journalism. The point here is not to dwell endlessly on autobiographical detail but to establish, in the famous phrase of the sixties, "where we come from" when we approach *Human Sexuality*.

Despite the fact that Mayo's college years preceded Vatican II and Patty's followed it, we are both products of what was, for the most part, a pre-Vatican II education. That has its advantages: even if both of us had not been pressed into a continuing familiarity with current theology through Mayo's work as *Time* religion editor, the stiff course requirements in theology and philosophy of those disciplined old days might still have brought the heavier chapters of *Human Sexuality* within the range of our vocabulary. But discipline had its price, as the authors of *Human Sexuality* surely must remember. Their book would have been on the Index of Forbidden Books, and any unrepentant authors would have been literally excommunicated—not just rhetorically read out of the Church by conservative critics.

Sexual ethics of the time seemed to exist in a vacuum, unable to straddle the gap between the innocence of one age and the emerging license of another. In the spring of 1965, when the Vatican Council was winding to a close and a panel of papal experts was already convened to discuss the pros and cons of birth control, a teacher in a "Christian Marriage" course in Patty's high school in Minnesota was solemnly warning the young women in his audience about the grievous sin of French kissing. Some of these high school seniors listened earnestly, considering it an ultimate question—and according to the theology of the day so it was. For others the warning came a bit too late. At least several of the listeners, all unwed, were already pregnant. And this would be the last formal Catholic sex education of their lives.

By no means were all the troublesome or exasperating teachings of the era sexual. At Xavier, a certain overscrupulous religion teacher, whom Mayo strenuously avoided, ruled that *Life* magazine was inimical to the faith because it presented a favorable view of Protestantism in its Great Religions series. To be fair, that teacher was considered to be something of a nut even by his own colleagues. But tougher, much brighter minds on the faculty could produce rather more unsettling encounters. Mayo, then a political science major, vividly remembers debating in 1954 with a young Jesuit philosophy teacher on the issue of religious liberty. The professor hewed faithfully to the traditional doctrine: "error has no rights." Even if error had no rights, Mayo countered, people do have a right to freedom of conscience, and to the forms of worship and evangelizing that freedom entails. The professor told him flatly that he was "a heretic." Some years later the teacher (now an old friend) conceded the point. Vindication, especially by the Second Vatican Council, was sweet, but at the time the accusation was unnerving.

It was not as if we really needed heresy to endanger our souls. There were mortal sins aplenty without it. Not just the sins themselves—the necking, the petting (rather rarer in those days than some of us would have liked), the masturbation (one disconsolate fellow used to pray nightly for wet dreams)—but the occasions of sin, too. As *Human Sexuality* makes abundantly clear in its quotations from fairly recent moral manuals, putting oneself into the proximate occasion of sin was a mortal sin as well, unless there was serious reason for doing so. Somehow it seemed like double jeopardy—damned if you do, damned even if you get a chance to —or even triple jeopardy. Could there not be occasions of occasions of sin? Why get up in the morning at all? On the grounds of avoiding such "proximate occasions," one Catholic college in Pennsylvania in the mid-1950s forbade steady dating among its students, under penalty of expulsion. It seemed a strange prohibition, and was not widely emulated. At Xavier, students interviewed by a local newspaper hooted at the idea. Where was a young Catholic man or woman to begin looking for a Catholic spouse, if not at college?

There were exceptions. One generous-minded counselor at Xavier told a scrupulous student that people often accuse themselves of serious sexual sins when they are in fact not quite so serious. At Notre Dame, a student of those same years remembers, one quite radical priest-professor was going considerably further, and urging engaged couples to become increasingly intimate to get some idea of one another's sexuality.

Such teachers were rare. On matters of sex (as well as on matter of "doctrine" long since displaced) there was simply too much thunder and lightning. Some of us more or less yielded to our inclinations and prayed for mercy—or hoped that the rules were not quite so rigid as we were taught. One immensely popular story circulating in our graduate years at Xavier concerned a terrible disaster on earth that had dispatched thousands to summary judgment at St. Peter's Gates. A long line of worried, fidgeting sinners waited to hear their sentences, when suddenly, from the head of the line, a great cheer began to rise, rippling backward through the crowd. A reprieved sinner, beaming from ear to ear, was running down the line shouting: "Sex doesn't count! Sex doesn't count!"

Of course it does count—or *Human Sexuality* would be without meaning and purpose. It was the gravity of the sins that we argued with—not the value of the virtues. Even the backsliders among us relished the anecdote about a husky Xavier football player who was in summer ROTC camp with officer trainees from other colleges. One morning a young man from an Ivy League college complained that he hadn't "had any" for three weeks. "Mister," said the Xavier man, "I haven't had any for twenty-one years." We noticed another phenomenon too. Sinners though we were, we often found on trips to secular campuses that we kept a distinguishably tighter rein on the sins we permitted ourselves than did some of our secular counterparts. One Xavier man, embarking for military service, astonished his non-Catholic date for the evening when he declined a rather intimate going-away present. It was not that she was not desirable, he explained; it simply wasn't fair to her.

Yet that act of Christian gallantry was accomplished by a student who was under a wide, leaden cloud of sexual gloom—the perpetual threat of mortal sin. It was a threat that did not vanish with Vatican II, a worry that could degenerate into the most ridiculous sort of scrupulosity. As late as 1963, Patty remembers, the students at her high school were warned that patent leather shoes might give a boy a forbidden peek up a girl's legs (that is *not* a legend). The same nun cautioned that girls entertaining boys at dinner should avoid white tablecloths: they might be suggestive of bed sheets. This sort of teaching could only elicit mockery, and it did, which simply made more critical sexual teachings all the more suspect to the students.

The mortal sin label on every consciously willed act of sexual pleasure has haunted Catholics and other Christians for centuries. How many angry defections from the Church can be traced back to a deep despair over this needlessly stern teaching? James Joyce's defection, thinly disguised in his persona as Stephen Dedalus, is harrowingly portrayed in a passage of spiritual terrorism in *A Portrait of the Artist as a Young Man*. James T. Farrell slips away in *Studs Lonigan* Kate Millett, self-avowed bisexual and feminist author of *Sexual Politics* and *Flying*, was Mayo's classmate in parochial school. She blames her religious teachers—at least some of them—for stifling the early feelings of affection she found outside of the misery of a broken home. Often it was the deep thinkers, the ruthlessly logical, who left. As Caryl Rivers observed in her warmhearted *Aphrodite at Mid-Century*, it was the congenital doubters among us who seemed to keep the faith. If something we were told seemed patently foolish we simply rejected it; to us, it had nothing to do with the core of our belief: with the fact of a God who died to redeem man, and who rose again from the dead to give us hope that we might one day do the same.

Other souls, more conscientious, played a counting game. At St. Catherine's in 1969, Patty recalls, *Humanae Vitae* had reduced smoker bull sessions into the most abysmal moral mathematics; if taking birth control pills was a mortal sin each time, and abortion a single mortal sin, why not risk the one sin of an abortion against the twenty-eight sins of a month on the pill? The ethics scholar can answer that easily in terms of the gravity of the offenses, but the mortal sin syndrome had a powerful and debilitating effect on common sense.

It also led to some strange mental gymnastics. One philosophy professor at Xavier (long since gone) suggested that mortal sin, paradoxically, might almost be necessary for salvation: that for most people, apart from saints, only the experience of falling from grace and regaining it through God's forgiveness could inspire a saving love of God. That somewhat tortured reasoning certainly has a measure of empirical proof in the lives of many believers, and it did give a sort of metaphysical importance to the trap that many of us felt we were in.

But trap it remained. Theologians tried to help in various ways. Marc Oraison, considering the classic formulation of mortal sin, wondered whether most people had a truly full and free consent of the will in matters of sex, and asked therefore whether serious sin, at least in this area of behavior, was possible for them. The hypothesis was rejected by the Vatican, but a hint of it at least remains in the new guidelines for confessors, included in the *Declaration on Certain Questions Concerning Sexual Ethics*. In section ten of that document, it is conceded that "in sins of the sexual order . . . it more easily happens that free consent is not fully given." Another, more useful approach, perhaps because it was less demeaning to what the Vatican Declaration called "people's moral capacity," was the concept of the fundamental option, and its application to sexual sins. As widely interpreted, this concept did not challenge the doctrine that violations of a sexual nature were serious sins, but suggested rather that within the context of a generally good life they might well *not* be "mortal."

Though the precise words of the theological formula—"the fundamental option"—may never have occurred to ordinary Christians through the ages, the idea surely did. From the time the question was raised in early catechism classes, most of us were horrified at the thought that a person might live a basically good life and then get caught up by an ill-timed mortal sin just before some horrible accidental death. Such tales were the ghoulish stuff of high school retreats, but they inspired not the love of God but an unhealthy and even angry fear in which some of us (to reshape the imagery of Jonathan Edwards) envisioned ourselves in the hands of a cruel and whimsical God. However well intentioned the warnings of some earnest moral teachers, the threats of damnation for the slightest sexual infraction colored the moral lives of Christians out of all proportion to the sin's importance. For some they distorted the message of Christianity so grotesquely that the only answer was apostasy. Fundamentalist Christians, further forbidden yet other pleasures of the world that Catholics were still allowed, often found the pressures even harder to bear.

*Human Sexuality* is a brave, pathbreaking book, an extraordinary compendium of the development of Catholic sexual morality that strives to use that teaching as a foundation for further thought, discussion, and ethical refinement. The chapters on sexuality in the Scriptures, in Church tradition over the centuries, and as seen by modern empirical sciences are masterpieces of concise yet thoroughgoing information. The chapters that seek to work out a fresh theology and apply it to pastoral guidelines are less satisfactory only because they raise almost as many problems as they solve. We will address those problems further on: what concerns us here is what the book does not say. It does not raise adequately the question of the gravity of sexual sins. To those of us who are still on the penitent's side of the confessional screen (or room, as the case may be), that is still *the* key issue. It is especially so for us who are parents, who do not want to raise our children in the same milieu of guilt in which we were schooled, but who at the same time do want to give them a solid and positive appreciation of sexual values.

Their turn comes sooner these days than it did for us. In a nearby parochial school (not ours as it happens, but too close for comfort), one of the associate pastors was called by a frantic principal to break up a group of third-graders who had skipped off to a nearby abandoned building to remove their clothes and have a try at a little fledgling fornication. They were stopped, fortunately, before the experiments could proceed. But such incidents, plus the news that both the age of puberty and the minimum age of unwed mothers are declining, warn us that we will soon be faced with something more serious than infantile masturbation.

To deal with adolescent sexuality we need something more graduated than a catalog of serious sexual sins. The 1976 Vatican pronouncement on sexual ethics still affirms that "the moral order of sexuality still involves such high values of human life that every direct violation of this order is objectively serious." Why? Is it because the Church is still, at this late date, trying to exercise some sort of sexual totalitarianism, as Catholic psychologist Eugene Kennedy suggests in his 1972 book, *The New Sexuality: Myths, Fables and Hang-Ups*? There he observes that "churchmen . . . were a clever lot because . . . they understood man's vulnerabilities and they knew if they could control his sexual attitudes they could effectively control him."[1] Kennedy acknowledges further on that "the power the Church has had over [man's] behavior is not something he has given to it in a completely unwilling fashion. When we are wiser we will understand that he needed the authoritarian attitudes he allowed the church to exercise over him."[2]

Perhaps. In the fluid, unpredictable society of medieval Europe, when there was no effective contraceptive method; when the common people knew little even of the process of conception; when communities (unlike those of Margaret Mead's South Seas) cared little or nothing for the fate of their bastards; when venereal disease could rapidly eat away a man's or a woman's life, perhaps the threat—if not the fact—of damnation was a necessary social control. And the very consequences of the sins could make them more serious than they might seem now. Yet one wonders how many lives collapsed in despair at the prospect of a Boschian hell. The witnesses are mixed. To read the *Penitentials* is to visualize half of society forever on bread and water. To read Chaucer is to visualize a world in which most people paid little attention to the jeremiads of monks. There was always a jolly fat friar to ease one's conscience—at least in the literature of the day.

For all the excuses that can be offered, the conviction persists that the Church has not played fair in assessing the gravity of sexual sin. No one puts it more eloquently or more angrily than the eminent Latin American Jesuit theologian Juan Luis Segundo. In his five-volume masterwork, *A Theology for Artisans of a New Humanity,* Segundo (who wrote in collaboration with the Peter Faber Center of Montevideo) attacks the proposition that sexual sin is by its nature grievous:

> Consider the great physical and psychic pressure that sexuality exerts directly on the individual and then consider the general situation of most people on a continent such as Latin America. For the vast majority of the people, sexual pleasure is the only pleasure possible for them. It is the only one compatible with their economic status. It is the only one cheap enough for people who have been deprived of the economic resources to afford others. . . .
>
> What interests us here is what is said about sexuality *in the name of Christianity.* And that does cease to strike us as very odd indeed. In the moral manuals absolutely every kind of sin, except one, varies in seriousness depending on the magnitude of what one does or plans to do. You can kill, but you can also wound someone seriously or slightly, or you can simply refuse to help them. And the gravity of the sin will have a relation to the gravity of the harm done. A lie that does serious

harm is a serious sin; a lie that does not have serious consequences is a venial sin.

But what happens when we enter the domain of sexual morality? A single slip, in thought alone and independent of any
harm done to one's neighbor, is grave enough to merit hell with
its endless sufferings and eternal separation from God. Pious
literature paints numerous examples of spectral apparitions from
hell whose sufferings are the result of a single sexual sin which
they did not have time to confess or be sorry for. . . .

There is no doubt that when sexuality is viewed in this light,
it leads morally to a most dangerous moral dissociation. Sex is
the wellspring of countless serious sins until suddenly, thanks to
some document or matrimonial ceremony, it is transformed
into an advisable, holy, and even obligatory thing. But when we
consider the power of sexuality, we can clearly see that it must
become an integral part of our psychic life before marriage is really possible. . . .

Now if sexuality is such a pervasive psychic element on the
one hand, and we maintain this moral chasm between premarital life and postmarital life on the other, then the only "social"
defense against sexuality we can put up is to label it in all sorts
of irrational ways. It becomes something "dirty," "impure,"
"unmentionable," "harmful" and so forth. [*Here, in a footnote,
Segundo points out that Christianity did, for centuries, defend
sex within marriage against those who found sex of any kind
evil.*] But how are we going to constructively integrate sexuality into our psychic life if we do that? Sexuality becomes taboo.
And this taboo, within the framework of a morality that claims
to be rational, either atrophies the whole complex or else is violated. . . .

The sexual part of what is called Christian morality has a
debilitating impact on overall Christian praxis as well. Man's
outlook on sexual matters is in large measure a solitary affair,
particularly in the light of the surrounding eroticism of society.
Now if his eternal destiny is constantly at stake in his attitude
toward sexuality, then Christ's single commandment to love
one another must drop into the background and suffer severe
distortion. The Christian moral life is an eminently social one
designed to create solidarity in society. But it is now devalued

and turned into an individual struggle to preserve one's chastity. It is as if chastity were something valid for its own sake instead of being meant to serve the social morality of Christianity. Paul's description of this social morality is completely opposed to the morality currently practiced by average Christians: "The person who loves his brother has fulfilled the whole of the law."

It is not just Christian morality that suffers from this terrible lack of balance. Faith itself is affected. For centuries the prevailing Christian morality has demanded that Christians regard this earthly life as a *test* in a game plan decreed by God. Quite understandably these Christians came to feel that the logicality or illogicality of the sexual moral code confirmed the fact that the whole business of life was a test and nothing but that. Morality certainly could not be meant to lead people to a progressively more coherent line of moral conduct.

And how were they to picture this "test"? It can only be regarded as the most gratuitously cruel and universally horrifying test imaginable. . . . How can we possibly picture a good God testing man in this way? How can we believe God is testing man's eternal destiny on the basis of the most despotic and ubiquitous instinctive force of all? How can we believe that the test is based on each and every single act or deed in this sphere, fleeting and private as they may be, rather than on man's gradual effort to dominate and integrate this force into his overall life?

Is it not time to ask to what extent the phenomenon of modern unbelief may be rooted subtly and implicity in this classic Christian conception of sexual morality and its taboos—which does not seem to be backed up by any portion of the New Testament?[3]

It is important to note that Segundo is a systematic theologian whose sympathies lie with Latin America's "liberation theologians," though his total canon of work goes well beyond the political, social, and economic concerns that dominate their books. His coruscating view of traditional Catholic sexual ethics is thus colored by his concern that it overrides a Christian's social consciousness. But it is nonetheless on the mark. He does not advocate license, but encourages growth toward sexual maturity ("to dominate and integrate this force into his overall life") without reinforcing the anxieties of guilt that overtake so many of us, young and old, in our quest toward that elusive goal of a full *and* fully Christian sex life.

The underlying mood of *Human Sexuality* seems certainly to share the feeling of Segundo and other writers that sexual sins need to be reclassified into the ranks of other sins, where they can be judged by the extent of their malice, and thus be treated with more compassion in counseling and in the confessional. But it could have and should have been far more forceful and explicit. On page 173 it is somewhat timidly suggested that "the moral approach of the past that regarded every wilful enjoyment of pleasure before marriage as . . . mortal sin needs to be re-examined." On the same page is the warning that "expressions or approaches that are . . . sin-centered should be avoided." And on page 179 the gradations of sexual morality are suggested in a passage that allows that a certain kind of non-marital relationship may be "less immoral" than relations in a selfish marriage. But the statement on page 159 ("it seems an exaggeration to hold that even the smallest degree of incomplete venereal pleasure involves necessarily a complete inversion of the purpose of sexuality . . .") must either be irony or the year's most timorous adventure in challenging the traditional magisterium. Perhaps the strongest statement is by indirection on page 167: "Sexual behavior for a Christian must be guided by the same values and norms as all other human behavior." In other words, no more rigorously than other actions. Apart from those references, the book seems mostly to disagree by quoting from classical moralists at their worst. Poor Henry Davis has the same passage quoted ("a serious perversion of nature has taken place, etc.") more than once.[4]

The importance of removing sexual aberrations (i.e., outside of marriage) from the automatically grievous cannot be exaggerated. Without moral gradations in sexual life the worst sort of irresponsible habits can be encouraged in the name of committing fewer mortal sins. We have already noted the specious argument that a single abortion was less immoral than a month on the pill. Consider another case: in his capacity as a naval base department head in Japan, Mayo had the authority to approve or disapprove requests from young rated men to live off base. This generally meant they wanted to move in and set up housekeeping with some Japanese girl. Mayo and most of his fellow officers ordinarily approved the requests, because they meant that the men in question would at least be living in a stable, usually caring relationship, rather than prowling the bars in search of an available hostess. But one seagoing Catholic chaplain took violent issue with this policy, arguing that it would be better to force the men to live on base, letting them go to town for casual sex with a prostitute, than allowing them to live in "a state of mortal sin." He failed to convince us. Then and now, the argument made neither Christian nor common sense.

If the theological reflections of *Human Sexuality* are to be heeded, gradations of sexual virtue—or the lack of it—will be all the more necessary. The now-celebrated septet of sexual values suggested for judging an act are rigorous tests, and there are few human acts of any kind that can be, at a given moment, "self-liberating, other-enriching, honest, faithful, socially responsible, life-serving and joyous." If those tests were applied to business, commerce would fail on at least one count ("other-enriching") and quite often on several others. Indeed, the book does not make sufficiently clear that these are guidelines for reflection on one's sexual life and direction, not a checklist to be hung on the bedstead. Using the septet as a checklist would for one thing automatically eliminate one of the values: there would be nothing joyous about the process at all.

(A small, perhaps picayune aside. Some of the seven values, quite sound and thoughtfully provocative when they are fully discussed, carry the abrasive ring of jargon when they are simply rattled off. Hyphenated words have a long history from the *Aeneid* to *Time* magazine, but several hyphenations here seem jarring. If "self-liberating" is self-fulfilling, why not say "self-fulfilling"? The word is still hyphenated, but more familiar and congenial, less resonant of est. Instead of "other-enriching," why not simply "generous"? It seems to cover the same bases. A truly generous heart would insist that his or her sexual relationship helped the partner grow. "Life-serving" poses more problems. "Creative" would be better were it not already pre-empted as one of the basic aspects of sex. A priest who is a good friend of ours

once counseled us that our marriage must remain "open to life."
At least that would avoid the San Quentin flavor of "life-serving.")

Translating this septet for the young is yet another problem.
The study seems positively naive in its confidence that the
Church has the resources to reach the young and that the young
have even the basic theological language to carry on a productive
conversation if and when they can be reached. The book calls for
a "patient, persistent and personal effort . . . to help youngsters
discern the fundamental moral values at stake." Where, how, and
by whom is this task going to be undertaken? In *some* Confrater-
nity of Christian Doctrine (CCD) classes, perhaps; but too few
attend and those that do not are the ones who need to be reached
most of all. In parochial school religion classes, of course, but too
few young Catholics are in parochial schools. At home? That is a
possibility, but it would entail a massive adult education program
to teach the parents how to teach their children. Even then, too
many parents would rather go bowling or watch Monday night
football. Perhaps sex needs to be brought back to Sunday sermons.
That audience is smaller than it once was, but it cuts across all
classes and ages still. Parents are frankly afraid about how their
children will grow up in an age of permissiveness. The problem
with this tactic, of course, is that it is so public. Compassionate
advice suitable to individual cases in the confessional could be interpreted as permissive license if enunciated from the pulpit. One
complaint to the bishop and the short course in *Human Sexuality* would be over. Only if the bishops themselves realize that the
old formulas will no longer do, that a responsible new approach to
sexuality is needed, will such a public campaign become possible.

Even Catholic education today is too often producing a large
crop of theological illiterates, mixed with smaller crops of earnest
and articulate youngsters. Patty is the daughter of a man who has
taught for four decades in a Catholic prep school; Mayo taught
both in a Jesuit prep school and in CCD: we keep up with the
news of the trade, and it is not encouraging. Working on a *Time*
cover on Catholicism two years ago, Mayo was impressed with the
hard core of young people at the Sunday youth Mass and the dialogue sermon in a parish he visited. But there were scarcely
twenty present. Where were the others? And how many would

have understood the questions suggested on page 174 of *Human Sexuality?* "Are you personally comfortable with what you are doing? . . . Does it express genuine respect for the other? Are you using or exploiting one another? Do you consider it an honest and fitting expression of the degree and depth of your relationship? . . . Does it show respect for legitimate family and community expectations? Does it lead to greater mutual trust, support, and fidelity? Does it reflect an awareness and sensitivity to the life-serving function of human sexuality?" Those questions would glaze the eyes of most adults, let alone youngsters. The Dead End Kid to Spencer Tracy: "What do all them big woids mean, Fatha? All I want to know is if it's OK." Spencer Tracy to the Dead End Kid, quoting the final leading question from *Human Sexuality:* "Does it result in genuine peace, joy, and happiness, without regrets or misgivings?" The Dead End Kid, now thoroughly puzzled: "Listen, Fatha, if I wasn't a little worried, I wouldn't be here in the foist place."

There are scores of other kinds of people who will need the language of *Human Sexuality* translated: truck drivers with tenth-grade educations, making a catch-as-catch-can sex life for themselves in shabby places on the lonely road; pretty, bright-minded girls in Manhattan whose last sex education was in eighth grade but who have to cope with the singles morality of a sexually predatory society; couples in crowded apartments with too many kids who have neither joy nor self-liberation nor truth nor faithfulness in what is left of their "life-serving" marriage.

Finding the proper forum to reach most of these people is a problem so vast that it can (and should) consume another study itself. But the manner of the approach need not be so difficult. Jesus used parables: the written and visual media are full of parables—some of them positive, some of them negative—that could be used effectively as teaching tools. Consider *The Great Gatsby*, either novel or movie. The novel is of course far better: romantic though Scott Fitzgerald was, he saw through the blur of romanticism's self-deception to its often bitter fruit. Yet the recent movie, disappointing as it was, could serve in its place. It has already been on television, and doubtless will be again; there are few better examples in modern American literature of people who exploit others sexually or romantically, then blithely walk away to continue their lives. At the end of the story, Tom Buchanan's paramour Myrtle Wilson is dead, Jay Gatsby unjustly slain as her suspected killer. The two who caused the tragedy, Tom and Daisy Buchanan, are untouched, even unmoved. Nick Carraway, the narrator of the tale, muses sadly:

> They were careless people, Tom and Daisy—they smashed up things and creatures and then retreated back into their money or their vast carelessness, or whatever it was that kept them together, and let other people clean up the mess they had made.

*Roman Holiday*, William Wyler's gentle 1953 romantic comedy, is an old favorite on the late show; it makes a rather more positive appeal for sexual responsibility. The heroine, played by Audrey Hepburn, is a ruling princess from some small, unidentified European country, who escapes for an incognito spree on the town. The hero, played by Gregory Peck, is an American newspaperman who needs a story—and finds her. At one point he has to let her sleep in his room, and quite matter-of-factly spends the night in a nearby chair. They fall very much in love, but do not marry: she must go back to her crown and her people. It is an old-fashioned story, almost wistfully so, with its gallantry and self-sacrifice, but there is hardly a more cogent demonstration of the "socially responsible" element argued in *Human Sexuality* on page 94: "a willingness to forego personal benefit and growth in order to preserve or promote the greater good of society."

*Human Sexuality* at one point discourages a "consequence-oriented" approach to sexual guidance of the young. We do not entirely agree, at least where those consequences concern out-of-wedlock pregnancies. The pathos of such pregnancies was recently demonstrated in an unusually serious episode of the television situation comedy "One Day at a Time." In it an unmarried friend of the family turns up with a new baby, explaining that the father does not know (she does not want him to quit school), and that she is giving up the baby for adoption. The unsuspecting father, it turns out, does show up: he is now dating one of the daughters in the family. Naturally, he offers to quit school, marry the girl, and raise his son properly. The two review the future: bleak, perhaps jobless, a marriage made bitter by lost opportunity. Reluctantly the young man agrees that adoption is the best thing. In a moving scene, he says farewell to his child, and then cries disconsolately. "I'll always know," he reflects, "that somewhere out there I have a son—and I'll never know who he is." That kind of show could provide fruitful discussion for any class of high school students: it is one consequence they need to consider.

Even science fiction these days can provide the key to a pointed discussion of sexual morality. Robert Heinlein, a science fiction author who became something of a cult figure in the late 1960s with his novel *Stranger in a Strange Land*, published in 1973 a long, discursive novel in his "future history" series called *Time Enough for Love*. Interjected in the novel is a collection of aphorisms and reflections by a character named Lazarus Long, "the oldest living member of the human race." At Christmastime in 1978 those sayings were published in a separate collection, and they are almost certain to become hugely popular among young people. Many of Lazarus Long's thoughts involve sex, marriage, and how to woo women (one concise recommendation: "Rub her feet."). Some could provoke lively debate on the nature of sex in general and certain sexual acts in particular. Consider:

> Masturbation is cheap, clean, convenient and free of possibility of wrongdoing—and you don't have to go home in the cold. But it's *lonely*.[5]

(Discussion question: If it is so lonely, why is it so certainly "free of any possibility of wrongdoing"?) Here is Heinlein once again, sounding not unlike parts of *Human Sexuality*, but saying it somewhat differently:

> Copulation is spiritual in essense—or it is merely friendly exercise. On second thought, strike out "merely." Copulation is not "merely" even when it is just a happy pastime for two strangers. But copulation at its spiritual best is so much more than physical coupling that it is different in kind as well as degree.
>
> The saddest feature of homosexuality is not that it is "wrong" or "sinful" or even that it can't lead to progeny—but

that it is more difficult to reach through it this spiritual union. Not impossible—but the cards are stacked against it.

But—most sorrowfully—many people never achieve spiritual sharing even with the help of male-female advantage; they are condemned to wander through life alone.[6]

That one brief passage contains enough dicta on the human sexual condition to keep a class in active discussion for a week or more. Some may object to our comparing *Human Sexuality*, a painstaking work of scholarship, with the wit and wisdom of popular media, even serious novels like *The Great Gatsby*. They should not. The age has made sex its preoccupation, at least in the Western world, and now we are paying the piper and worrying about it. The language and the audience may be different; the concern is not. What characterizes the best of all these works is a sense of compassion informed by a concerned conscience.

*Human Sexuality* brims with compassion, and, if read carefully, is a stern call to a reinformed sexual conscience among Catholics. Perhaps because of its view that "sex is seen as a force that permeates, influences and affects every act of a person's being" (an unusually sweeping interpretation), it finds compassion for those who are seldom mentioned in moral manuals, most especially those whom the book calls "involuntary singles." The world is full of such outcasts, but it took Victor Hugo to bring them to life in *Notre Dame de Paris* in the full poignancy of Quasimodo. Few of the "involuntary singles" are grotesques like the hunchbacked Quasimodo, but inside or out they often bear a similar stigma. It is refreshing to hear "such individuals cannot and should not be expected to live as asexual or nonsexual beings." Yet the book refuses to face the inevitable question: what kind of sex can they have? Masturbation, with the aid of fantasies from pornography? Casual couplings with others of their kind? (Damien's Molokai lepers, to his perpetual distress, found surcease in such encounters.) Prostitutes? Whether it was true or not, Henri de Toulouse-Lautrec was convinced that his own crippled body could be loved only by prostitutes; we have, by way of his thank-you, his own compassionate portrayal of that demimonde. We might be profitably reminded that Jesus sat and ate with similar outcasts.

Just as it is compassionate because of its mystical view of sex,

*Human Sexuality* seems unusually harsh when sex seems to fulfill
a lighter, more transient function: the "recreational sex" that is
the only realistic outlet for many people: what Heinlein calls a
"happy pastime." The authors are right to be suspicious of patterns that can lead to a demeaning promiscuity (*Looking for
Mr. Goodbar* is a horrific parable in this regard), but they seem
convinced (page 168) that such sexual relations "are simply forms
of exploitation, at best a matter of casual play unworthy of the
seriousness of sex. Such exploitation certainly falls short of the
command of love enjoined by Jesus Christ upon his followers." Is
recreational sex always so exploitative? On page 65 the authors declare that "the consensus would seem to be that sex can be for fun
in a context of mutual respect and caring." Is this simply a report
of the consensus in the empirical sciences? Or is it a value judgment? If the latter, it contradicts, at least to a degree, the conclusions on page 168. At the same time, it is difficult not to agree
that casual sex almost always "falls short of the command of love
enjoined by Jesus Christ." Most of our actions, in bed or out, do
fall short of that commandment. Even so, a condemnatory note
seems self-defeating. For some, it will be the only sex they ever
have. If they can be led gently to a more stable, lasting relationship, all the better. If they cannot, they need not be threatened with hellfire and brimstone. The natural sanction enunciated by Heinlein is enough: "to wander through life alone."

In some passages, *Human Sexuality* seems too permissive, in
others too strict. The lengthy discussion on masturbation will
probably provoke accusations of both, because it seems in fact
somewhat contradictory. Most categories of masturbation are
dismissed as matters of minor moral malice, if any; even "masturbation of necessity" involving "reasonable relief from excessive
sexual tension" may be under certain circumstances "a matter of
prudent choice of values." But "hedonistic" masturbation "simply
for the sake of the pleasure involved" is viewed with a horror
scarcely paralleled anywhere else in the book. To be sure, the authors are careful to delineate this aberration as an exclusive, consistent, self-absorbing preoccupation, but there remains an almost
amusing dichotomy between it and "masturbation of necessity."
It is as if there were some sort of puritanical usefulness to the lat-

ter that is lacking in the former. The implied message: do it if you have to, but don't enjoy it.

Quite apart from its critical view of recreational sex, the book is too vague in its view of what constitutes sexual immorality and what does not. Boundaries, as the authors point out, are not easy to define, but in discussing the limits of permissible intimacies in a developing sexual relationship (e.g., between the engaged) they state on page 168 that "there are intimacies that are not signs of affection but simply a stimulation of sexual gratification." What sort? Intimacies *involve* sexual gratification, and if it can be argued that there is a "masturbation of necessity," those who would permit graduated intimacies among the unmarried must realize that at some point in the game there will develop an orgasm of necessity. Some, perhaps young women especially, need to be warned about this. Persons rightly resent a sexual tease, and those who play that role deliberately commit one of the cruelest sexual jokes. On the other hand, some do not know how easily such intimacies as prolonged necking sessions can arouse another. When they then refuse to go further, they earn an unfair reputation as a tease. Couples should know that a certain level of intimacy will fairly demand release for one or both of them.

*Human Sexuality* asks too much of the young when the authors expect them not to try to "prove their respective masculinity (or) femininity" in their encounters. Early dating, even at well-chaperoned dances or parties, involves just such preening. They need such proof, but they should be encouraged to grow out of that need.

We worry about one area in which the authors' warnings are not strong enough. The section on "child-free" marriages fails to take note of a galloping danger to American society, and probably others in the Western world. We find no particular fault with the authors' reasoning in this regard that purposely child-free marriages "should rightly become more acceptable." We concede, under the careful conditions outlined, that even a couple quite capable of having and raising children "might live out its marriage commitment in a truly Christian way, contributing to its own growth and that of the community at large, without necessarily including child-bearing in that process." Elsewhere the authors make it sharply clear that such an intention could *not* include the intent to abort if a child were conceived.

What concerns us is the growing number of such marriages in our society, marriages that are beginning to take their economic and social toll. In our city, two-career, childless couples are earning extraordinary incomes, enabling them to outbid larger families for the limited space in the apartment market. The result, abetted by an influx of monied people from abroad, is a soaring, record-high apartment market. They are shaping the market for consumer goods—and raising the prices there as well. And they are holding down two jobs where some families hold none. Against such a developing trend, the Christian child-free couple must be convinced that their vocation is, as the authors warn, "life-serving"—and not an exploitation of society.

We note in several places in *Human Sexuality* that both the young married and the growing number of voluntary singles are worried about the population problem. Latest projections are not as horrendous as they once were, but the population of the world will nonetheless probably double by the year 2000. That is certainly cause for worry, but it is not a good rationale for the educated Christian who wants the ideals of Jesus to have a place in this burgeoning world. A teeming planet will create vast new problems, and some of the decisions to be made will be crucial moral choices. We no longer need to compete for Mother of the Year with sixteen or eighteen children, but neither is it time to abandon the procreative role of sex altogether. The next generation, too, will need its thoughtful Christians, and the problems may even be bigger than sex. For our part, we have two children so far. We intend that they will not be our last.

## NOTES

1. Eugene C. Kennedy, *The New Sexuality: Myths, Fables and Hang-Ups* (Garden City, N.Y.: Doubleday, 1972), p. 11.
2. Ibid., p. 37.

3. Juan Luis Segundo, Vol. 5: *Evolution and Guilt* (New York: Orbis Books, 1974), pp. 91–93.
4. Pp. 159, 252; for another view of Davis, see Chapter Six above, nn. 17, 26.
5. Robert A. Heinlein and D. F. Vassalo (illus.), *The Notebooks of Lazarus Long* (New York: G. P. Putnam's Sons, 1978), unpaginated.
6. Ibid.

*Chapter Eight*

※

# DIALOGUE WITH
# AN ARCHBISHOP

An Interview with
JOSEPH L. BERNARDIN, D.D.

When he graciously accepted the invitation to participate in
this project, Archbishop Bernardin chose the option of having
questions sent to him in preference to an oral interview. Accordingly, I thought it advisable to concentrate on topics with lead-
in observations followed by a series of questions pertinent to
each topic. I suggested to His Excellency that he should feel
free to answer the questions in summary form, or even selec-
tively, since they are intended to help him focus and precise his
remarks on each topic. Hence, the present format. The questions which follow include my own in addition to those submit-
ted by some of the other contributors to this volume and are
meant to reflect the honest concerns of many theologians and
members of the People of God at large. These are some of the
concerns which, as noted in the Introduction above, ordinarily
pass without comment in most theoretical treatises. I know
from phone conversations that Archbishop Bernardin would
have preferred, understandably enough, to contribute an essay,
positive in tone, on human sexuality instead of being "locked
into this framework" (Reply to Question 10) of direct questions some of which accentuate positive concerns only indi-

rectly. To my reading, his straightforward replies, which are unedited, make concrete his deep pastoral concern to "take advantage of opportunities to present the Church's teaching in a credible way" (from correspondence, noted in Question 9) —*Editor.*

## 1. *Episcopal Reaction to the CTSA Report*

The American bishops were quick to react to the CTSA Report on human sexuality (some even in advance of its publication). On balance, how would you assess that reaction, including your own? By way of comparison, if it had been a Report urging absolute pacifism, do you think the hierarchy would have responded as quickly and as forcefully? Or is sexual morality in a category all by itself?

REPLY: It is true that many American bishops were quick to react to the publication of *Human Sexuality.* In my view, they offered their reactions out of a sense of pastoral responsibility—it was not their intention to enter into a theological dialogue with the authors of the CTSA Report, but rather to point out to the faithful that the concerns of the book did not reflect the teaching position of the Church but constituted a whole new approach to that teaching. Such a reaction by the bishops was particularly urgent in view of the fact that the CTSA Report offered itself not just as an exercise in speculative moral theology but as a concrete set of guidelines for immediate pastoral practice. A more technical and theologically sophisticated critique of the Report was forthcoming later in the fall of 1977 from the Bishops' Committee on Doctrine.

Another component governing the quick response of many bishops was the fact that the Report had received a great deal of publicity even before its publication. Indeed, it was the subject of a high-powered marketing campaign, including news conferences and media interviews by the authors. In such a situation, it would have been irresponsible, in my view, for bishops to have sat back and said nothing.

If the Report had dealt with an issue like pacifism, it would have deserved careful and studied response, just as this Report does. Admittedly, it would not have received the same kind of

quick and forceful response from the bishops. Neither would it
have received the same kind of sales campaign and the same
amount of media attention. There is no way to compare issues
like sexual morality and pacifism and rate them on a scale of absolute priority and importance. But everyone knows that questions
pertaining to sexual morality have as a matter of fact been particularly urgent and sensitive in Catholic circles for the last fifteen
years. Hence the nature of the promotional effort on behalf of the
CTSA Report and of the kind of attention it received from the
media. Hence also the nature of the bishops' response.

## 2. Prior Consultation with Bishops

The chapter on pastoral guidelines understandably occasioned
the most criticism because of the practical ramifications of the
theory which the authors articulated. Some bishops have objected
that there should have been prior consultation with members of
the hierarchy. Would you care to speculate on how such consultation—or "collaboration," as one archbishop has referred to it—
might have changed things for the better? Would that chapter, in
order to meet with episcopal approval, have had to favor only the
teachings that are approved?

REPLY: There are at least two different ways of thinking of consultation or "collaboration" in a matter such as this. They are not
mutually exclusive, but they do deal with different questions and
have different ends in view.

The first kind of consultation takes place at a very early stage—
before people have made up their minds, reached conclusions, decided on the answers to questions, perhaps even on the questions
themselves. The assumption is that all parties have something to
learn. This is not a negotiating process; it is a process of mutual
exchange and learning.

Nothing of the sort took place here as far as dialogue with
bishops is concerned. It did not take place because the people involved in the CTSA project did not choose for it to take place.
This is not said in criticism; it is simply a fact. Whether things
would have been changed for the better had such consultation
taken place, I do not know. It would at least have been worth exploring the question—a very valid one, to my way of thinking—of

whether "pastoral guidelines" have any place in a speculative theological enterprise which departs so much from what the Church
teaches.

The second kind of consultation takes place after one or both
parties to the consultative process have reached their conclusions,
made up their minds about what it is they propose to say or do.
The question at this point is procedural: *how* what has already
been decided is going to be done. In the case of the CTSA study,
for example, there might have been consultation about whether it
was a good idea—from the point of view of theology and scholarship, from the point of view of pastoral consequences, and from
the point of view of dialogue between bishops and theologians—
for a document like this to be published to the accompaniment of
a rather intensive media campaign or, for that matter, to be published at all. But consultation of this kind did not take place—
again, it seems, by the decision or oversight of those responsible for
preparing and issuing the report. That was unfortunate.

## 3. *Scripture in Church Pronouncements*

The conciliar *Constitution on Divine Revelation* (Art. 24)
reminds us that Scripture "is, as it were, the soul of sacred theology." According to the *Decree on Priestly Formation* (Art. 16)
the "scientific exposition [of moral theology] should be more thoroughly nourished by scriptural teaching." The Scriptures present
God's revelation not so much as a timeless statement but as the
result of a profound interaction among social conditions, past traditions, new questions, and supernatural hopes. Can these factors
be identified in the Church's teaching on sexual morality? According to many, *Humanae Vitae*, considered a key document in
Catholic sexual ethics, evidences very little reliance on Sacred
Scripture. If you agree with this claim by exegetes, do you find
such a lacuna explainable or perhaps regrettable?

REPLY: The statement "the Scriptures present God's revelation
not so much as a timeless statement but as the result of a profound interaction among social conditions, past traditions, new
questions, and supernatural hopes" is somewhat obscure. The four
"factors" noted hardly make up an exhaustive list, though they

have all played a role in the development of moral doctrine. They leave out what seems to be the most basic factor, human nature itself, with its sinful proclivities along with its "supernatural hopes." Later, in replying to Question 6, I shall discuss development of doctrine more specifically.

Probably most Scripture scholars would have preferred a more pervasive use of Scripture in *Humanae Vitae*. However, Father Eugene Maly, a Scripture scholar with whom I have discussed the encyclical, assures me that the texts which are used are not taken out of context and that most would have to be part of a more thoroughly scriptural treatment.

More to the point is the issue of "reliance on Sacred Scripture." Even if we grant that Scripture does not explicitly teach the immorality of contraception, does the encyclical manifest a reliance on Scripture? Three aspects of the encyclical seem to have particular relevance: the concern for human life, the close relationship between marriage and procreation, and the compassionate attitude toward those who fail to meet this standard. These are general principles (or Kingdom "ideals" as some have called them), which must be translated into particular situations. It is up to the Church, in the various periods of its history, to make the particular application of the biblical principles.

## 4. Empirical Sciences

According to Article 62 of the *Pastoral Constitution on the Church in the Modern World*, "appropriate use must be made not only of theological principles, but also of the findings of the secular sciences, especially of psychology and sociology." With this in mind, what is the magisterial understanding of the role of empirical findings, admittedly inexact, in scientific theology and in pastoral guidance? Does the conciliar passage mean that the findings of these sciences are not valid unless they corroborate official Catholic teaching—in context, in the area of human sexuality?

REPLY: In speaking of "appropriate use" of the secular sciences of psychology and sociology, Vatican II surely did *not* mean that corroboration of Catholic teaching is the norm by which the validity of their findings is to be tested. Otherwise, these behavioral sciences would lose their autonomy as empirical sciences.

Nor did the Vatican statement mean the reverse—namely, that the findings of these sciences are the test of the validity of Catholic doctrine. Yet this is the impression that some people derive from *Human Sexuality*.

The empirical findings of psychology and sociology are as valid as their methods. But bear in mind that we are speaking here about empirical findings—discoveries of patterns and connections in human behavior. They tell what is happening, not whether it is right or wrong, virtuous or sinful.

The Bishops' Committee on Doctrine referred to empirical studies in its statement on *Human Sexuality*:

> The Committee recognizes the importance and value of empirical studies (cf. Chapter 3), but it is also aware of the inadequacy of such studies by themselves to establish moral norms or alter them. Social scientific research has an important role to play in providing the raw material for theological reflection. It is one way of "consulting the faithful" about their problems and insights. However, no responsible social scientist claims that his efforts describe behavior as it in fact is. Moral values are not produced by social research and social research makes no claim that its findings are normative.

With regard to empirical studies, we can discuss more in detail their use both by scientific moral theology and in pastoral guidance.

1. Scientific moral theology can use empirical studies to understand better the real elements of human actions, their short- and long-range effects, the roles of conscience and moral education in modifying behavior, the interplay of emotions, passions, and social conditioning.

But the statistical incidence of a particular form of behavior— whether masturbation on the one hand or racial prejudices on the other—can hardly provide scientific moral theology with norms for moral goodness.

The authors of *Human Sexuality* do *not* take such a naive position; with reference to human sexuality they write that "the pervasiveness of sin and the often blind urgency of erotic impulse prohibit the mere frequency of some sexual behavior from becoming an acceptable determinant of sexual ethics" (p. 55). What the authors of *Human Sexuality* do propose, however, is that scientific moral theology compromise its claim to teach universal negative prohibitions about certain sexual expressions unless empirical data indicate that such actions are always and everywhere detrimental to full development of the human personality. In other words, they suggest that moral theology cannot universalize about immoral behavior without universal empirical data to demonstrate the negative consequences of such behavior.

Scientific moral theology does expect immoral behavior to correlate in some general way with a generally imperfect development of the human personality. But it does not look to the empirical sciences for clear, universal, and unambiguous data of the negative effects of universally evil sexual expressions. To expect such data assumes the impossible: that the empirical sciences can alone adequately measure and delineate the *full* development of human personality and adequately incorporate in their measurements the various shades of authentic and inauthentic guilt which in subtle and unperceived ways modify the effects of human behavior. To hope for such data seems to presume that sin will always take an empirically verifiable toll on human happiness, so that virtue and vice will immediately produce their own rewards. This is contrary to our common experience and to the Christian vision of life as a pilgrim-journey.

2. Secondly, pastoral guidance too can benefit from data provided by empirical studies about human behavior. But its use of the data is directed by the normative principles of scientific moral theology.

For instance, data which suggest that premarital sexual activity has a bad effect on the marriages of those who felt guilty about it indicate the long-range effects of guilt and moral compromise. Such data do *not* suggest that those who have no guilt about premarital sex are thereby performing good actions.

In a sinful world, the teaching of moral norms through pastoral guidance may stir up authentic guilt, but that is no reason to abandon moral norms. Rather, it is reason to cultivate conversion and virtue and to overcome sin with the redeeming grace of Christ.

Empirical data can show the level of conscience formation and the kinds of moral awareness present in human actions. They can also help make possible an assessment of the social pressures and internal psychological tensions which diminish freedom and responsibility for actions.

The Vatican *Declaration on Sexual Ethics* summarized the role of psychology and sociology in pastoral guidance about masturbation in two paragraphs which well exemplify the present point:

> Sociological surveys are able to show the frequency of this disorder according to the places, populations, or circumstances studied. In this way facts are discovered, but facts do not constitute a criterion for judging the moral value of human acts. The frequency of the phenomenon in question is certainly to be linked with man's innate weakness following original sin; but it is also to be linked with the loss of a sense of God, with the corruption of morals engendered by the commercialization of vice, with the unrestrained licentiousness of so many public entertainments and publications, as well as with the neglect of modesty, which is the guardian of chastity.

> On the subject of masturbation modern psychology provides much valid and useful information for formulating a more equitable judgment on moral responsibility and for orienting pastoral action. Psychology helps one to see how the immaturity of adolescence (which can sometimes persist after that age), psychological imbalance or habit can influence behavior, diminishing the deliberate character of the act and bringing about a situation whereby subjectively there may not always be serious fault. But in general, the absence of serious responsibility must not be presumed; this would be to misunderstand people's moral capacity. (※9)

These reflections indicate the "appropriate use" of the empirical sciences to which the Second Vatican Council referred. In no case do the empirical studies compromise the normative role of scientific moral theology. Yet that seems to be what happened in *Human Sexuality*.

## 5. Mortal Sin

The authors of *Human Sexuality* have been severely criticized for having rejected traditional absolutes, for allowing virtually any form of sexual expression as long as it promotes "creative growth toward integration." The traditional teaching insists that some things are intrinsically evil, that there are objective norms of morality, and that these are self-evidently clear with regard to sexual conduct. Traditionally, *in re sexuali* what is objectively normative is the procreative-unitive nature of sexual intercourse.

The concept of serious sin, associated with objective evil, is frightening. To commit one with full knowledge and full consent is to merit eternal damnation, the frustration of a person's very existence, which is the total rupture of friendship with God as this is understood biblically. According to the *auctores probati*, the officially recognized manualists, there are some two hundred occasions to commit mortal sin just in the administration and reception of the sacraments alone. Add to this transgressions against the virtues, the precepts of the Decalogue, the precepts of the Church, and the duties of one's state in life—the usual format of the manuals—and it would seem either that Catholicism is an extremely dangerous way of life, a living occasion of sin, or, what is more likely, that something is wrong with the teaching on sin. In this mind-set the Sixth and Ninth Commandments and the virtue of chastity understandably occasion a multiplicity of *sub gravi* prohibitions. And yet, even the approved authors recall the "general rule that to condemn any action as gravely sinful its grave malice must be obvious" (Aertnys-Damen).

Hence, does it really make sense to hold that an individual act of masturbation is such an objectively and intrinsically evil disorder that one's salvation is thereby negated, objectively speaking (apart from the question of subjective imputability)? If so, how can this be made credible to the teenaged parishioner in the pew? More generally, since an act said to be intrinsically evil is such *ex natura sua*, can the teaching Church designate certain acts as seriously sinful, if only for a time? (Abstinence from meat on Friday no longer binds *sub gravi*. Theologically, did it ever—really?) Monsignor F. Lambruschini, a papal spokesman, observed that

*Humanae Vitae* was "not irreformable." If he is correct, how can we explain pastorally that something is gravely evil in itself, of its very nature, but perhaps only for a period of time? In a word, what is the magisterial understanding of grave sin and how does it apply to sexual conduct? Would it not be more appropriate to hold up ideals, as did the prophets of old, rather than to preach mortal sin whose biblical basis in this regard is questionable at best? Isn't our approach at present more pedagogical than theological?

REPLY: An adequate response to this probing series of questions would require a whole treatise in moral theology. Let me simply make six specific points.

1. Enumerating hundreds of possible occasions of committing mortal sin obviously cannot be the primary role of moral theology. Moral theology must first of all emphasize the call of Christ to live a new life of continual conversion and to practice love of God, of self, and of neighbor. But this *is* a serious call; spiritually it is a matter of life and death.

It is not that Catholicism is "an extremely dangerous way of life," but that it is a way of life so intimately bound up with love of God that it is possible to find innumerable ways of violating that love. Fortunately, the same gift of love which can be violated in so many ways also supports the loving Christian in the face of temptation.

2. The notion of grave matter flows readily from the supreme importance of eternal salvation and the fundamental option of freely choosing to love God or to reject Him. The Vatican *Declaration on Sexual Ethics* repeated common Church teaching that one can reject God by choosing seriously disordered acts:

> A person therefore sins mortally not only when his action comes from direct contempt for love of God and neighbor, but also when he consciously and freely, for whatever reason, chooses something which is seriously disordered. For in this choice, as has been said above, there is already included contempt for the divine commandment: the person turns himself away from God and loses charity. (※10)

Hence the theological concept of grave matter refers to those
actions which, if performed freely and knowingly, are capable of
rupturing one's relationship with God. In order to form truly
Christian consciences, moral educators must necessarily teach
what are grave matters in the light of Christian revelation and tradition. The *General Catechetical Directory*, published by the Sacred Congregation for the Clergy with the approval of Pope Paul
VI in 1971, referred to this role:

> Christian freedom still needs to be ruled and directed in the
> concrete circumstances of human life. Accordingly, the con-
> science of the faithful, even when informed by the virtue of
> prudence, must be subject to the Magisterium of the Church,
> whose duty it is to explain the whole moral law authoritatively,
> in order that it may rightly and correctly express the objective
> moral order. (※63)

This is the sense in which the Church seeks to teach what is
the will of God in practical decisions of moral life, in obedience
to Jesus' words, "It is not those who say to me, 'Lord, Lord,' who
will enter the kingdom of heaven, but the person who does the
will of my Father in heaven" (Mt. 7:21).

3. The moral teaching of the Church has strenuously defended
the sacredness of human life and the human power of procreating
life. That is the context in which even a single act of masturbation constitutes grave matter. The Vatican *Declaration on Sexual Ethics* repeated this in 1975: "In fact both the Magisterium
of the Church—in the course of a constant tradition—and the
moral sense of the faithful have declared without hesitation that
masturbation is an intrinsically and seriously disordered act"
(※9).

In responding to the previous question on empirical sciences, I
quoted at length the discussion in that same Vatican document of
what sociology and psychology teach about masturbation. This
discussion was filled with indications of how full subjective responsibility for this act may be diminished. But the Church still
upholds the sacredness of the human power of procreative sexuality and teaches with the Second Vatican Council that its only

morally acceptable expression is found in a relationship which re-
alizes the "total meaning of mutual self-giving and human procreation in the context of true love; all this is possible only if the
virtue of married chastity is seriously practiced" (*Church in the
Modern World*, Art. 51).*

With reference to conscience formation among teenagers on
this issue of masturbation, an analogy may help. We teach that it
is a serious matter to curse someone to hell. We cannot modify
this teaching in the face of casual attitudes toward such language,
nor can we approve of such language. Neither can we modify the
teaching on masturbation in the face of casual attitudes toward it,
nor can we approve of it. In the misuse of our life-power we find a
graver disorder than in the misuse of language.

4. The notion of grave matter cannot be restricted to actions intrinsically evil. An action of itself only slightly sinful or perhaps
not sinful at all can become grave matter if it causes grave scan-
dal.

When the Church teaches about grave obligations in matters
like the administration of the sacraments or the precepts of the
Church, our assurance of the gravity of the matter arises from the
Church's authority given her by Christ to bind and loose. The
Church can legitimately teach that a given matter is of such grave
importance that one's relationship to God can be broken in that
matter.

The Church must use this power in a truly responsible way.
The change in Church discipline about fast and abstinence *did*
disturb many Catholics. But it represented a change within the
competence of the Church and need not lead to a rejection of the
Church's power to specify grave matters.

5. It is not altogether clear what Monsignor Lambruschini
meant in saying that *Humanae Vitae* was "not irreformable."
Presumably he meant that Pope Paul VI's encyclical was not in
and of itself an infallible statement. But the degree to which a
"reform" of the encyclical could include a "reform" of the doc-

* All quotations from and references to Vatican II documents in the
*Replies* in this chapter are to *Vatican Council II: The Conciliar and Post
Conciliar Documents*, ed. Austin Flannery, O.P. (Northport, New York:
Costello Publishing Company, 1975).

trine about the grave evil of contraception is highly controversial. Those who assert that the universal prohibition of directly contraceptive acts can give way to justifiable exceptions in marriage would see such a "reform" of *Humanae Vitae* as possible. I doubt that Pope Paul VI himself saw this as possible.

6. In conclusion, it must be emphasized that the Church's moral teaching is both theological and pedagogical. In the best tradition of the biblical authors, the Church not only teaches general moral truths or Kingdom ideals but lists specific kinds of actions which are spiritually "deadly" or mortal. When the rich young man asked Jesus for the way to eternal life, He did not simply call for faith and conversion but replied with a form of the Decalogue (Mk. 10:17–19).

Surely St. Paul was not simply talking about ideals but specific moral conduct which must be avoided when he wrote: "You know perfectly well that people who do wrong will not inherit the kingdom of God: people of immoral lives, idolaters, adulterers, catamites, sodomites, thieves, usurers, drunkards, slanderers and swindlers will never inherit the kingdom of God" (1 Cor. 6:9–10).

The important biblical teaching about sin, however, is the antithesis of sin and love. Ultimately, wherever sin occurs there is found a violation of authentic love for God, for self, or for neighbor. Just as surely as sin violates authentic love, so love drives out sin.

## 6. Doctrinal Development

When you spoke at the fourth annual Archdiocesan Parish Councils Congress at DeSales Preparatory Seminary in Milwaukee on October 25, 1975, you discussed the issue of women priests. The Milwaukee *Journal* the next day quoted you as saying that the official position on women priests could be changed only by a "contrary theological development." With reference now to the official teaching on sexual ethics, what would constitute a "contrary theological development"? Or, from a magisterial standpoint, when is such a development arrived at? Do you see *Human Sexuality* as a contribution to such a development? More pointedly, perhaps, is such a development possible? Is this what Monsignor Lambruschini (referred to in the preceding question) meant when he observed that *Humanae Vitae* was "not irreformable," at least with regard to contraception? And, from the standpoint of the sociology of knowledge, what can we say to those who charge that the Church's teaching on sexuality is exclusively determined by unmarried males, a teaching therefore that reflects the interests of a particular group, and hence that the inclusion of women in the work of theology necessarily means that our teaching on sexual morality (among other areas) is theologically reformable? Or, what is the role of dissent in the evolution of the Church's moral teaching, in establishing a contrary theological development? In context, sexual norms have not been directly revealed by God; in Scripture God enabled the people Israel through religious leaders to discern what was acceptable or non-acceptable in their contemporary age. Do you see Church leaders interacting in such a way today?

REPLY: Quite a difference exists between development in sexual ethics and development on the issue of women's ordination. The Church's practice of ordaining only men cannot be rooted in the natural moral law in the way its teaching on sexual morality is. In fact, the Sacrament of Orders totally transcends the order of nature, since it is a gift and a grace made possible by the redemption of Christ.

The fact that the Church's teaching on sexual ethics is rooted in the natural moral law does not prevent authentic development of that teaching. The early Church developed specific moral doctrines on issues like contraception and abortion which it faced in the pagan world and which are not treated specifically in the Bible. Since developing those doctrines it has held them with remarkable clarity and continuity throughout twenty centuries. The application of those teachings to contemporary forms of contraception and abortion and to the contemporary cultural justification of those practices has added to this authentic development.

The Church has developed its doctrine of sexual morality throughout its history in the face of challenges from both rigorists who condemned marriage itself and laxists who permitted divorce and remarriage.

In the last hundred years there has developed within the

Church a new appreciation of the mutual rights of spouses in marriage and a rejection of the chauvinist view that husbands are justified in treating their wives more like property than as partners. Thus we have developed a more profound appreciation of the interpersonal relationship which spouses must be able to establish and must intend in order to enter a valid marriage. The Second Vatican Council authentically accepted this development when it said:

> But marriage is not merely for the procreation of children: its nature as an indissoluble compact between two people and the good of the children demand that the mutual love of the partners be properly shown, that it should grow and mature. (*Church in the Modern World*, Art. 50)

All this development has taken place within a framework of sexual ethics built on the divinely designed finality of human sexual powers. However, the moral methodology employed in *Human Sexuality* would modify this framework in a substantial way. It would suggest that in given circumstances genital activity may be morally good even though it involves homosexual activity or masturbation, for example.

Such a modification is proposed as an authentic development by some theologians today. Others find this to be a deviation from the moral teaching of the past and hence inauthentic. The critical issue facing the Church today, therefore, is not the question of development or non-development, but rather of authentic or inauthentic development.

The kind of moral methodology used in *Human Sexuality* and the conclusions which it reaches were already being proposed when the *Declaration on Sexual Ethics* was published on December 29, 1975, by the Sacred Congregation for the Doctrine of the Faith with the approval of Pope Paul VI. That *Declaration* firmly rejects the positions on premarital intercourse, masturbation, and homosexuality which were subsequently proposed in *Human Sexuality*. Hence the authentic magisterium of the Church has judged this kind of development inauthentic.

Could publications such as the 1977 study, which dissent from a recent and firm teaching of the magisterium, stimulate fresh analyses and at least some modification of the traditional teaching? Certainly this *could* happen. But this is not to approve either the manner in which this book was published or its attempt to formulate pastoral guidelines contrary to Church teaching.

Could the views expressed in *Human Sexuality* even contribute to an eventual situation where the magisterium came to regard those views as authentic? While those who published those views presumably think so, I find it virtually impossible to situate such views in an authentic process of development.

Responsible and prudent dissent may be useful in the authentic development of moral doctrine. In past generations, however, such dissent was rare. Now, by contrast, it has reached significant proportions and created profound doubts and confusion.

The suggestion is made in the question that "the inclusion of women in the work of theology necessarily means that our teaching on sexual morality . . . is theologically reformable." Two suppositions underlying this are that 1) unmarried males have exclusively formulated the Church's teaching, with no significant appreciation of the insights women have on human sexuality, and 2) a feminine approach to human sexuality would significantly "reform" our sexual ethics. I strongly question both these suppositions, while I welcome the increased involvement of lay theologians, both men and women, and of women religious in the theological reflections of the Church. Their efforts will enrich the theological climate in which the official and authentic magisterium must discern authentic development in the Church's moral doctrine.

In conclusion, the statement that "In Scripture God enabled the people Israel through religious leaders to discern what was acceptable or non-acceptable in their contemporary age" seems to me an incorrect description of what really happened. I would prefer to say that religious leaders, ranging from Isaiah and Jeremiah through the New Testament authors, taught moral truths to the people under divine inspiration. It is true, of course, that the people had to discern the application of these truths to their own situations.

The magisterium functions today in continuity with these biblical teachers. It still teaches moral truths. Through human experience and theological reflection under the guidance of the Holy

Spirit development has occurred in the understanding of those moral truths. The magisterium does not teach in a timeless vacuum from the lofty heights of Mount Sinai, but neither is it a mere instrument of communal discernment nor the expression of a collective consensus.

## 7. Divorce and Remarriage: Adultery

On the same occasion referred to above you are reported as saying that you foresee no change in the Church's doctrine on divorce, and quoted as saying "there has been and there can be more development in determining when a marriage is actually valid." To many Catholics and others this annulment route, humane as it is, is a back-door approach to divorce. But more to the point, terms have to be defined carefully. According to Roman Catholic teaching, persons divorced and remarried and now living conjugally are said to be living in adultery and hence are denied participation in the Eucharist. At the same time, Vatican II's *Decree on Ecumenism* emphasizes (Art. 15) that we should all "venerate, preserve, and foster the exceedingly rich liturgical and spiritual heritage of the Eastern Churches." That heritage tolerates divorce and remarriage. Accordingly, what can a pastoral counselor say to those who accuse us of a double standard in our teaching? That is, can divorced and remarried Roman Catholics truly (objectively) be said to be living in adultery while our Eastern Orthodox brethren are not?

REPLY: The reference to annulment proceedings as a "back-door approach to divorce" seems to suggest that these proceedings imply an unacknowledged acceptance of divorce and remarriage. However, the enlarging of grounds for annulment because of the doctrinal development on marriage which I noted in replying to the previous question is just the opposite of an acceptance of divorce. Instead of trying to dissolve sacramental marriages, this marriage tribunal procedure insists so strongly on the sacredness of marriage that it declares null and void those which lack adequate consent and dispositions.

In fact, the very reason the Church cannot accept the dissolubility of consummated sacramental marriages—namely, the reality of the marriage relationship despite obstacles to common life—

stands at the heart of annulment proceedings. Every formal case tried by a marriage tribunal uses the best human wisdom and prudential judgment available to test whether such a sacramental reality actually exists between a married couple.

My comments on ecumenism in replying to the next question also apply to the problem posed here about Roman Catholic attitudes toward Eastern Churches which tolerate divorce and remarriage. However, it should be pointed out that there is a particular gratuitous assumption here: namely, that the statement of the Second Vatican Council urging veneration and fostering of the *liturgical* and *spiritual* heritage of the Eastern Churches includes approval of their toleration of divorce and remarriage. There is no reason to speak of a double standard, as if the Roman Catholic Church approved of divorce and remarriage for others but not for Catholics.

It is not my task to justify or even articulate the position of other churches regarding divorce and remarriage. All I can do is explain our position. The Catholic Church has consistently maintained its belief in the objective validity of sacramental marriages even after couples have divorced and taken other partners. On these objective grounds, such persons are living in adultery. However, two very important comments must be added.

1. In the teaching of the Church, objective adultery is a grave matter but not automatically formal sin. The sin of adultery involves a person's knowledge of and consent to objective evil. Some divorced and remarried persons may well be acting in a form of "good faith" before God and hence may not be subjectively guilty of sin. It is not difficult, for example, to believe this of Christians whose churches tolerate divorce and remarriage.

2. If a supposedly sacramental marriage were null and void from the beginning, the person who divorced and remarried could not be guilty of objective adultery, even though a marriage tribunal had not declared the first marriage null and void.

So far, I have tried to set forth the Church's teaching on marriage as I understand it. I hasten to add, however, that the pastoral concern of the Church must be extended to everyone, regardless of marital status. Certainly we should be sensitive to the deep suffering and sense of alienation frequently experienced by those who are separated, divorced, or divorced and remarried.

In many instances, our marriage tribunals can be of assistance to those whose marriages are irreparably broken. But even in cases where the marital status cannot be rectified, we must reach out to the persons involved with Christ's love and mercy, striving to lead them to deeper faith, to genuine hope, and a realization of God's continuing love for them. They should be encouraged to pray and made to feel welcome in the community of the Church. At the same time, they should be helped to a fuller understanding of the doctrine of Christian marriage and of any necessary limitations on their participation in the sacramental life of the Church.

The ministry to the separated, the divorced, and the divorced and remarried requires of the Church's ministers a high degree of personal maturity, spiritual sensitivity, and loyal obedience to the authority of the Church. We must avoid the extreme of keeping them at arm's length as pariahs; but also we must avoid the essentially non-pastoral approach of appearing to reconcile all such persons with the Church, regardless of the objective realities of their case. Moreover, we need to instruct our people not to sit in judgment, but to help the divorced and the divorced and remarried by their prayers and compassionate understanding. "You should carry each other's troubles and fulfill the law of Christ" (Gal. 6:2).

## 8. Ecumenical Dialogue

That same *Decree on Ecumenism* states (Art. 23) that "the ecumenical dialogue could start with discussions concerning the application of the gospel to moral questions." What is your understanding of the value of insights by other Christians? Are these values authentically Christian even though others "do not always understand the gospel in the same way as Catholics, and do not admit the same solutions for the more difficult problems of modern society" (ibid.)? As you know, contraception and premarital sex between engaged persons, for example, are not regarded as sinful by most other Christians. Must they accept our official view in these regards if reunion is ever to be achieved? Or, in a way parallel to the divorce-remarriage issue in the last topic, is our teaching in these regards a matter of Church discipline rather than revealed doctrine? In the Vatican *Declaration on Sexual Ethics,* in the contexts of value-judging and rejecting homosexual relations and masturbation, an appeal is made to "the moral sense of the Christian people" and "the moral sense of the faithful" (nn. 8, 9). Since contraceptive birth control is not offensive to the "moral sense" of the Christian community, can you recognize a legitimate appeal to this to justify contraception for Roman Catholics?

REPLY: Ecumenism does not mean abandoning one's own beliefs for the sake of reunion, nor does it mean taking the position that it makes no difference which interpretation one makes of the moral teaching of the Gospels and the Church.

First, in reference to your specific questions, I do not feel comfortable with generalizations about what "other Christians" do and don't believe. On many matters, the official positions of other churches vary a great deal from one another, and the actual beliefs and attitudes of individual members of those churches no doubt reflect even greater variations. Some non-Catholic Christians are quite traditional on matters of sexual morality; others are not. So there is not much to be gained by starting with the proposition that the Catholic Church holds one position and all other Christian churches hold another. It just isn't so.

On the specific issues mentioned—contraception and premarital sex—one also has to bear in mind that most other Christians as a matter of fact did hold very much the same position as the Catholic Church until quite recently; this was the "moral sense" of the Christian community.

Now, to the extent that other Christian churches have changed their positions, I suppose one could argue that the Catholic Church should learn from them and do likewise. But there is nothing in logic to compel one to this conclusion. Simply within the framework of this discussion, going no further at all, one can just as well argue that in these matters the Catholic Church has remained true to the Christian tradition, and the other churches should learn from it. In short, the discussion strikes me as a dead-end street.

I hasten to add, however, that I do not consider discussion of moral questions, including sexual ethics, with other Christians to be fruitless. Such discussion plays a role in the authentic development of moral doctrine. But arguments based simply on the fact that some churches have changed their moral teachings are not conclusive.

As far as Christian unity is concerned, it is one thing to recognize the authentic faith in Christ and baptism of separated Christians and another to assume that the different moral teachings which various groups profess are equally as authentic as the moral teaching of the Catholic Church. Reunion can, hypothetically, come about in various ways, and I would not anticipate the unifying work of the Spirit. But I disagree that the moral teaching of the Catholic Church is a mere disciplinary matter, since it is rooted in the Church's understanding of the gospel and gospel values. Hence, in general terms, I cannot envisage full ecclesial unity between the Catholic Church and another communion whose official position included positive approval, at least in some circumstances, of such things as sexual intercourse outside marriage, abortion, contraception, and other acts concerning which the authentic teaching of the Church is so clear. Are there legitimate, intermediate forms of unity short of full ecclesial union? Will continued dialogue show us a way out of what now appears to be an impasse? On matters like this I cannot play the prophet.

## 9. Casuistry and Counseling

Since casuistry is part of our tradition in moral teaching, and indeed our immediate heritage as you will recall from your own seminary days, perhaps we can become casuistic for a moment. In that tradition, with St. Thomas Aquinas, unnatural sins (e.g., masturbation) are said to be more gravely evil than natural ones (e.g., fornication or adultery). You say in your letter to me that you wish "to present the Church's teaching in a credible way"—as you have been endeavoring to do in your responses so far. Now, although evil is never to be condoned, it seems only logical to favor the lesser of two evils in a conflict situation. Is it credible, therefore, to argue that, granted the evil of both natural and unnatural sins, fornication is preferable to masturbation and, more casuistically yet, that adultery open to the transmission of life is preferable to contraceptive fornication? Must a pastoral counselor, if asked, endorse this reasoning? Or, is the traditional distinction between natural and unnatural sex acts (based on the procreative orientation as intended by nature) and their moral gravity no longer intelligible (if it ever was)?

REPLY: While no counselor could honestly endorse anyone's choice of a moral sin, it is not idle speculation to discuss the comparative gravity of mortal sins. Furthermore, it seems to me that, if St. Thomas were writing today, he might well revise his rankings. For instance, he might consider fornication as grave as masturbation because it misuses sexual intercourse (using a natural sign of total self-giving where no such commitment is present) even though it does not violate physical nature. And he might consider adultery open to the transmission of life as grave as contraceptive fornication because it violates the proper use of the sign of total self-giving and the rights of at least one other party, even though it does not violate physical nature as contraceptive fornication does.

The important point for our discussion is that because of developments in moral theology in the last fifty years the Church does recognize, as I mentioned in replying to Question 6, the significance of mutual love as part of human genital activity.

This is not to say that such development necessarily entails the legitimization of contraception and sterilization for reasons of love. Taking that step might well allow love to replace procreation as *the* primary end of marriage. This was not the teaching of the Second Vatican Council.

In conclusion, the most significant point of this discussion may be one made originally by St. Augustine and quoted by St. Thomas Aquinas in the *Summa*: "Every sin, insofar as it is a sin, is against nature" (I–II, q. 71, a. 2, sed c.).

## 10. *Homosexuality*

Since homosexuality is such an explosive issue these days, from a theological standpoint how can we convincingly preach that those who are homosexually oriented must, in order to practice virtue and avoid sin, embrace the charism of celibacy? A heterosexual who desires to be sexually active at least has the option of marriage. Since this is "unnatural" to a homosexual, how do we know that his salvation must be worked out by a life of complete sexual abstinence?

REPLY: As a practical matter, I doubt whether it is possible to preach celibacy convincingly to anyone, whether heterosexual or homosexual, for whom not only sexual abstinence but chastity itself is a virtually meaningless notion, or who considers it axiomatic that to be sexually active is essential to self-fulfillment. Of course, there are many people to whom, in a sense, it is not necessary to "preach" chastity and celibacy because they already perceive important values in them. But there are many others who are totally persuaded by the contemporary view that fulfillment is not possible in the absence of sexual activity. This is, to say the least, a problem.

It is, for example, a very real problem even in the context of marriage. Not a few heterosexual persons suffer greatly because they have not found an altogether suitable sexual partner in marriage. Does this make their marriages an "unnatural" way of life for them, so that they should attempt to dissolve their marriages and find a more suitable or congenial sexual partner? I think not.

Many heterosexual persons are simply not psychologically capable of profound intimacy and interpersonal relationships in marriage. Others do not find a suitable partner for marriage. Others lose their spouse through death or divorce. But rather than offer these persons a kind of pseudo-fulfillment by genital activity without benefit of true marital love and the marital relationship, we must help them with the practice of chastity. The virtue of chastity can be strengthened, like any virtue, through the interior life of prayer and growth in the divine gift of charity.

What I have said about such heterosexual persons applies also to homosexual persons. It seems to me that, for all alike, we must call attention to the Paschal mystery as central to Christianity. I mean dying to self in order to rise with Christ. This is a hard saying at a time when the gospel of self-fulfillment predominates; but it is also a necessary saying.

Without claiming to know much in a clinical way about homosexuality, I must say that I feel uncomfortable with easy generalizations: "*all* homosexuals react in this way," "*no* homosexual is capable of that." To put it in layman's language, it appears that there are different degrees of homosexual orientation and different ways in which people with such an orientation deal with it. At the very least, pastoral counseling, as well as theology, ought to be aware of the complexities of real-life situations. Why tell a homosexual who is quite capable of living a celibate life that he isn't? Even in human terms, is it a kindness to put psychological pressure on such a person to be sexually active? I doubt it.

I don't think anyone has ever said that salvation depends on *accomplishing* certain things; rather, it is *trying* to do God's will—sincerely, persistently, perhaps in the face of many difficulties and failures—that counts. To put it another way, one works out one's salvation by doing the best one can in one's circumstances—celibate or married, homosexual or heterosexual. If one falls, God's forgiveness and mercy are infinite and readily accessible to those who are willing to seek them out and continue trying to meet the seemingly "impossible" demands of Christian morality —demands which by worldly standards *are* "impossible," not just in regard to sexual morality but in regard to much else.

Of course, none of this makes sense if one accepts the idea that homosexual activity is simply one more acceptable form of sexual self-expression (provided, I suppose, that it is loving, enriching, growth-producing, etc.). But there are profound reasons to support the Church's teaching that homosexual actions "are acts which lack an essential and indispensable finality" (*Declaration on Sexual Ethics*, ✕8). No amount of love and tenderness can make up for that deficiency. I am certain Christ does not want us to ridicule or ostracize homosexual persons because they suffer a genuine form of privation as real as blindness or lameness. But neither can I find any indication that Christ wants us to preach to these persons a modern-day gospel of compromise, offering them a morality of their own.

With regard to what is at issue here, we need to get back to basics. In this at least I agree with the authors of the CTSA Report: the Church and the churches have not done a distinguished job lately of explaining and proclaiming Christian sexual morality. The emphasis is so often on the negative—on what one *can't* do. Even in this discussion I have found myself locked into this framework by the nature of the questions—very pertinent and valid ones, to be sure—put to me.

In discussing sexual morality, like other areas of morality, it is, of course, essential to be clear about what constitutes immoral behavior, but it is also essential to identify positive values which underlie negative prohibitions. If celibacy, for example, simply means doing without sexual activity, there is little reason to propose it to anyone—priest or lay person, homosexual or heterosexual—as a way of life. If, on the contrary, celibacy is understood as an eschatological sign and a privileged way of following Christ, it takes on meaning and value. But I would not pretend that this is easily explained or that it has been explained with outstanding success in the recent past.

## 11. *Authority*

Perhaps the magisterial approach can be brought into clearer focus with a few questions relating to the topic of authority. Mention is always made by bishops and others of that "special assistance of the Holy Spirit" which members of the hierarchy are said to be promised in arriving at truth. Exactly how does it work? Does anyone really understand it? Theologians, who seem to lack that assistance, must be content with the force of probable opinions, according to the individual's own lights. The CTSA Report has reintroduced probabilism into the area of sexual ethics. As an Ordinary, how do you advise confessors regarding the use of probabilism on issues such as contraception? If I may phrase this next question rather indelicately, is it accurate to assert that the bottom line of the magisterial approach is: "Obey. These prohibitions and moral imperatives are the will of God—at least for the time being"? (The earlier teachings on usury and religious liberty come to mind right away.) More generally, as the "authentic teacher" of your diocese (*The Church*, Art. 25) do you uphold official teachings because you are intellectually convinced of their intrinsic worth (e.g., that the rhythm method of birth control is open to the transmission of life), or do you do so because it would be pastorally imprudent (and perhaps politically unwise) to disagree openly? Finally, is it possible for anyone to be an authentic teacher in any regard who is content to pass on unquestioningly past doctrines—or must he or she, rather, be in active dialogue with the issues of the times (as referred to in Question 6)?

REPLY: This series of questions reflects a view of the magisterium and of probabilism which I find somewhat confusing and unsatisfactory. Historically, probabilism meant the system of finding working principles in areas not explicitly covered by Church teaching. But when theologians and others disagree with an actual Church teaching, the proper word for their position is "dissent"— which was discussed briefly in my response to Question 6. Dissent may then be evaluated in terms of its intellectual cogency and the validity of its claim to represent an authentic development of Church doctrine.

Thus it is more accurate to say that *Human Sexuality* introduced a rather significant and systematic form of dissent, not probabilism, into the arena of Church teaching on human sexuality. And granted that dissent may have a healthy influence on the teaching magisterium, this could be accomplished without the massive confusion introduced among unsophisticated people by the practice of "press conference theology."

In the same way, the problem confessors face regarding contraception is better described as dissent than probabilism. Confessors can hardly give people permission to dissent. Instead they must help penitents recognize the implications of dissent and remind them that God judges them on the basis of their own integrity and willingness to respond to the Church and its teaching.

This series of questions also contains familiar references to usury and religious liberty as examples of developing moral teaching. Some theologians have been suggesting for a number of years that comparable development will legitimize contraception. But the Church has not adopted their view. And that is why their opinion remains in the category of dissent. Responsibility for distinguishing authentic from inauthentic development of moral doctrine rests with the magisterium.

How does the magisterium accomplish this? It does not work either in a timeless vacuum or as a mere instrument of communal discernment. Rather, the Church authentically teaches the doctrine of Christ as applicable to present-day life and problems. The Church does not receive new revelations. It must consult the real

experience of the faithful, the scholarly and reflective studies of
theologians, the doctrinal formulations of the past, and the original teaching of Scripture and tradition in order to discern authentic development of doctrine. Thus, even when a teaching is not
proposed as infallible or *ex cathedra*, it calls for a religious submission of will and of mind simply because the Church *is* Christ
teaching in the world today (cf. *The Church*, Art. 25).

It is highly desirable to uphold the Church's teaching because
of its intrinsic worth and attractiveness. But another—and complementary—reason why bishops and priests uphold magisterial
teaching is their perception that this is Christ's teaching and
their respect for the privilege of teaching and pastoring in His
name. In this sense, a bishop or pastor who rejected magisterial
teaching would not only act with pastoral imprudence but actually
undermine the work of Christ.

Obviously an authentic teacher does not "pass on unquestioningly past doctrines." That is why the magisterium must constantly search for authentic development or moral doctrine. But
individual bishops and pastors cannot set themselves up as individual judges of authentic or inauthentic development.

## 12. *Space-Age Catholicism*

The late Pope Paul VI will be remembered for many things. If
press reports are accurate, he counted among the highlights of his
papacy the encyclicals *Coelibatus Sacerdotalis* and *Humanae
Vitae*. Be that as it may, would it not be refreshing if we could
somehow shed the image of a Church overly concerned with sexual matters! Surely there are more issues that are more pressing
than warmed-over arguments on papal infallibility and sexual
morality. By way of a couple of direct questions, why can't the
teaching Church simply recognize the rightness of striving Christians in different societies to work out their own code of sexual
conduct "in the light of the gospel and of human experience"
(*Church in the Modern World*, Art. 46) without a "guilt trip
being laid on them," as the popular expression has it? Why can't
the Church be hailed for leadership in terms of inventiveness and
imagination and creativity and daring in helping to resolve issues
proper to an era on the verge of space colonization? The casuistry

of our sexual code is well known. Why can't we have a teaching on social justice that is at least as equally certain regarding objective norms and as notoriously casuistic regarding moral gravity in such issues as the distribution of wealth, the allocation of resources, the equal rights of men and women, the inhumanity of war, the violence of exploitation, etc.? As a by-product, wouldn't the Church's credibility then be restored?

REPLY: A lot of people share the sense of frustration which underlies this question, and I am one of them. But I don't think we should let the experience of frustration blind us to the causes of frustration.

Start with what's said about the Church's social doctrine. Although the evolution of this doctrine can be traced back to the Old Testament, its present elaboration has obviously been a relatively recent phenomenon. Why? Because social doctrine necessarily deals with highly contingent social, economic, and political realities. One could hardly expect Augustine to anticipate the conditions of the post-Industrial Revolution era which Leo XIII addressed in *Rerum Novarum* or Aquinas to foresee the circumstances of the post-colonial period which inspired Paul VI to write *Populorum Progressio*. The social doctrine of the Church has developed enormously in the past century or so. I expect this to continue. My principal regret is that more people are not familiar with this doctrine. If they were, they would find in it more inventiveness and creativity and boldness than they may suspect.

As for the Church's alleged preoccupation with sex, I have two observations to make. First, whatever one's view of sexual morality may be, it is impossible to ignore the fact that sexuality is a central element in human personality as well as interpersonal relations. We did not need Freud to tell us that, but he and his successors have underlined it and worked it out in far greater detail than ever before. Now if this is so—if sexuality is such a crucial element in human life—why shouldn't the Church be highly concerned with it? I see nothing unusual in the fact that the Church has a great deal to say about sexual morality; I would find it odd if it didn't.

Second, I wonder whether it is the Church which is excessively concerned with sex or whether it is the contemporary secular society. I won't indulge in rhetoric about a "sex-saturated society," but it does seem clear that Western society in our day is obsessed with the subject and entertains some very strange notions about it. That being so, I am not sure that this is precisely the time for the Church, which has a long tradition of teaching on sexual morality, to back away and leave the field to those whose views on sexuality, whatever else might be said of them, are certainly not shaped by Christian principles and values. As a matter of fact, I believe the opposite to be true. Now is the time for the Church to re-present its heritage on love and intimacy and to do so in a way which will capture the attention of our contemporary society. The real riches of our Catholic tradition in this crucial area of human concern have too long been hidden by the noisy confrontations of recent years. To bring those riches into focus, bishops must work with theologians and other scholars, and with married couples themselves whose insights are needed in a venture of this kind. In this connection, I commend the authors of the CTSA Report for at least trying to deal with the subject from a Christian point of view, even though the results leave a great deal to be desired.

## 13. Whatever . . .

Is there anything else you would care to comment on at this time?

REPLY: There are two general comments which I would like to make. First, in the previous question I was asked whether the Church was preoccupied with sex. I answered that the Church's interest in the subject is legitimate and necessary and suggested that perhaps our contemporary secular society is excessively concerned. I would like to go back to that question now and answer it from a different perspective: if the leadership of the Church has been too preoccupied with the moral dimensions of sex, cannot the same thing be said about the theologians who wrote *Human Sexuality*? Granted that moral theology is important and that there are many complex moral problems which impinge on human sexual behavior and which it is the province of moral theologians to study, I was nevertheless disappointed that the theologians did not also turn their attention to doctrinal and ascetical issues, which seem to me to be far more important. The doctrinal section of the volume is short and neither very insightful nor very original. There is nothing at all about what I would like to call the "spirituality of human sexuality," yet it seems to me that here is both an important challenge and the most important opportunity for the Catholic theological heritage.

Let me put the matter this way: suppose that the teaching authority were to agree completely with the moral positions taken in the book, would all problems of sexual relationships be solved for Catholics in the modern world? Indeed, would the sexual lives of most Catholics be changed or enhanced at all? Most sexual intimacy occurs between married heterosexuals who are permanently and faithfully committed to one another. What does the book provide for them?

It seems reasonably clear that the excessively flexible view of sexual morality as presented in *Human Sexuality* does not suffice to sustain the kind of courage, patience, sensitivity, and forgiveness that are necessary for a mature and developing sexual relationship. Studies of the life cycle problem, for example, point to painful ambiguities in sexual relationships at the various turning points in life. With the average marriage lasting four times longer than it did just a mere century ago, a capacity for forgiveness and reconciliation seems to be immensely important for any sustained pleasurable relationship between man and woman. There is no dearth of elaborately detailed "practical" material available in bookstores nor of competently staffed sex clinics. Still it is not obvious that people find any more fulfillment—or any fewer problems—in the area of sex now than they did in the past.

Without wishing to minimize the importance of either education or therapy, I would submit to theologians that, like all human behavior, sex is ambiguous. Unlike other animals, we humans must attach interpretations to our sexual activity and must seek from our interpretative systems the resources and motivations necessary to sustain us through the dilemmas and the ambiguities of this most poignant, most pleasurable, and most challenging of human intimacies. A sustained and developing sexual relationship requires extraordinary openness and vulnerability. Such orientations, as we all know, place great demands on our courage and our faith. If one permits oneself to be vulnerable to another human being, one runs the risk of getting badly hurt. More than that, if the relationship is both extremely intimate and of a long duration, it is certain that one will hurt and be hurt, will be called on to forgive and be forgiven, will find it necessary to reconcile and be reconciled. Death and rebirth, cross and resurrection, dying to the old self and being born again to the new self are essential paradigms for successful sexual intimacy.

If one is to commit oneself to such a relationship in which so much is chanced, one will almost certainly fall back at least implicitly on one's basic world view. Do we live in a cosmos in which it is safe to take such kinds of chances? Is the power or Power at work in the universe such that one can run the risk of trusting another to invade as much of one's life space as a sexual partner does? Do human relationships have any significance beyond the realm of the purely human?

These are religious questions par excellence. I do not understand why the scholars of the CTSA did not realize that these questions are of critical importance for the sexual lives of modern human beings, and that the Church has in its traditions an abundance of resources from which responses might be drawn.

I realize that bishops must address themselves to these opportunities, but in this matter as in so many others we need the help of professional scholars in theology and in the social sciences. I hope bishops will devote attention in the future to the question of the spirituality of human sexuality. I invite theologians to do the same.

My second general comment addresses itself to the institutional question. Most institutions in recent years have suffered from a credibility problem. People no longer accept at face value their pronouncements or the rationales which institutions give for their policy or programs. People have become much more independent in their thinking. They want to know all the reasons for adopting a certain position and they reserve the right to decide for themselves whether or not they will accept it.

As the foregoing dialogue clearly affirms, the Church today faces a similar situation in the area of doctrine. We believe that one of the Church's most important responsibilities is that of teaching. And we hold that the teaching authority of the Church, as exercised in an official way by the Holy Father and the bishops in union with him, receives special guidance from the Holy Spirit so that God's message will be understood correctly in every era. It is that teaching which forms the core of religious education's doctrinal content. Today, however, much of the Church's teaching is challenged and even contradicted. This is especially true in the area of morality. The Church's teaching concerning human sexuality, marriage, and social justice, for example, simply does not have the impact it should on many people.

I simply want to reflect for a moment on one aspect of this difficulty and then make a suggestion. I am convinced that too many people look on our moral teaching as a laundry list of do's and don'ts based more on some vague tradition or institutional concern than a gospel mandate. So they pick and choose what they want. I believe that in confronting this problem a greater evangelistic effort is needed on our part. While not minimizing the intellectual approach, that is, the necessity of developing well-reasoned arguments for our teaching, I believe that a prior step is needed. People must first come to know and love the Lord. They must experience Him in their lives; His love, mercy, understanding, and compassion must be a reality for them. Only then will they be willing to commit themselves to Him and accept the demands that He makes of all of us. Only then will they be ready to make that surrender which is expected of every Christian. When this happens, they will discover that His demands are much more radical than many of the do's and don'ts on our list of moral teachings. They will begin to understand that we are all called to a totally new way of life, one that runs counter to many of the values of our contemporary culture; they will also find that, humanly speaking, the gospel and its demands are impossible. Only God's grace and strength make them possible and indeed something that we can accept willingly and joyfully. Seen in the context of Christ and our living, personal relationship with Him, doctrine takes on a deeper, richer meaning. Indeed, learning more about His message can become a very exciting adventure because we then see more clearly that fidelity to Christ's teaching is an important measure of our personal fidelity to Him. Indeed, infidelity or indifference to what He teaches calls into question the authenticity of our commitment to Him.

*Chapter Nine*

# OF BEGINNINGS, NOT ENDS: A REJOINDER

ANTHONY R. KOSNIK

At the outset of this concluding chapter I should like to emphasize that the response herein reflects full collaboration with Fr. Ronald Modras and consultation with Dr. William Carroll, members of the committee commissioned by the Catholic Theological Society of America to author *Human Sexuality*. On behalf of the entire committee we wish to thank Doubleday & Company and the contributors to this volume of essays for the investment of critical reflection, energy, and resources that went into it, and for the invitation to respond. Our response itself is intended as both a reaction to the views of the present writers and a fuller development of our original approach.

Few books have been deemed seminal or significant enough to warrant a subsequent volume of debate. In recent theology one thinks of Bishop John Robinson's *Honest to God*, Harvey Cox's *Secular City*, Joseph Fletcher's *Situation Ethics*, and Hans Küng's *Infallible?: An Inquiry*. For *Human Sexuality* to occasion a special volume of scholarly appraisals is a rare compliment which we genuinely appreciate.

Indeed, we are grateful to all the commentators and critics who have written about *Human Sexuality* since its publication in June 1977. Although some saw fit to form opinions and publish judgments before reading the book carefully, many have given it serious and thoughtful consideration and, even when their conclusions did not agree with our own, were willing to come to grips with the same issues. The invitation we made to our colleagues in the theological and other sciences to serious criticism and scholarly dialogue has been taken up energetically. We expressed in *Human Sexuality* the hope that our study would provide for "the kind of theological discussion that will contribute to a better understanding and more effective articulation of the Christian values we share in common" (p. 241). That hope is being realized as the discussion, exemplified by these essays, continues. It is leading to a clearer understanding of the questions, a sharper focus on the differences that divide opinions, and a keener appreciation of the creative thinking that still needs to be done. We welcome this volume of essays as an important contribution to the evolution unfolding in the field of Catholic sexual ethics.

This is the first opportunity any of us, as the authors of *Human Sexuality*, has taken to reply to any extent to those who have written about our study. The criticisms, naturally, have been varied in nature and uneven in quality. If there has been one kind of criticism that has been leveled against the book with any kind of consistency, however, it has not been that of an error of fact or an unfounded judgment but an omission of one sort or another. So it is that our critics have faulted *Human Sexuality* for not giving consideration or more emphasis to: the theology of the Elohist (C. Stuhlmueller);[1] the Old Testament prophets and wisdom literature (J. Jensen; C. Stuhlmueller); Jesus' sexuality (T. Driver);[2] 1 Corinthians 6 (W. May and J. F. Harvey);[3] hermeneutics (E. LaVerdiere);[4] the historical development of Catholic sexual ethics (J. Gaffney);[5] Alexander of Hales and Albert the Great (D. Doherty); the medieval tradition and literature of Romantic Love (R. Haughton);[6] the critical phase of the late enlightenment (G. Baum); the Catholic tradition of casuistry and early personalist theologians like Herbert Doms, Bernhardin Krempel, and Dietrich von Hildebrand (D. Doherty); depth psychology and the sociology of sexual mores (G. Baum); the gravity of sexual sins (M. and P. Mohs); the relationship of sexuality to Christian spirituality (J. Bernardin); and the translation of the theology of *Human Sexuality* into language easily accessible to young people (M. and P. Mohs). For us to have attempted all the above would obviously have required another committee, working another three years on another three hundred pages, producing an entirely different book of encyclopedic proportions.

Our intentions, of course, were much more modest. The commission given by the Catholic Theological Society to our committee was to provide "some helpful and illuminating guidelines in the present confusion" in the area of sexual morality. We were not commissioned to produce a biblical theology, a history of Christian sexual ethics, or a survey of empirical data on sexuality. The commission given us and the intention we had in writing *Human Sexuality* was much more restricted. The call for "helpful and illuminating guidelines" suggested a study that would be primarily pastoral in nature. As we stated in the Preface, the readership for whom the study was intended was not primarily the community of professional theologians, who were already well aware of the new directions Catholic moral thinking is taking, but rather pastors, educators, and counselors, professional "leaders in pastoral ministry." That is why pastoral theology constitutes well over two thirds of the book. Biblical, historical, and empirical data were reviewed in summary fashion to demonstrate the validity and propriety of attempting to articulate a Catholic sexual ethics within a framework of Christian personalism.

With these general observations, we can now respond to the contributors in this volume. We cannot answer all of them in detail, but will attempt to address the more important questions and objections they raise.

## The Bible and Sexuality

Writing on "The Relevance of the Old Testament," Joseph Jensen accuses the report of being "superficial and tendentious" in its use of Scripture, and of putting emphasis "almost solely on legal texts" instead of reading them synchronically and diachronically. He charges that in the light of the "extended discussion of the Old Testament," the attempt to separate what is revealed and lasting from what is time- and culture-conditioned begets results that are "meager and disappointing in the extreme." *Human Sexuality* seems to "leave very little for the Bible to say to us in the area of sexual morality," and Jensen wonders why we "spent so many pages on it."

There are twenty-six pages in the chapter entitled "The Bible and Human Sexuality," eleven pages devoted to the Old Testament. Even if a critic did not read the Preface to our study with its stated purpose, it should seem quite obvious that nothing like a comprehensive study of sexuality in Scripture was ever intended. Within that limited amount of space, there was, of course, no question of going into any specific topic to any degree of depth or detail, let alone presenting a variety of opinions available on the interpretation of a particular text. We described our brief treatment of sexuality in Scripture as "schematic" (p. 29). Eugene LaVerdiere describes his own longer contribution in this volume as selective. Jensen seems to prefer the more pejorative term "superficial." (One is reminded of a regular feature in Sidney Harris' column, entitled "Antics with Semantics.")

The emotive rhetoric of his presentation rather weakens Jensen's case in charging us with being tendentious and lacking objectivity. Contemporary philosophy and psychological research have demonstrated rather convincingly that none of us approaches a text with complete objectivity. We all come with certain predispositions and biases. There is no choice between being biased or unbiased, but only between being conscious or unconscious of our biases, explicit or implicit in our predispositions. *Human Sexuality* was quite explicit in the formulation of the question which it brought to contemporary biblical exegesis: does Sacred Scripture "approve or reject categorically any particular sexual act outside of its contextual circumstances and intention" (p. 31)? Even our schematic review of Scripture (admittedly emphasizing the legal tradition in the Old Testament) proved sufficient to answer that question in the negative. Fr. Jensen neglects to confront the principal conclusion of the entire chapter on the Bible and sexuality: "In view of the weight of contrary historical evidence, anyone who maintains that the Bible absolutely forbids certain forms of sexual behavior, regardless of circumstances, must likewise bear the burden of proof" (ibid). Are we to assume *qui tacet consentire videtur?* If he does not give his tacit assent, Fr. Jensen still has to prove the contrary.

Carroll Stuhlmueller attempts to do just that, at least insofar as the Old Testament prophets are concerned. His contribution is a detailed exposition of "Prophetic Ideals and Sexual Morality," for which he deserves to be congratulated. We appreciate his approach inasmuch as it confirms and amply illustrates our statement (p. 17) that "under the impact of the prophets, cultic notions of purity were interiorized and transformed into profound moral concepts. Without lessening the need to observe all the laws of the Torah, ritual precepts became subordinated to moral requirements."

Stuhlmueller goes on to conclude, however, that the "prophets condemned all adultery and prostitution, literally as such." In making that judgment, Stuhlmueller directly contradicts no less a biblical scholar than his colleague in the Catholic Biblical Association, John L. McKenzie, from whose work A *Theology of the Old Testament* we quoted: "It is remarkable that the entire Old Testament never manages a clear and unambiguous moral condemnation of prostitution" (p. 16). Since the appearance of *Human Sexuality*, Fr. Raymond Collins of the University of Louvain has made a further study of the subject and has come to the conclusion that "McKenzie's declaration would seem to be a valid assessment of the available data."[7]

There seems to be serious disagreement among some rather eminent Catholic biblical scholars, one which certainly cannot be resolved by systematic or moral theologians. We can only see the inconclusiveness of the data and dissent among the scholars and repeat our conclusion that critical biblical scholarship, at least up to this time, "finds it impossible on the basis of the empirical data to approve or reject categorically any particular sexual act outside of its contextual circumstances and intention."

But there is still Jensen's rather serious criticism that *Human Sexuality* leaves "very little for the Bible to say to us in the area of sexual morality." The Committee on Doctrine of the National Council of Catholic Bishops similarly faulted *Human Sexuality* for "a rather impoverished concept of the role that the written Word of God must play as a foundation for theology."

Eugene LaVerdiere answers this objection for us in his welcome contribution to this book. In approaching the Gospels from the standpoint of redaction criticism, he confirms our own conclusions, drawn from the perspective of what we can say with assurance about the historical Jesus. There is nothing in his essay with which we would disagree, nothing which we find incompatible with our own survey of the biblical text. Of course, LaVerdiere goes radically beyond *Human Sexuality* with his view that present Church practice regarding the indissolubility of marriage stands at variance with Matthew's Gospel, which LaVerdiere sees as open to the possibility of a marriage relationship dissolving.

If Fr. Jensen and the Bishops' Committee on Doctrine believe that we leave the Bible too little to say, we can only refer them to LaVerdiere's "hermeneutical interpretation of the New Testament's teaching on Christian sexuality." He states there, as we did, that sexual issues are in no way at the heart of the Church's central message. He finds, as we did, that "human dignity and respect for other persons are constants of New Testament teaching concerning sexuality." LaVerdiere seems to go on to imply, however, without being specific, that sexual ethics are somehow materially different for Christians than for other human beings. If we are correct and LaVerdiere actually does maintain this, he is taking a position almost universally rejected today among moral theologians as to the existence of a materially distinctive Christian ethic. Does Christian faith possess concrete norms and values beyond those afforded to human reason? Or does faith provide us instead with a transcendent vision (the Kingdom of God) and a supernatural motivation (the love of God) for observing a natural law accessible to the consciences of all people, not only Christians?

The fact that Scripture offers little with respect to concrete norms to regulate sexual behavior should come as no surprise, since Catholic tradition from the very beginning sought moral guidance from extrabiblical sources such as Stoic philosophy. Catholic moral theology has never depended upon Scripture to the same extent Protestant moralists have. The strong reliance upon natural law in Catholic moral tradition arose precisely because Scripture does not provide us with complete or concrete moral guidance.

If Sacred Scripture offers us little in the way of concrete instruc-

tions or norms regarding moral sexual behavior, it offers us a
wealth with respect to values and motivation. Fr. Jensen fails to
make the distinction between norms and value and thus fails to
understand the stated purpose and message of *Human Sexuality*.
At the end of his essay Fr. Stuhmueller comes close to admitting
that that distinction is verified in the Scriptures themselves. After
concluding that the prophets "condemned all adultery and prostitution, literally as such," he implicitly contradicts himself by making a distinction between "apodictic laws," which sustain ideals
and summon us to heroism, and "casuistic laws," which interpret
and apply those ideals because, as Stuhlmueller puts it, "such
drastic and vigorous demands cannot become daily obligations."

We agree completely with the distinction Fr. Stuhlmueller
makes, but would like to point out that he uses categories and terminology which may be part of the stock-in-trade of Old Testament exegesis but are quite foreign to that of contemporary Catholic moral theology. Could it be that Catholic biblical scholars,
systematic and moral theologians, in concentrating on their own
fields of specialization, have lost touch with one another and are
now speaking past each other instead of to each other? Is misunderstanding the result of insufficient dialogue and interdisciplinary
collaboration? If this is so, then it is certainly time to reconsider
the traditional practice of the Catholic Biblical Association and
the Catholic Theological Society of America sponsoring separate
conventions. Catholic biblical exegetes cannot afford to ignore the
existential questions and issues being confronted by moralists and
pastors, any more than systematic, moral, and pastoral theologians
can afford to ignore the present state of biblical research.

Fr. Jensen claims that his personal disappointment is shared by
a number of his Scripture colleagues at not finding a treatment of
the Bible and sexuality that would be extensive and detailed
enough to stand above the charge of harboring glaring lacunae or
misplaced emphases. Surely he did not expect the Catholic Theological Society to assume what would be the proper task of the
Catholic Biblical Association. If *Human Sexuality* did nothing
else, it would be a contribution much to its credit to encourage
the Catholic Biblical Association to sponsor a comprehensive
study of the Bible and sexuality. And it would be a contribution
much to the credit of this present discussion if it could lead to a

closer association and collaboration between our two respective organizations. Joint meetings of the Catholic Biblical Association and the Catholic Theological Society, with the bishops of the United States in attendance and active participation, could only serve to improve the ministry all of us owe, pastors and scholars, to the Church in America.

## Christian Tradition and Sexuality

Dennis Doherty describes our treatment of the Church's historical tradition generally as "commendable," our appraisal of some aspects of it as "diplomatically gentle and generous." He faults us for certain "glaring lacunae," however, most notable our omission of the Church's tradition of casuistry, which Doherty sees as buttressing the directions we take in *Human Sexuality*. While praising us for being consistent in applying our personalist principles, he demonstrates the inconsistencies present in the tradition. Turning that tradition upon itself, Doherty invokes Catholic casuistry to justify certain cases of masturbation, premarital intercourse, heterologous artificial insemination, and even comarital relationships for the elderly.

We welcome Doherty's insights and their confirmation, in some instances, of our own conclusions. At the same time, we must confess discomfort with his methodological approach. His facile use of the casuist tradition proves, in our opinion, not the possibility of a new, more humane casuistry, but rather the need for a moral methodology which is less abstract, less juridical, less aprioristic, a methodology which is more phenomenological, more personalist, if you will, one more along the lines taken by *Human Sexuality*.

Doherty's contribution stresses the pessimism of traditional Catholicism concerning sexuality and the negative influence of St. Augustine. He excuses his concentration on the basis that the mentality which regarded sexual activity as shameful still pervades consideration of current questions in sexual ethics. Be that as it may, we admit, as James Nelson has pointed out,[8] that in our own summary of our history we preferred to accent more of the positive aspects of St. Augustine and the Catholic tradition. Precisely because it was our intention to show that there is much of value and wisdom in the tradition, we strove to highlight the positive and to explain (if not excuse) the negative on the basis of historical and cultural influences extraneous to Catholicism, such as Stoicism and an antiquated biology.

If some of the Church's past teaching on sexuality embarrasses us today, it is because the Church, despite its divine origins, is human in nature. It is not above the social and historical forces which affect all human institutions and communities. The eyes of faith view the Church as the people of God, as the human response to a divine revelation; but it is still people, still human, and as such susceptible to all the weaknesses and failings that flesh is heir to. There is no need to berate the past at any great length. And we agree with Doherty when he says that history is something not only to be studied but meant to be made. We would add only that sometimes history needs to be overcome.

## The Empirical Sciences and Sexuality

Gregory Baum's comments are eminently useful. He shared some of them with us prior to the publication of our Report. We were much tempted to give the attention he recommended to the Freudian-Marxian critique of sexuality. Again, we decided that it would be more suitable to the limited purposes of the Report simply to acknowledge their contributions to our growing understanding of the pre-reflective influences that shape our ethical thinking. This decision was prompted by Occam's rule of parsimony: Take on only those problems you have to. Our limited objective did not seem to require committing ourselves to the insights of depth psychology or, for that matter, ego or cognitive psychology. In our chapter on the empirical sciences we expressly state our purpose to limit ourselves to observed phenomena and not to indulge the various theories of developmental psychology. In the intellectual world we addressed, there are many who are impressed only by the rational demonstrative model of a science. They view the theoretic constructs of Freud, Adler, and Jung (or the currently popular Piaget) as imaginative scenarios but not verifiable. For them the same behavior, even the demonic dimension of sexuality, can be explained in other ways.

We saw no reason to take on this debate. For the most part,

however, we do agree with Baum that this left our Report impoverished. It is good he has enriched the discussion by his present contribution.

## Nature of Personhood

William May's basic criticism of *Human Sexuality* is that its theology builds on a false and dualistic understanding of human personhood. It is that precise charge we want to address in the comments that follow.

The concept essential to our understanding of sexuality and personhood is that sexuality is a constitutive factor of human existence. We say this unambiguously in the topic sentence introducing the chapter on personhood (p. 83). We say further that sexuality, far from being a subsidiary characteristic of human existence, pervades the totality of our human existence as being in the world. We so define sexuality (p. 82). And because we so understand human sexuality, as a central constitutive factor of all concrete human bodily existence pervading the total reality of the person, we can say in the same discussion that our "definition broadens the meaning of sexuality beyond the merely genital and generative." We caution the reader that this meaning of sexuality "is to be understood in all that follows." Indeed this understanding is critical to all our subsequent reasoning. Professor May is in accord with this much of our understanding of sexuality in that he observes in his critique that "sexuality is thus integral to the human person." It is then agreed. But we wonder whether Professor May has grasped the implications of what he says.

A related notion that is central to our position on sexuality as a person is our understanding of the relation of body to subjectivity. We express our position clearly and unambiguously where we state, "we *are* our bodies" (p. 83; emphasis in original). At the same place we refer to our personal existence as "our fleshly reality." We intend by this forthright language to say that body and person are one in the reality of concrete human existence. The body itself is subject. The body perceives, gives meaning, communicates, through its own subjectivity and not through a principle that, while distinct from it, is somehow present within and shares an intimate union with the body. We expressly reject this dualism. It is precisely because we are persuaded that personal existence is one with bodily existence that we stress the importance of bodily experience, of sexual reality, in the development of the person. From our definition of sexuality through our discussion of sexuality in personhood this position is abundantly clear to a reader free of preconceptions. It is gratifying to note that May echoes our statement "we *are* our bodies" when he observes, "the body I am." Immediately before, he had stated "the *body* of the human person is not something other than the person but is rather constitutive of the *being* of the person." He is therefore in accord with us. We are in further agreement as to the importance of the biological dimension of sexual expression. May insists that "the procreative dimension of human sexuality is not . . . a merely biological given or function; rather it is a personal sexual power." This language is not far from our observation that "sexuality is not just an isolated biological or physical phenomenon accidental to human beings but an integral part of their personal self-expression" (p. 82).

In view of the apparent agreement between ourselves and Professor May, even to "similarities of language," on the centrality of sexuality in regard to the person and on the unity of body and person, it is surprising that May sees crass dualism as the philosophic error lurking at the foundation of our thesis.

This distortion of our position seems purposeful. In view of our unacceptable conclusions perhaps he wishes to identify us with a position that is more easily attacked. However, he does not develop his argument other than by referring to certain choices of language we have made from time to time. When taken out of context these expressions suggest to May that we are rudely separating body and person or subject. He notes that we say that subjectivity is "embodied." Elsewhere we use variations of the expression. This, he concludes, negates all else we have said, and indicates we have in mind a Platonic principle held captive in lumpish matter, the body. He apparently would find it convenient if this were our position. It clearly is not. Our true position is manifest from the full context of our discussion. If we were so inclined, we might accuse Professor May himself of dualism for his use of the expression "the body of the human person." That is, we could understand May to intend that the body is a spiritless thing possessed by the distinct person. From the context of his remarks, it is evident that this is quite the opposite of his true meaning. Our meaning is likewise evident.

The language selected by May for criticism appears in our discussion (p. 84). The language is appropriate to that focused discussion. Its meaning must be derived from our total explication of the relation of body and subject. For the latter we have leaned on the reflections of Merleau-Ponty. His development of the concept of body and subject is expressly intended to overcome both Cartesian dualism and that of medieval and classical philosophy. By our adaptation of Merleau-Ponty's term "body-subject" (p. 83) we confess this indebtedness.[9] However, even Merleau-Ponty acknowledged the difficulty of discussing the two concepts of "body" and "subject" without using language that derives from our dualistic past. The unprejudiced reader makes allowance for this limitation of language.

It is somewhat ironic that May should select language from our discussion of the significance of sexual differentiation to support his suspicions of our dualistic leanings. The burden of that discussion is our opinion that the reality of sexual differentiation must be given proper weight. This is a position very congenial to May as apparent from the remainder of his critique. However, May's refusal to acknowledge our position is not without purpose. He apparently wishes to put us in the camp of those who minimize the differentiation in complementarity of the sexes. He gratuitously states that we favor such a position; in fact, we merely report this position. We describe with equal intention the quite contradictory position embraced by other philosophers (p. 64).

The direction of May's argument appears to be that we are able to justify, e.g., contraception, because we are dualists who use the "subject" as a principle distinct from and superior to the body. For us, as May would have it, the logic of the body and its function can be distinct from the behavior of the person. Interfering with the procreative function of the body, therefore, in no way touches or modifies the person. May apparently cannot entertain the possibility that one might hold the body and the person to be a unity, reject crass dualism, and still, under given circumstances, judge contraception to be harmonious with the "body-subject" unity.

A final distortion of our position by May must be corrected. May suggests that our use of the term "subjectivity" requires us to hold that only the free and conscious subject is a human person. On the contrary, we do not feel that such a position is essential to our thesis. Merleau-Ponty's notion of "body-subjectivity" does not suppose such developed consciousness but the body as subject has a pre-conscious power of dialogue with the world before arriving at consciousness. The relational functioning of the body-subject is not restricted to deliberate conscious activity. The pre-conscious existence of the body-subject has meaning and fundamental worth. We appreciate Professor May's comments but, as indicated above, regard his attempts to categorize our understanding of personhood as dualistic without foundation.

## Moral Evaluation and Sexual Conduct

Daniel Maguire is generous in his praise of *Human Sexuality* and its achievements. As a good critic, however, he does not hesitate to point out areas of incompleteness and to make several important contributions of his own to the present discussion. Perhaps his greatest tribute to our study is that it has dramatically changed the status of the question by fostering open and public dialogue.

One of the important contributions Maguire makes is the call for a distinction between species and individual needs in defining the relationship between the procreative and unitive aspects of human sexuality. He contends that the relationship between the procreative and unitive would be better maintained if it were recognized that the sexual encounter is always unitive and hence serious but that "the species-need for reproduction is not inseparably conjoined as a moral condition to sexual exchange." The distinction between individual and species-needs is a helpful one. But as Maguire himself inclines to admit, the distinction is not altogether neat and tidy since the procreative does at times serve both individual and species needs and vice versa. Furthermore, Maguire's explanation would hardly satisfy those who insist on an inseparable connection between the procreative and unitive aspects of sexuality.

His claim that "the unitive demands of sexuality which are part of every sexual expression would provide sufficient safeguard for assuring the marital orientation of sexual exchange" is sure to be seriously challenged by many theologians, particularly in view of his contention that "the marital orientation of sexual exchange" could include a responsible homosexual union. This is pouring such new wine into the old wineskins of "unitive" and "marriage" that the terms could not help but burst at the seams. This is precisely why we felt it necessary and preferable in our study to introduce the new wineskins of "creativity" and "integration."

Throughout the remainder of his essay it is fascinating to observe Maguire maneuver back and forth, trying on the one hand to provide a basis for more specific and firm judgments, and on the other hand to avoid anything that would resemble an inflexible and rigid imposition of absolute norms. In a word, Maguire seems to be seeking a way to render what in moral tradition was recognized as "the moral imponderable" more ponderable. He suggests, for instance, that a greater reliance on the deontological approach incorporating "mystical and affective *appreciations*" would have permitted *Human Sexuality* to reach a more firmly negative judgment on swinging. To say, as our study does, that swinging is "generally dehumanizing" is too mild for Maguire. He is more inclined to categorize it as the "unimaginable exception." His firm judgment would proceed, as he puts it, from "my pluriform moral consciousness—from my practical reason, from historical experience, from creative imagination, from affective appreciation, from judicious reliance on religious and other cultural authorities, etc."

It is surprising to us that the same deontological method does not lead him, as it does other moralists, to demand a firmer judgment on homosexual behavior. Quite the contrary, he clearly rejects the position of those who, on the basis of evidence from sources similar to those he cites, regard homosexual acts as always ontically evil, not a human expression at full term, or as falling short of the full meaning of human sexuality. It would seem Maguire needs to get a better handle on these deontological arguments if he is going to draw firm judgments. Otherwise he opens himself to the accusation of being inconsistent. For this reason we preferred with regard to many conclusions in our study to remain less conclusive, and more tentative but consistent with the available data.

While encouraging greater use of the deontological method to capture the mystical elements of a moral experience, Maguire cautions against an overmysticalization of sex. He expresses some prudent reservations regarding the use of the social sciences, but at the same time presses for contextualized moral principles that would derive from the particular specific behavioral one we are studying.

All observations Maguire makes are valid and need to be made. But it would seem that the more specific one becomes in making moral judgments about particularized behavior, the more imperative it is to test those judgments against empirical data. We do not maintain that the empirical sciences are infallible. But it does seem that their input becomes more valuable and telling the more concrete and specific the behavior we are evaluating. Although empirical data cannot definitively resolve our moral question, they can help keep our deontological intuitions from going too far astray. For this reason, we believe that it is important to remember the caution of St. Thomas that the more one moves away from the self-evident principles of the natural law, the less certain and definitive one can be.[10]

## A Word to the Home Front

The "Word from the Home Front" by Mayo Mohs and Patricia Turbes Mohs should be made compulsory reading for any bishop or priest ordained over fifteen years. Much to our embarrassment, they remind us of the kind of advice we used to give, the kind of attitudes we used to inculcate into our students, congregations, and penitents. The Mohses' forthright description of young adults in the 1950s and '60s living in constant dread of falling into mortal sin because of sexuality lends weight to the terrible indictment made by Segundo, to which the Mohses allude. There is no reason to believe that the Mohses' Catholic education was exceptional in conveying to them a specter of a "cruel and whimsical God," as they put it. Segundo's troubling question deserves serious pondering: to what extent is modern unbelief subtly rooted in the taboos of classic Christian sexual morality?

We appreciate the valuable suggestions the Mohses make regarding the use of literature, movies, and television for moral education. And we sympathize with their perplexity, and that of other parents and educators, on how to translate pedagogically a personalist Christian sexual ethic for children, young adults, and also those adults who prefer to be told what to do. Christian educators have a difficult challenge to face, and we hope that they will become actively involved in the present discussion being carried on by theologians and representatives of other sciences regarding sexuality.

At the same time, we cannot help but point out sadly that, in asking us for more about the gravity of sexual sins and for a clearer classification of those sins, the Mohses betray how much they are still a product of their education and era, an education whose traces long remain, and an era which is not altogether past. Their early Catholic conditioning remains with them, as it does with most of us. The unfortunate thing is not that embarrassing advice along with destructive attitudinal conditioning was given in the past, but that it is still being given in the name of Catholicism today.

## Continuing the Dialogue

We are particularly grateful to Archbishop Joseph L. Bernardin for becoming part of this dialogue and communicating through his observations the concerns of the chief pastors of the Catholic Church in America. His comments touch upon some of the basic and divisive issues regarding human sexuality, areas in which our study often takes a point of view significantly different from official Church teaching. Because of their fundamental importance, the answers given by Archbishop Bernardin will be addressed at greater length than those of other contributors. Among those issues, we would single out the following as the most important:

1. moral/pastoral theology
2. the magisterium and moral/pastoral pronouncements
3. probabilism
4. mortal sin, grave matter, and intrinsic evil
5. the media and moral dialogue today

6. empirical sciences and morality
7. spirituality and human sexuality
8. Christ—the ultimate norm.

1. *Moral/Pastoral Theology.* Archbishop Bernardin indicates that one of the reasons the bishops reacted so quickly and vehemently to *Human Sexuality* was the fact that it presumed to suggest pastoral guidelines rather than remain simply an exercise in speculative moral theology. This remark, it seems to us, goes to the very heart of the matter; it touches the very definition and meaning of moral theology. There are a number of serious, highly respected moral theologians (particularly in Europe) who would agree with the archbishop in defining moral theology primarily as a speculative science of absolute and unchanging principles. They maintain at the same time, however, that, alongside moral theology, there is the closely related science concerned with the application of moral principles to individual persons and particular situations, namely, pastoral theology. Although moral theology and pastoral theology are regarded as closely allied and complementary sciences, they are also viewed by these theologians as essentially distinct.

Fr. Jan Visser, one of the authors of the Vatican *Declaration on Sexual Ethics,* is a prominent exponent of this school of thought. As a moral theologian, he does not hesitate to state categorically that homosexual acts are absolutely and intrinsically immoral. When ministering pastorally to homosexual persons, however, Fr. Visser's primary concern is to help them live as stable a Christian life as possible in their particular situations. Thus, in a magazine interview he remarks:

> When one is dealing with people who are so deeply homosexual that they will be in serious personal and perhaps social trouble unless they attain a steady partnership within their homosexual lives, one can recommend them to seek such a partnership, and one accepts this relationship as the best they can do in their present situation.[11]

Those who follow this line of reasoning see no incompatibility between such a humane pastoral attitude and the rigid adherence to the general principle that homosexual acts are always intrinsically evil. Such an approach enables them to maintain a moral principle that defines the ideal, and, at the same time, in pastoral practice, to make compassionate accommodation for individuals in their particular circumstances. This accommodation, they insist, however, is not moral but pastoral theology.

Many equally prominent theologians find this sharp distinction between moral and pastoral theology somewhat arbitrary and often misleading. They prefer to approach morality in terms of persons and personal relationships instead of in terms of theoretical and abstract principles. We who authored *Human Sexuality* would align ourselves with this latter group and agree with Maguire when he states in his essay, "moral theology is pastoral by its nature." Varying circumstances, intentionalities, and complexities of human existence all constitute an essential part of moral judgment. Moral theology pertains to flesh-and-blood people in time and space, not to an ideational sphere of Platonic abstractions. For this sector of the theological community, there is no moral theology that is not at the same time inescapably pastoral.

Whichever definition of moral theology one ultimately prefers, it would be incomplete to approach so complex and delicate a subject as human sexuality by simply taking cognizance of abstract, absolute principles without reflecting at the same time on their implications for human living. Throughout the Church's moral tradition, theologians regarded this kind of reflection as an integral part of their task. This was precisely the charge that was given to the committee by the Catholic Theological Society of America when we were asked to provide some "helpful and illuminating guidelines in the present confusion."

It has never been Catholic tradition to see Church pronouncements as assuming the task of pastoral theology. Individual circumstances are simply too varied and complex to expect anything like this from the magisterium, and it is commonly accepted Catholic opinion that Church pronouncements do not intend this. Fr. Visser's statement, quoted above, clearly indicates that official, magisterial declarations need to be tempered with pastoral theology before an appropriate individual decision can be made. This is the proper task and inalienable right of individual persons in the exercise of their consciences, together with the pastoral counselors who assist them in their decision-making process. Both the individuals and their counselors have a right to expect from moralists the kind of serious and competent reflection that will aid them in their particular concrete decision. For this reason, we find it difficult to appreciate Archbishop Bernardin's concern that *Human Sexuality* was proposed "not just as an exercise in speculative moral theology but as a concrete set of guidelines for immediate pastoral practice" (*Reply to Question 1*).

Whatever methodological school one follows in pursuing morality, one cannot avoid the pastoral implications. There is abundant evidence from history that Catholic moral theologians have never limited their efforts in this way. From the Fathers, through the *Penitentials*, from the schoolmen and the manualists, from the Council of Trent to Vatican II, Catholic moralists have recognized it as their responsibility to address the practical as well as the theoretical aspects of morality.

The College of Bishops together with the Holy Father certainly have the responsibility and right to articulate clearly and forcefully the basic moral values that constitute Christian living. They also have the duty to provide specific directions as to how these values are best realized in the Christian community which they serve. But to imply that these pronouncements of the official Church are the only guidance deserving of consideration by the Catholic conscience appears unduly restrictive. Individual Catholics have the responsibility of taking magisterial pronouncements seriously and according those pronouncements a priority and presumption of truth in the formation of their consciences. But the magisterium is not the only source of truth. In complex situations especially, individuals have the responsibility to open their consciences to every possible source of truth. Catholic tradition has always recognized the evidence of science and the reflected thought of theologians as particularly valuable in this regard. To deny any pastoral validity to such sources goes contrary to a long Catholic tradition.

Granted, the pastoral value and import of the guidance from such extra-magisterial sources will have only as much weight as their arguments can support. This is far from claiming, though, that they have no validity at all or that moralists ought not even attempt to speak pastorally to issues. In the last analysis it is the well-formed individual conscience that must accept responsibility for the pastoral decision that is made. The magisterium, theologians, and science must serve conscience, not usurp it. One of the conclusions we might draw from the point raised by the archbishop is the need for a continuing dialogue to further clarify the respective roles of bishops, theologians, and pastors in the pastoral care of God's people.

2. *The Magisterium and Moral/Pastoral Pronouncements.* The volume of literature that has appeared on this topic in the last decade has undoubtedly stamped this question as one of the principal theological issues of our generation. It is not surprising, therefore, that the issue should surface again.

Our difficulty with Archbishop Bernardin's articulation of the role of the magisterium in moral matters is that it all too easily conveys the impression that the magisterium has a monopoly on moral truth. There is no doubt that many Catholics hear and understand the message of the bishops in this way. The chapter by Mayo and Patricia Mohs graphically illustrates how well-meaning Catholics felt absolutely bound to the most exact observance of Church prescriptions in the moral area. Archbishop Bernardin and many of his colleagues in the episcopal college clearly strive to make the impression that any decision not in complete accord with magisterial directives is objectively immoral and subjectively a manifest sign of ignorance, weakness, or sin. The archbishop does not state this explicitly but there seems no room left for any other conclusion. We respectfully wish to point out that such a conclusion is clearly in contradiction to the best of the Church's moral tradition, whether one uses the more historical principles/pastoral accommodation approach or the more contemporary personalist approach.

The archbishop strengthens this impression when he insists that the responsibility for distinguishing authentic from inauthentic development of moral doctrine rests with the magisterium. The ultimate criterion that separates inauthentic moral development is that "the Church has not adopted their view" (*Reply to Question 11*). To be sure, the archbishop modifies his remark with the condition that a thoroughly comprehensive and responsible process of discernment involving consultation with the experience of the faithful, the reflection of theologians, the formulations of the past, and the original teaching of Scripture and tradition has occurred. The implicit assumption, of course, is that such a comprehensive process of discernment lies behind every magisterial statement on moral matters. Dissent from such teaching is then rendered unacceptable. But this assumption is precisely what is being questioned in the literature on this topic during the last decade. The question does not disappear simply by assuming that it is so!

This same impression is further confirmed in the statement by the archbishop that "the Church *is* Christ teaching in the world today" (ibid.). This is a rather generous paraphrase, not altogether accurate, of the celebrated article 25 of the *Dogmatic Constitution on the Church*. Placed in a fuller context of other conciliar documents dealing with this topic, the archbishop's statement may not be a totally accurate reflection of Vatican II's understanding of the relationship between Christ and the magisterium. The careful wording of article 50 in the *Constitution on the Church in the Modern World* deserves to be considered, especially in the way that it cautions against an overly simple identification of the teaching of the Church with the teaching of Christ.

The *Dogmatic Constitution on Divine Revelation* likewise expresses the relationship of the magisterium to Christ more precisely when it states: "This teaching office is not above the Word of God, but serves it" (Art. 10). To claim otherwise is to make Christ responsible for the burning of heretics, the use of torture by the Roman Inquisition, the persecution of witches, and the condemnation of Galileo—all grievous moral failings of a fallible human Church not attributable to Jesus. Our day is no different, and it is dangerous and misleading to speak of the Church simply as the continuation of Christ. Such an identification all too easily leads to the identification of Church teaching with God's teaching.[12] Human directives are given out as divine directives, the commandments of bishops and popes as the commandments of Christ. This is virtual ecclesial monophysitism. It exalts the Church into an idol assuming the Lordship of Christ instead of pointing to it. From our vantage point it would seem wiser and

truer for the magisterium, when speaking on complex moral issues, to acknowledge the limitations of our knowledge and make
more modest claims to truth.

3. *Probabilism.* Catholic moral tradition has had a long history of
dealing with the question of limited knowledge and uncertainty.
Daniel Maguire has sketched this history masterfully in his
remarks on probabilism and saw fit to accord probabilism a high
point in Catholic moral thought. He joins the authors of *Human
Sexuality* in a call for a return to probabilism or rather neo-
probabilism that would include ecumenical thought as well. He
sees probabilism as the most satisfactory way of dealing with the
moral pluralism of our day.

Archbishop Bernardin rejects the approach of probabilism on
these issues, maintaining that, historically, this approach was restricted to areas "not explicitly covered by Church teaching"
(*Reply to Question* 11). A review of the history of probabilism, as
found in such standard and acknowledged authors as Noldin,
Tanquerey, Merkelbach, Sabbetti-Barrett, and Henry Davis,
would indicate disagreement with the archbishop and confirmation of Maguire's conclusion that only defined Church teaching—
of which there exists none in the moral area—would constitute
such an exception. The archbishop prefers to label any opinion
that departs from official Church teaching as "dissent" (ibid.),
which in his understanding has validity only when it is accepted
by the magisterium. This neat arrangement completes the vicious
circle and leaves the magisterium completely and exclusively in
command of what is supposed to be moral truth. In our estimation, Catholic moral tradition had a better approach to truth
in the system of probabilism which more candidly admitted
limitations to our knowledge, fostered mutual respect for diver-
gent views, encouraged a more honest pursuit of truth, and
showed great respect for the integrity of the individual conscience.

4. *Mortal Sin, Grave Matter, and Intrinsic Evil.* Archbishop
Bernardin's response to the questions on mortal sin, grave matter,
and intrinsic evil (Question 5) reveals a fidelity to the best in traditional thought in this area. He deserves to be praised for the
extra effort—not always found in the tradition itself or its popular

presentation—to bring out the personal and relational dimensions inextricably connected with each of these concepts.

As he explains, the essential element of mortal sin is the free and deliberate rejection of a friendship with God. Grave matter is described as referring to those actions which, if performed freely and knowingly, are capable of rupturing one's relationship with God. Intrinsic evil is not explicitly defined but, in his remarks about the evil of a single act of masturbation, it becomes clear that the basis for his judgment is its violation of the sacredness of human life and the human power of procreating life—again relational realities. All of the above indicate that Catholic moral tradition, in its best form, did not entirely lose sight of the personal and relational dimension crucial to these moral concepts. It is thus unfair to accuse traditional morality of being purely biological, mechanical, or legalistic in its dealing with sin and morality. Many popular presentations of traditional morality because of their almost exclusive emphasis on act and neglect of these personal dimensions certainly leave this impression and they deserve to be rejected as caricatures of the authentic tradition.

The personalist approach to morality prefers, on the other hand, to highlight the relational and intentional aspect of human moral behavior. For this reason a person's orientation and direction in life receive more attention than individual acts. This does not mean that individual acts are insignificant or without meaning. There is no serious personalist theologian who would not consider the act as part of the total moral evaluation of human behavior. It is equally unfair, therefore, to accuse personalism of reducing morality to pure intentionality and sin to attitude and orientation. These are distortions of authentic personalism that are wide of the mark.

The difference between traditional and personalist schools of thought is not that either one of them rejects elements that are essential to the concept of morality and sin. The difference is more subtle than that. It consists rather in the way that these various elements are interrelated and the priority, at least in terms of emphasis and presumption, that is accorded one or other of these essential elements. Traditional moral theology highlights the importance of the individual act. It focuses its moral evaluation on individual acts and in certain cases judges these acts to be gravely immoral by their very nature. The unexpressed assumption here is that the person is responsibly carrying through an action that is utterly irreconcilable with the friendship of God. This obviously implies a matter of extreme importance. A second assumption is that, ordinarily, this action will involve the individuals to the very depth of their personalities to such an extent that they realize they are in a life-and-death confrontation with God. That is why it is often stated in traditional theology that exceptions to such total personal involvement may occur but they are not to be presumed. If in an individual case, such a life-death encounter does not occur it is only because subjectively various elements interfered with the person's full freedom to realize or choose what was at stake.

Thus, in the case of masturbation, for example—even masturbation for medical reasons of fertility testing—the logic of the traditional system would presume that this single action is of such consequence that if a person were truly conscious and free, it would break that person's relationship with God. The only explanation as to why sin may not occur in such an instance is that the person was not fully free. Traditional moralists hesitate to draw out so severe a judgment in a concrete, particular instance; that is why they turn to pastoral theology and its excusing causes to escape the judgment of serious sin. The presumption, however, remains in favor of moral sin even though extenuating circumstances may mitigate responsibility partially or completely, in the vast majority of cases.

It is precisely at this point that we believe the logic and consistency of the traditional approach to morality turn against themselves. Why attribute to an action the presumption of consequences of such magnitude when admittedly, at least with regard to some intrinsically evil actions, this reality does not occur in the vast majority of cases? There appears here an inconsistency that is not only misleading but laden with potentially harmful consequences of fear and guilt especially when such a position is proclaimed repeatedly and forcefully. Such inconsistency has the further damaging effect of casting suspicion and doubt about other statements of grave moral consequence and results eventually in a profound credibility gap between the teaching Church and its listening faithful.

The personalist school, on the other hand, places its emphasis on persons and their relationships rather than on the act. This does not mean that the act is incidental or unimportant. We do express our relationship with others through acts. But the deeper question that interests the personalist is what is occurring within the relationship. This difference of focus has profound implications. As Cardinal Joseph Ratzinger, the Archbishop of Munich, has pointed out: "It is simply not the same, whether a person asks himself if his actions are 'in accord with nature' or whether he must ask whether his actions are responsible in the view of other persons and in view of the Word of the personal God."[13]

Archbishop Bernardin reveals in his comment on these topics a continuing commitment to a morality heavily biased in favor of nature and acts though not excluding the necessary relationship to person and intentions. We find it more convincing and consistent to approach moral judgments with a bias in favor of persons and intention though not disregarding the implications of nature and act.

It is difficult to overestimate the importance of the difference between these two approaches. As in the case of masturbation, so also in many other areas of human sexuality, how one focuses on the questions and where one places the emphasis lead to a radically different formulation and expression of sexual ethics. It is our firm conviction, and we have repeatedly indicated this in our study, that it is precisely this change of focus from nature to person that has been most responsible for the new directions and conclusions that emerge there. Archbishop Bernardin and others regard this development as incompatible with authentic Church teaching. From our point of view, it was Vatican II's *Pastoral Constitution on the Church in the Modern World* that provided us with this principle. *Human Sexuality* was simply an attempt to unfold some of its many implications and ramifications in the area of sexual ethics.

There is a spirit of personalism that breathes throughout the entire *Pastoral Constitution*, but most perceptibly in its opening chapter, entitled "The Dignity of the Human Person." In that chapter, the Council accepted as its own six essential principles of personalism:

1. The *centrality* of personhood. All thought, all ideas, all judgments ought to be related to persons. In its opening statement in Chapter One, the *Constitution* states: "all things on earth should be related to man as their center and crown" (Art. 12).

2. The *relationality* of personhood. The human person is defined in terms of relationships. A person can never be known, can never become himself or herself, except in intercommunion with other persons: "God did not create man as a solitary. For from the beginning 'male and female he created them' (Gen. 1:27). Their companionship produces the primary form of interpersonal communion. For by his innermost nature man is a social being, and unless he relates himself to others he can neither live nor develop his potential" (Art. 12).

3. The *unity* of the human person. In contrast to a body-soul dualism which exalts the spiritual at the expense of the physical, the Council taught that "man is one in body and soul" (Art 14). This wholistic view was the point of departure of the *Constitution:* "the pivotal point of our total presentation will be man himself, whole and entire, body and soul, heart and conscience, mind and will" (Art. 3).

4. The *corporality* of human persons. Rejecting classic dualism means affirming the human body. A human person not merely has a body but is a body. As a result, the Council declared: ". . . man is not allowed to despise his bodily life. Rather he is obliged to regard his body as good and honorable since God has created it and will raise it up on the last day" (Art 14).

5. The *freedom* of the human person. Freedom is not a danger to be distrusted but a value to be protected as integral to human dignity. In the words of the Council: "Only in freedom can man direct himself toward goodness. . . . Man's dignity demands that he act according to a knowing and free choice" (Art. 17).

6. The sacredness of personal *conscience*. As human freedom requires a person to act responsibly, human dignity accords inviolable rights and duties to personal conscience. The *Pastoral Constitution* states that "Man has in his heart a law written by God. To obey it is the very dignity of man; according to it he will

be judged. Conscience is the most secret core and sanctuary of a man. There he is alone with God, whose voice echoes in his depths" (Art. 16).

These personalist principles, together with a new and deeper appreciation of the personalism of Jesus in the gospels, constitute the basis for the personalist ethics of sexuality and marriage espoused by the Second Vatican Council. A preliminary draft of a statement on sexuality and marriage had been prepared for the Council which rejected this draft and the Augustinian tradition it espoused. In fact, rather than *natura*, the Council deliberately showed preference for the word *indoles*, meaning natural disposition, a term less freighted with biological Stoic connotations.

The *Pastoral Constitution* in its chapter on marriage explicitly made "the dignity of the human person" the basis of its consideration (Art. 46). Its opening statement on marriage calls it a "community of love" and relates it to "the well-being of the individual person and of human and Christian society" (Art. 47). So, too, conjugal love is described in personalist terms as "eminently human." "Directed from one person to another . . . it involves the good of the whole person," and "is uniquely expressed and perfected" through sexual intercourse.

This break with our Stoic and Augustinian past extended as well to the Thomistic teaching that placed human sexual activity in the category of the generic natural law we share in common with the animals. The *Pastoral Constitution* explicitly rejected this doctrine, when it declared that the characteristics of human sexuality "wonderfully exceed the dispositions of lower forms of life" (Art. 51). Implicitly, but unmistakably, the Council also broke with the more recent tradition of subordinating the unitive to the procreative purpose of marriage. Granted, children are "the supreme gift of marriage," and conjugal love is by natural disposition "ordained toward the begetting and education of children." Yet, at the same time, "marriage is not instituted solely for procreation" and "the other purposes of matrimony are not of less account" (Art. 50). While married love and fostering life are not separate and unconnected realities, neither are they in competition with each other.

The *Pastoral Constitution* likewise affirmed human freedom and personal conscience in the realm of sexual ethics. In determining the number of children for their family, spouses are "interpreters of divine love," called to make a conscience decision "thoughtfully," with "responsibility," and "ultimately in the sight of God." This decision should take into account the welfare, spiritual and temporal, of the spouses, their family, church, and society (Art. 50). In other words, a conscience decision must look to the totality of circumstances, not primarily biology.

The Second Vatican Council recognized that harmonizing the unitive and procreative elements of marriage is not always easily accomplished. Spouses have a right to express their love sexually, even when it may be morally imperative for them not to have any more children. With a statement disarming in its simplicity, the Council enunciated a principle revolutionary in its significance. On the issue of integrating the procreative and unitive aspects of marriage, the *Pastoral Constitution* asserted that the morality of any act does not depend on sincere intentions or motivation alone, so-called subjective criteria. Morality "must be determined by objective standards." Traditionally, that objective criterion had been the nature of the sexual act. The Council broke with that naturalist tradition and adopted a personalist basis instead. The objective morality of a sexual act must be "based on the nature of the human person and his acts" (Art. 51). To avoid any uncertainty on the exact meaning of this text, the commission that drafted it attached the following explanatory note: "These standards mean the acts are not to be judged solely by their biological aspects but as acts proper to the human person, and the latter is to be fully envisaged in its total reality" (*Modus* 104).

In our judgment, the present tension between the act-centered and person-oriented approaches to morality is not all bad. Both approaches have their respective strengths and weaknesses. If we can only restrain ourselves from rash condemnation of one another, seriously strive for a better understanding of each other's position, and dialogue toward a resolution of the areas of tension, the future of moral theology will surely provide better guidance than either system can presently guarantee by itself.

5. *The Media and Moral Dialogue Today.* In several places (*Replies to Questions 1 and 11*), Archbishop Bernardin refers to the publication of *Human Sexuality* as being accompanied by a "rather intensive media campaign," the "subject of a high-powered marketing campaign," and introducing "massive confusion

. . . among theologically unsophisticated people by the practice of 'press conference theology.'"

For the record:

1. The study was originally commissioned to provide some helpful guidelines "in the present confusion." Obviously, the existing confusion was the cause for the study—not its consequence. Numerous surveys confirm this fact.

2. The "high-powered marketing campaign" was limited to one press conference scheduled after much deliberation and consultation to clarify some serious misrepresentations of the study sensationalized particularly in the Catholic press even before the book's release. The promotion of the book by Paulist Press has been minimal. As noted in one account: "Paulist Press canceled a substantial advertising campaign for the book last fall and currently is not promoting it in any other way than through a listing in its catalogue."[14] This can hardly be called a "high-powered marketing campaign."

3. The "rather intensive media campaign" consisted of appearances on "The Today Show," "The Phil Donahue Show," and "The Good-Morning Canada" program in an attempt simply to set the record straight and diffuse the sensationalism created mostly by certain elements of the extreme right-wing Catholic press. Many invitations to appear on the media were refused because it was the committee's conviction that this was not an appropriate forum for a serious discussion of the contents of our Report. On the other hand, we have welcomed and invited serious criticism of the Report from competent professionals in various disciplines.

The widespread publicity and reaction given to the Report signal not "press conference theology," but rather an age where, as Maguire so aptly states, "moral theology is no longer a clerical preserve." An enlightened laity and modern means of communication provide the Church with an unprecedented opportunity for engaging all the faithful in their rightful mission of sharing in Christ's prophetic office. If we are to accomplish the Church's frequently stated goal of forming believers who respond freely out of inner conviction rather than from simple conformity to imposed rules, we believe they must be involved in the dialogue and dialectic and not simply be subjects of indoctrination. The many positive responses our efforts have received from responsible and committed lay people give us hope that our confidence has not been misplaced.

6. *Empirical Sciences and Morality.* One of the surprisingly frequent criticisms of *Human Sexuality* lies in its use of the empirical studies. In this series of essays alone, Gregory Baum, William May, Daniel Maguire, and Archbishop Bernardin have expressed their observations on the topic. As we indicated in our study, the debate on the relationship of the empirical data to moral theology was initiated long before *Human Sexuality* was written and will continue for a long time after.

Archbishop Bernardin has been fairer than many of our critics when he acknowledges that we do not simply equate statistical incidence with moral goodness. As he reads us, however, our treatment of this topic suggests that "moral theology cannot universalize about immoral behavior without universal empirical data to demonstrate the negative consequences of such behavior" (*Reply to Question 4*). Perhaps the best response to this impression is simply to ask whether the authors of *Human Sexuality* do universalize about immoral behavior. At the level of principle and values, we had no hesitation in universalizing about sexual behavior (p. 96). At the level of norms and concrete decision-making which deals with specific individual acts we agree with many contemporary theologians that one cannot securely universalize negative absolutes. Those who presume to do so ought to indicate on what basis they make their claim. Our contention was simply that empirical sciences do not furnish the proof for such a claim. This does not mean that there can be no general norms; rather, that they cannot claim universal validity.

The archbishop refers to several paragraphs from the Vatican *Declaration on Sexual Ethics* which he commends as an "appropriate use" of the empirical sciences. The paragraph cited (※9) links the frequency of masturbation with "man's innate weakness following original sin; but it is also to be linked with the loss of a sense of God, with the corruption of morals engendered by the commercialization of vice, with the restrained licentiousness of so many public entertainments and publications, as well as with the neglect of modesty, which is the guardian of chastity."

Actually, there is little empirical evidence that can support this analysis. The scientific and empirical studies provide other explanations for the frequency of masturbation. If the reasons cited were the principal causes for frequent masturbation, one would expect masturbation to be a constant throughout a person's life, since the factors indicated are quite constant. On the contrary, the empirical data reveal a remarkable fluctuation in frequency that can hardly be explained by a fluctuation in the above factors.

The Vatican document further maintains that psychology helps us understand how the immaturity of adolescence and other factors can diminish the deliberate character of the act, but it persists in insisting that the absence of serious responsibility must not be presumed. It seems to us that the empirical data and an overwhelming majority of psychologists would draw a quite contrary conclusion, namely that serious responsibility, as moral theology understands it, ought not be the presumption in the case of adolescent masturbatory behavior. The norm advocated in the Vatican's *Declaration*, and held up by the archbishop as a model, is contrary to the empirical data and hardly an "appropriate use" of such data. Obviously, here too, much interdisciplinary dialogue and communication will need to occur before a proper relationship between moral theology and the empirical sciences can be established.

7. *Spirituality and Human Sexuality*. Archbishop Bernardin expresses disappointment that greater attention was not given in *Human Sexuality* to doctrinal and ascetical issues and that he found nothing at all that would deal with what he calls the "spirituality of sexuality." His comments surprise us. Some of the more gratifying responses we have received to the study from a diverse cross section of readers have congratulated the committee for the deeply Christian and spiritual approach to the subject. What the archbishop found as an excessively flexible view of sexual morality, others found far more morally and spiritually demanding than anything they had known before. What the archbishop claimed to be a source of confusion to many, many felt enabled them to make sense of sexuality for the first time in their lives. What accounts for such contrasting impressions? There are many places in *Human Sexuality* where the mysteries of Christianity have undoubtedly influenced the approach, where asceticism, discipline,

and prayer are called for and encouraged, where the integration of sexuality is regarded as indispensable to spiritual wholeness. Perhaps, these are too few, not explicit enough, or in a language unfamiliar to the archbishop's spiritual vocabulary. Perhaps, too, the difference is even deeper than that. Others have noted that there are radically different understandings in the Church today as to what constitutes spirituality. Throughout our approach we have sedulously sought to avoid all traces of the Augustinian-Platonic dualism that has been the bane of Catholic spirituality and sexuality for many centuries. This has profound implications for where one finds the spiritual. The diverse reactions to the spirituality or unspirituality of our Report certainly support the archbishop's call for further theological investigation and reflection in this area!

8. *Christ—the Ultimate Norm.* In the closing paragraphs of his response Archbishop Bernardin touches a chord absolutely central to Christian morality. Christ is the source, the center, the touchstone, the soul, of Christian morality. Fidelity to him is what the Christian moral enterprise is all about! Here, there can be no disagreement! But even here we must be wary of speaking for Christ prematurely. We find Karl Rahner's reserve in his response to the Vatican *Declaration on the Question of the Admission of Women to the Ministerial Priesthood* a most fitting conclusion to our remarks:

> The Roman declaration says that in this question the Church must preserve fidelity to Jesus Christ. That is in principle clearly correct. But the question of what loyalty in this case actually consists of still remains open.
>
> For this reason the discussion must proceed. With discretion, amid mutual respect, with criticism of the bad arguments on both sides, with criticism of the inappropriate emotionalism also expressly or secretly at work on both sides. Above all it requires the courage to face a historic change which is part of the fidelity the Church owes its Lord.[15]

## Conclusion

Since the publication of *Human Sexuality* the field has been further enriched with the appearance of a number of noteworthy studies and works. We think it important to call attention to the following:

Philip S. Kean, SS., *Sexual Morality* (New York: Paulist Press, 1977).

Andre Guindon, *The Sexual Language* (Ottawa: The University of Ottawa Press, 1977).

James B. Nelson, *Embodiment* (Minneapolis, Minn.: Augsburg Publishing House, 1978).

The United Church of Christ, *Human Sexuality* (New York: United Church Press, 1977).

The United Presbyterian Church, *The Church and Homosexuality* (The General Assembly of the United Presbyterian Church in the United States of America, 1978).

Although these works are not treading the identical path of *Human Sexuality*—each of them makes its own distinctive contribution—there is no doubt that they are all moving along the new directions pointed out in our Study. We find this encouraging and hopeful.

The serious work of developing a consistent, coherent, and comprehensive theology of sexual morality is just beginning. Our dialogue with each of the contributors to this volume makes it clear that much remains to be done. The experience of sharing in this exchange of views has been most profitable and enriching.

## NOTES

1. C. Stuhlmueller, "*Human Sexuality*: A Biblical Appraisal," *The Bible Today* 93 (1977), 1438.
2. T. Driver, "A Stride Toward Sanity," *Christianity and Crisis* 37 (1977), 246.
3. W. E. May and J. F. Harvey, *On Understanding Human Sexuality* (Chicago: Franciscan Herald Press, 1977), pp. 36-41.

4. E. LaVerdiere, "*Human Sexuality*: A Biblical Appraisal," *The Bible Today* 93 (1977), 1442.

5. J. Gaffney, "A Brace of Controversies," *America* 137 (1977), 14.

6. R. Haughton, "Toward a Christian Theology of Sexuality," in *Doctrine and Life* (Dublin: Dominican Publications, July 1978), pp. 326f.

7. R. Collins, "The Bible and Sexuality," *Biblical Theological Bulletin* (Oct. 1977), 163.

8. J. Nelson, *Embodiment* (Minneapolis, Minn.: Augsburg Publishing House, 1978), p. 278, n. 33.

9. M. Merleau-Ponty develops this notion in his *Phénoménologie de la Perception* and *La Structure du Comportement*. These appear in translation as *Phenomenology of Perception* (London: 1962) and *The Structure of Behavior* (Boston: 1942). A further description of the "body-subject" is contained in his last published article, "L'Oeil et l'Esprit." For a perceptive discussion of this whole topic, cf. R. Kwant, *The Phenomenological Philosophy of Merleau-Ponty* (Pittsburgh: Duquesne University Press, 1963), Chapter 1. Kwant considers the "body-subject" to be Merleau-Ponty's fundamental contribution to philosophic thought. Kwant, however, criticizes Merleau-Ponty for not attending to the truth for which classical dualism attempted to provide (Chapter 13).

10. *Summa Theol.* I–II, 94, 4 c.: "Sed ratio practica negotiatur circa contingentia, in quibis sunt operationes humanae: et ideo, etsi in communibus sit aliqua necessitas, quanto magis ad propria descenditur, tanto magis invenitur defectus."

11. *L'Europa*, Jan. 30, 1976.

12. H. Küng, *The Church* (New York: Sheed and Ward, 1967), pp. 238f.

13. J. Ratzinger, *Theological Highlights of Vatican II* (New York: Paulist Press/Deus Books, 1966), pp. 167f.

14. *National Catholic Reporter*, June 30, 1978.

15. *Ibid.*, Oct. 7, 1977, p. 14.

# EPILOGUE

If it is true that every end marks a new beginning, the conclusion of a work such as this should occasion further probing or, in the words of Fr. Kosnik, "a keener appreciation of the creative thinking that still needs to be done." Every writer, by the very fact of publishing, invites reaction. Fr. LaVerdiere expressly invites "the scholarly and pastoral community to join in an ongoing exploration and discussion." I should like to repeat here the hope which I expressed in the Introduction, that other members of the hierarchy might address themselves to the issues that Archbishop Bernardin has spoken out on. In conjunction with other members of the original committee Fr. Kosnik encourages the Catholic Biblical Association "to sponsor a comprehensive study of the Bible and sexuality" and he sees the value of joint meetings of the Catholic Biblical Association and the Catholic Theological Society including active participation by the American bishops. I might observe that, with Martin Luther King, Jr., on the steps of the Lincoln Memorial, it's good to "have a dream"!

I think here of the 1968 presidential address to the Catholic Theological Society delivered by Fr. Walter Burghardt, S.J. He began by recounting some of the changes in the Society over the years and lightly observed that "to the horror of all that is Roman, we have stopped talking in dreadfully precise Latin; we are doing our thing in gloriously ambiguous English." But his concluding remarks are in dreadfully unambiguous English: "In a word, can we, in hard-nose reality, justify our actual, independent, relatively unproductive existence? I say no." One of the reasons for this honest conclusion is, according to Fr. Burghardt, that "Catholic theology in America is *not collaborative*. In an age characterized by co-operative effort, where teams attack the atom and isolate the virus, where organized expeditions track down the footsteps of man and re-create the birth of his world, where it takes thousands of human beings to launch one astronaut into space, where men march arm-in-arm for justice and bread, we walk alone. No scholar is an island—except the Catholic theologian. The closest approximation to collaboration happens every fifty years: a Catholic encyclopedia; . . . At this challenging, frightening moment in American history there is not a single gut issue of human existence that has summoned our theological fraternity to a systematic effort, to bring its many-splendored resources to focus in creative agony. We each do our little thing, . . . we skirmish with Roman congregations elusive as Vietcong; and the world passes us by . . . because we have so little to say."[1]

Human sexuality is a "gut issue," one that admittedly is not the most important of the day (as noted in Question 12 to Archbishop Bernardin) but certainly of common and current (because perennial) interest. Ironically enough, the publications of the Report did little to unite the Society. Some members threatened to withdraw their support, and the Board of Directors voted only to "receive" the Report (an action which implies neither approval nor disapproval).

Because publication of the Report has in fact aroused such interest, perhaps it could serve as a modest occasion for joint endeavors not only between the Catholic Theological Society and the Catholic Biblical Association but the American Catholic Philosophical Association, Psychologists Interested in Religious Issues (formerly the American Catholic Psychological Association, now Division 36 of the American Psychological Association), the Guild of Catholic Psychiatrists, and other scholarly organizations whether Catholic or not. Authentic scholarship transcends sectarian and non-religious camps.

Active participation by the American bishops is certainly something to be devoutly wished. At the very least this might help mute somewhat an honest lament made by the respected Scripture scholar Fr. Bruce Vawter. Writing on the divorce issue in the New Testament, Fr. Vawter's "terminal animadversion" is "a certain feeling of frustration." He recalls that the Commission for Canon Law of the National Conference of Catholic Bishops encouraged the Canon Law Society of America to sponsor an interdisciplinary symposium to study the question of indissolubility. In 1968 the results of that symposium were published. And yet, as Vawter rightly complains, "It would be hard to demonstrate from any ecclesiastical pronouncement" that even semiofficial gatherings "or any unsolicited scholarly contribution mentioned here or elsewhere has had any appreciable influence on hierarchical thinking about divorce and remarriage in the Catholic church and/or the pastoral care of the divorced Catholic." And he concludes: "As far as practical utility to the church is concerned, therefore, the biblist often feels pushed to the sidelines, puttering about with his colleagues regarding the niceties of Greek vocabulary when he would prefer to assist the church to grow under the instruction of the inspired word. If he cannot be allowed to lend his voice to the ear of him who would hear what the Spirit is saying to the churches, however, at least he must be permitted to continue to putter with his peers."[2]

In one sense the views expressed by Frs. Burghardt and Vawter are not exactly compelling invitations to younger persons in the Church to take up the task of the theological enterprise. But in another they are challenges of freight-train impact to all of us to continue to speak out. For it is still true that what one sows another may reap.

It is not the task of an editor of a volume to evaluate in the same forum what his contributors have written. Critics can best do that. His own evaluations and suggestions were made prior to publication. But it is his pleasant prerogative to thank them all publicly. I do that now with pleasure, and in so doing I include Fr. John Breslin, S.J., our editor at Doubleday, and Ms. Deborah McCann, his assistant, for their continuous and gracious assistance.

D.J.D.

# NOTES

1. W. Burghardt, "Towards an American Theology," *CTSA Proceedings* 23 (1968), 20–27, *passim*.
2. B. Vawter, "Divorce and the New Testament," *The Catholic Biblical Quarterly* 39 (1977), 528–42, at pp. 541f.

# CONTRIBUTORS

GREGORY BAUM, S.T.D. (University of Fribourg, Switzerland)
Professor of Theology and Religious Studies, St. Michael's College, University of Toronto. Author of *Man Becoming, Religion and Alienation, Truth Beyond Relativism: Karl Mannheim's Sociology of Knowledge*, among numerous other books and articles. Past President of the Canadian Theological Society; editor of *The Ecumenist*. Resides in Toronto with his wife.

JOSEPH L. BERNARDIN, D.D., M.A. (Education, Catholic University of America)
Archbishop of Cincinnati (since 1972); immediate Past President of the National Conference of Catholic Bishops and the United States Catholic Conference (1974–77); one of four U.S. delegates elected by NCCB to the World Synod of Bishops in Rome (1974, 1977); elected by Synod delegates in Rome to Permanent Council of the Synod (1974, 1977); appointed by Pope Paul VI as Consultor for the Sacred Congregation for Catholic Education (1978); Chairman of the Board of Directors of the National Catholic Educational Association (1978). Author of *Prayer in Our Time* (pastoral letter), *"Let the Children Come to Me"*: A Guide for the Religious Education of Children. Contributor to *U.S. Catholic, St. Anthony Messenger, L'Osservatore Romano,* the New York *Times*.

DENNIS J. DOHERTY, DR. THEOL. (University of Würzburg, W. Germany)
Associate Professor of Moral Theology, Marquette University. Author of *The Sexual Doctrine of Cardinal Cajetan, Divorce & Remarriage: Resolving a Catholic Dilemma*. Contributor to *Continuum, The Jurist, Chicago Studies, The American Ecclesiastical Review,* and other books and periodicals. Married, two children.

JOSEPH JENSEN, O.S.B., S.S.L., S.T.D. (Catholic University of America)
Associate Professor of Sacred Scripture, Catholic University of America. Author of *God's Word to Israel, The Use of tôrâ by Isaiah: His Debate with the Wisdom Tradition*. Contributor to *The Catholic Biblical Quarterly, Novum Testamentum, The Bible Today*, and other periodicals.

ANTHONY R. KOSNIK, S.T.D. (Angelicum University, Rome)
Dean of Theology and Professor of Moral Theology, Saints Cyril and Methodius Seminary, Orchard Lake, Michigan. Chairperson of the CTSA *Human Sexuality* Report. Contributor to *The Jurist, Linacre Quarterly, The Catholic Mind*, and other periodicals.

EUGENE A. LAVERDIERE, S.S.S., S.S.L. (Pontifical Biblical Institute, Rome), PH.D. (University of Chicago)
Associate Professor of Biblical Theology, Jesuit School of Theology, Chicago. Author of *Introduction to the Pentateuch, Trumpets of Beaten Metal, Finding Jesus Through the Bible*. Contributor to scholarly and popular journals. Associate Editor: *The Bible Today, Emmanuel*.

DANIEL C. MAGUIRE, S.T.D. (Gregorian University, Rome)
Professor of Moral Theology, Marquette University. Author of *Death by Choice, The Moral Choice*. Contributor to *Cross Currents, Commonweal, Christian Century, Anglican Theological Review*, and other books and periodicals. Married, two children.

WILLIAM E. MAY, PH.D. (Marquette University)
Associate Professor of Moral Theology, Catholic University of America. Author of *Christ in Contemporary Thought, Becoming Human: An Invitation to Christian Ethics, On Understanding "Human Sexuality."* Contributor to *Communio, Faith and Reason, Homiletic and Pastoral Review, Linacre Quarterly*, and other books and periodicals. Former editor of religious books for Newman Press, Bruce Publishing Company, and Corpus Instrumentorum. Married, seven children.

MAYO MOHS, M.A. (Political Science, Xavier University, Cincinnati)
Associate Editor, former Religion Editor (1969–75), *Time* maga-

zine. Author of *Other Worlds, Other Gods: Adventures in Religious Science Fiction.*

PATRICIA TURBES MOHS, B.A. (College of St. Catherine, St. Paul, Minnesota)
Researcher for *Time-Life* Books. Co-editor of *Time-Life Legal Guide.* Contributor to other books. Husband and wife with two children.

CARROLL STUHLMUELLER, C.P., S.T.L. (Catholic University of America), S.S.D. (Pontifical Biblical Institute, Rome)
Chairperson of the Department of Biblical Languages and Literature and Professor of Old Testament Studies, Catholic Theological Union, Chicago. Author of *The Prophets and the Word of God, The Books of Jeremiah and Baruch, Thirsting for the Lord: Essays in Biblical Theology,* among more than a dozen other titles. Editor of *Women and Priesthood.* Contributor to *The Catholic Biblical Quarterly, The Thomist, Biblical Research, Verbum Domini,* and many others. Current President of the Catholic Biblical Association of America. Associate Editor: *The Catholic Biblical Quarterly, The Bible Today, Old Testament Reading Guide.*

# INDEX